# The Evolving Pacific Basin in
# the Global Political Economy

# The Evolving Pacific Basin
in the
# Global Political Economy

## Domestic and International Linkages

edited by
## Cal Clark and Steve Chan

Lynne Rienner Publishers ▪ Boulder & London

HC
460.5
E94
1992

Published in the United States of America in 1992 by
Lynne Rienner Publishers, Inc.
1800 30th Street, Boulder, Colorado 80301

and in the United Kingdom by
Lynne Rienner Publishers, Inc.
3 Henrietta Steet, Covent Garden, London WC2E 8LU

**Library of Congress Cataloging-in-Publication Data**
The evolving Pacific Basin in the global political economy:
   domestic and international linkages / edited by Cal Clark and Steve Chan.
      p.      cm.
   Includes bibliographical references and index.
   ISBN 1-55587-271-9 (hc : alk. paper)
   1. East Asia—Economic conditions.   2. East Asia—Politics and  government.
3. China—Foreign relations—1976- .     4. Japan—Foreign relations—1945–
5. Thailand—Economic  conditions.   6. Automobile industry and trade—Malaysia.
I. Clark, Cal, 1945–  .  II. Chan, Steve.
HC460.5.E94        1992
330.95—dc20                                                    92-4871
                                                               CIP

**British Cataloguing in Publication Data**
A Cataloguing in Publication record for this book
is available from the British Library.


Printed and bound in the United States of America

The paper used in this publication meets the requirements
of the American National Standard for Permanence of
Paper for Printed Library Materials Z39.48.

*To Janet and Jennifer*

# Contents

# Tables and Figures

## Tables

## Figures

# Preface

The Pacific Basin is becoming an increasingly vital center of world politics and economics. In the security/diplomatic realm, the end of the Cold War has dramatically rearranged the relations among the Great Powers in the region and their client states; in the economic realm, the extremely rapid growth in the Asian nations with Pacific shorelines has generated interest in their "model" of economic success as well as fear of these countries as overwhelming economic competitors. This book, then, examines the recent evolution of the Pacific Basin. In particular, the chapters explore two principal questions: What are the effects of the recent diplomatic revolution? And what are the central dynamics of these political economies?

Answers to both these questions should help the academic community move toward "new thinking." Clearly, the basic tenets of many nations' foreign policies must be rethought. Less obviously (but, we hope, convincingly shown in several of these chapters), a detailed look at the Pacific Basin political economies forces us to move beyond the current dominant but simplistic views of how "state" and "market" operate in the contemporary world. Thus, we hope (without meaning to be pretentious) that the reader will be stimulated to join the contributors in commencing an intellectual odyssey in reconceptualizing the international political economy—one whose first steps are represented by these chapters.

Initial drafts of most of these chapters were presented in panel sessions at the 1991 annual meetings of the International Studies Association and Western Political Science Association, which were held on the same weekend in late March in Vancouver and Seattle, respectively. As editors, we were impressed not just with the quality of the papers, but also with the authors' speed and sophistication in crafting final essays. We are especially thankful to Martha Peacock of Lynne Rienner Publishers for her support and encouragement in this project. We also are very grateful for the valuable help in manuscript preparation that we received from Karen Bowyer and Barbara Powell of the University of Wyoming's Political Science Department. Last, but far from least, we dedicate this book to our wives—Janet Clark and Jennifer Chan—for all their support, understanding, and love.

*Cal Clark*
*Steve Chan*

# 1

# Changing Perspectives on the Evolving Pacific Basin: International Structure and Domestic Processes

*Steve Chan & Cal Clark*

Since the sixteenth century, Europe has been the center of the modern world system (Wallerstein, 1974). With the rise of the United States as a major international power, especially after World War II, this center has shifted to the North Atlantic area (Deutsch et al., 1957). Recently, however, the Pacific Basin has assumed such an increased importance in the international political economy as to suggest that a further westward movement of the center of the world system may be in the offing. Some observers remark that we have already entered a new era, the Pacific century (Linder, 1986).

On the borders of the Pacific Basin are located most of the world's major countries—whether measured in territorial expanse, population size, economic output, military capability, or resource endowment. By virtue of their possession of these traditional assets for international influence, these nations—the United States, the Soviet Union, Japan, China, Indonesia, Australia, Mexico, and Canada—are or could potentially be key actors in shaping the regional as well as global political economy. The imposing size and rich resources of these countries, however, belie their rather heterogeneous positions in the international structure and the divergent processes characterizing their domestic and foreign adjustments. The role adjustments and policy shifts for some of these countries have been so sharp and swift that they could hardly have been anticipated barely a decade ago. Moreover, their changing status and niche in international politics and economics would also be quite unexpected from the perspective of one or more of the prevailing theories of political economy.

Thus, the positions of many Pacific Basin nations have changed considerably, if not dramatically, along a number of dimensions. First, the relative economic power of some has waxed, whereas that of others has waned; second, the alliances and ideological confrontations of the Cold War era are clearly being transformed into new patterns of diplomacy; and third, these international changes are closely intertwined with fundamental shifts in the domestic polities and economies of many of these nations. These changes are especially surprising, perhaps, because they challenge the conclusions of the three primary competing theoretical paradigms in contemporary political economy: (1) the developmentalist or modernization approach, which seeks to explain national status in terms of free market economics and cultural modernization; (2) dependency theory, which argues that a global capitalist economy dominated by a "core" of advanced industrial powers distorts and retards economic growth and political development in the "periphery" of the Third World; and (3) the statist perspective, which, unlike the other two, assigns government organization and policy the key role in accounting for social, economic, and political outcomes.

This introductory overview of the evolving Pacific Basin is organized around challenges to each of these theoretical perspectives. The first section of this chapter examines the changing role of the state within the region to indicate some serious shortcomings in the statist model, which is probably now the most popular framework for viewing the area's political economy. The second section then shows how the workings of the "international product cycle" have negated most of the dismal *dependencia* predictions about Third World economies, and have actually stimulated remarkable growth in many Pacific economies. The third section presents four models of the different political economies in the region and, in so doing, sharply challenges the laissez-faire assumptions of modernization theory. The final section summarizes the principal arguments of the chapters in this book and asks what they tell us about international structure and domestic processes in the Pacific Basin.

## The Changing Nature of the State in the Pacific Basin

The Pacific Basin nations have been a focal point for statist theory. The socialist countries were governed by extremely strong states, state industrial and trade policies are generally seen as forming a major ingredient of the "East Asian development model," the state has been alleged to be the primary influence affecting economic and social outcomes in many Latin American countries, and even the laissez-faire United States has played a leading role in the global economic order. This section, then, examines how some of these stereotypical ideas about the state have changed recently with the crumbling of state socialism in the Soviet Union and the People's Republic of China, the decline of the "economic hegemony" of the United States, and the questions that have been raised about the real nature of the presumed state-led growth in capitalist East Asia.

The domestic fragility of the socialist Chinese and Soviet regimes (as attested to by the 1989 Tiananmen Square disturbance in China and the pathetic 1991 abortive coup in the Soviet Union) must be recognized as a major surprise from the point of view of those theories that emphasize the efficacy of strong, autonomous, and "hard" states in mobilizing and directing socioeconomic resources in late industrialization (Evans et al., 1985; Gerschenkron, 1966; Myrdal, 1968). Just when Western scholarship was turning increasingly to statist interpretations to explain the rapid economic growth of the East Asian capitalist economies (Alam, 1989; Amsden, 1989, 1985, 1979; Barrett and Whyte, 1982; Deyo, 1981; Gold, 1986; Haggard and Moon, 1983; Johnson, 1982; Jones and Sakong, 1980; Wade, 1990, 1988), Mikhail Gorbachev undertook perestroika and glasnost to loosen the grip of the communist party and central bureaucracy in the Soviet Union. At the same time, Deng Xiaoping launched China's "second revolution," aimed at market liberalization and "taking the state back out" of economic planning (Harding, 1987).

This turn of events must also have been a major source of discomfort for proponents of dependency theory (Amin, 1974; Bornschier and Chase-Dunn, 1985; Cardoso and Faletto, 1979; Chase-Dunn, 1989; Evans, 1979; Frank, 1969; Leys, 1974; Moulder, 1977), whether they advocated socialism or autonomy as an alternative to dependency. Instead of following their advice to break away from the world capitalist system and to adopt an economic strategy of self-reliance, the Soviet Union and China have in fact opted for reintegration into this system. Thus, in spring 1991, Gorbachev traveled to Tokyo and Seoul to seek financial loans and technology transfer in an effort to resuscitate his moribund economy. As the Soviet Union disintegrated and its economy unraveled in late 1991 and early 1992, the new members of the Commonwealth of Independent States (CIS) became increasingly dependent upon western aid and investment.

Although in less dire economic conditions, socialist China has likewise reversed its traditional Maoist emphasis on self-reliance and import substitution during the past decade. Thus, Beijing openly appealed for international aid to alleviate the economic hardship caused by the devastating floods in summer 1991. For some time now, the Chinese government has also established export-processing zones and actively pursued foreign investment and technology. In 1987 (the latest year for which figures are available at this writing), China received the second highest net inflow of foreign direct investment in the developing world (US$1.8 billion, next to Mexico's US$2.5 billion). Imitating the examples of its fast-growing capitalist neighbors, Beijing launched a rather successful export-promotion program of its own (Harding, 1987). Consequently, since the late 1970s, southern coastal China has had the extremely rapid economic growth typical of Japan and the East Asian newly industrializing countries (NICs). This program brought a Chinese trade surplus with the United States of US$10.4 billion in 1990 and a projected surplus of US$15 billion in 1991. The latter estimate, if true, would place China (after Japan) as the second largest surplus country in bilateral trade with the United States—a development that would again be quite incongruent with traditional dependency expectations.

If recent events in China and the Soviet Union strongly challenge the efficacy of a command economy and autarchic development, all has not been well in the United States with its weak state and free market economics. The United States clearly dominated the world economy from World War II through the mid 1970s, when trade barriers were reduced and world growth was robust, giving rise to the "hegemonic stability" theory. The logic of this theory is that a strong world leader with substantial economic clout is necessary to create a liberal trade regime, to enforce more or less general adherence to its norms, and to provide subsidies to the system in times of crisis. The imputed motivation for the hegemon is that its industries are so competitive that they ultimately benefit from an open world economy (Gilpin, 1987, 1981; Keohane, 1980; Kindleberger, 1981, 1973).

Although its diplomatic leadership remains strong, especially in the wake of the Gulf War (Nau, 1990; Nye, 1990), the United States is clearly facing increasing economic challenges from Japan, the European Community, and the dynamic NICs. It also suffers from declining economic competitiveness and a stagnating standard of living (Gilpin, 1987; Phillips, 1990). Although scholars may disagree vehemently about the causes and extent of the economic crisis in the United States, many blame some type of state policy failure—misaligned macroeconomic policies (Hufbauer, 1990; Nau, 1990), timidity in trade negotiations (Prestowitz, 1988), or abjuring industrial and strategic trade policy (Tyson, 1990). In short, recent international changes suggest state "failure" in the United States as well as for the great powers adhering to state socialism.

Appeals to a strong state as the chief reason for rapid economic development have recently also come under challenge in the analysis of those East Asian capitalist economies that had originally motivated statist explanations. The co-occurrence of a laissez-faire state and a vibrant economy in Hong Kong has, of course, always presented a problem to such explanations (Rabushka, 1979). However, several recent studies have also argued that the role of the state has been exaggerated in countries such as Japan, Taiwan, and South Korea (e.g., Chan et al., 1990; Friedman, 1988; Lam, 1988; Moon, 1990, 1988; Okimoto, 1989). Flexible manufacturing, dynamic entrepreneurship, and what has been called "guerrilla capitalism" seem to have been crucial ingredients in these countries' economic performances. Thus, the greater export successes of the East Asian textile manufacturers relative to their Latin American counterparts cannot be accounted for by differences in state intervention or labor costs, but rather have to be explained in terms of the former's commercial adaptability and production flexibility in meeting changing market conditions (Morawetz, 1981).

As a further paradox of statist interpretations, the very successes of the East Asian late industrializers under the auspices of ostensibly strong states have initiated the process of "embourgeoisement" and brought about a post–material generation (Inglehart, 1990). Electoral competition, personal freedom, consumer rights, and environmental protection gain public salience relative to pocketbook issues. Pressure mounts on the authoritarian regimes to allow for more political participation and social freedom. The fist fights among Taiwan's parliamentarians, the protests by South Korea's students against police brutality, and the demonstrations of the Chinese demanding democratic reform at Tiananmen Square are symptomatic of such pressure. These examples conform to the adage that rapid growth can be politically destabilizing (Olson, 1963).

At the same time, incidents such as labor strikes at Hyundai's steel and shipbuilding plants, local opposition to the installation of additional nuclear reactors by the Taiwan Electric and Power Company, and critical public opinion in reaction to state intervention in family planning in Singapore all suggest that these societies are becoming more pluralistic and that their states can no longer be assumed to occupy the "commanding heights." The proliferation of interest groups—in Olson's (1982) terminology, distributional coalitions—in turn implies that these countries may face the increasing prospect of economic stagflation and political gridlock, two afflictions due to the type of "institutional sclerosis" that is particularly characteristic of advanced industrial democracies with numerous and entrenched distributional coalitions.

Thus, the role of the state is clearly changing throughout the Pacific Basin. The strong control of state socialism has probably suffered a fatal blow; the relative economic decline of the United States is raising important questions about its government's economic role and policies; new research has challenged the model of state-led growth in East Asia (ironically, the very growth that state policies stimulated there has undermined state power and autonomy); major powers, such as China and Japan, are facing the necessity for foreign policy reorientations (see the summaries of Chapters 3 and 4 below); and several examples of outright policy failure in East Asia (e.g., the Philippines and Vietnam) are easy to discern. This does not so much call for discarding the statist model, however, as for elaborating it by realizing that state policies can be both productive and harmful and that a state itself is intimately connected with its broader socioeconomic environment.

## The International Product
## Cycle and Economic Dynamism

If statist theories can be criticized because of government policy failure, dependency theory is challenged, ironically, by an unexpected success in state policy throughout much of the Pacific Basin. Although the states for the late industrializing countries are becoming less strong and autonomous relative to the various social interests, they have been gaining leverage over foreign economic interests. Despite misgivings on the part of dependency theorists with regard to the deleterious social and economic effects of foreign direct investment (e.g., Bornschier and Chase-Dunn, 1985), over time Third World countries have been able to assert greater control over and insist on more favorable terms in dealing with multinational corporations. In the larger developing countries, such as India, Brazil, Iran, Nigeria, and Venezuela, the host governments have begun to harness these foreign firms in a variety of crucial sectors, including automobiles, computers, petroleum, and banking (Biersteker, 1987; Doran, 1977; Encarnation, 1989; Evans, 1979; Grieco, 1984; Jenkins, 1987; Newfarmer, 1980; Tugwell, 1975).

Furthermore, statistical analysis of the sub-Saharan African countries shows that state intervention plays a major role in mediating the influence of foreign capital penetration (Bradshaw and Tshandu, 1990). Case studies pertaining to those Latin American countries on the eastern side of the Pacific Basin tend to reinforce this impression. Mexico's relations with foreign automobile and pharmaceutical manufacturers (Bennett and Sharpe, 1985; Gereffi, 1982); Chile's relations with the multinational copper corporations (Moran, 1974), and Peru's relations with U.S. mining and sugar interests (Becker, 1983; Goodsell, 1974; Stepan, 1978) indicate that the host state's policies, although far from always effective, are usually able to promote the development of indigenous manufacturing or the nationalization of ownership.

Similarly, capitalist countries located on the Asian side of the Pacific Basin are far from the easy preys for multinational corporations that classical dependency theorists are apt to imply. Even though they have been seeking foreign direct investment to contribute to their industrialization efforts, the developmental states of South Korea, Taiwan, and Singapore have hardly adopted an indiscriminate open-door policy toward multinational corporations (Huang, 1989; Mardon, 1990; Mirza, 1986; Wade, 1990). They have insisted instead on a variety of concessions—such as joint ownership, domestic content, export quotas, and technology transfers—in exchange for admitting foreign direct investment. In some countries, such as Indonesia, Thailand, Singapore, and the Philippines, state enterprises often enter joint industrial projects with foreign corporations and local capitalists in a manner similar to Evans's (1979) description of the Brazilian experience (Deyo, 1981; Hawes,

1987; Higgott and Robison, 1985; Hill, 1988; Robison, 1986; Rodan, 1989).

This "triple alliance" of state, foreign, and indigenous capital has sometimes been in part motivated by a desire to undermine the commercial status of non-native entrepreneurs such as the Indian community in Kenya and the Lebanese community in Nigeria (Biersteker, 1987; Leys, 1974). In a number of Southeast Asian countries (e.g., Indonesia, Malaysia, and Thailand), this coalition has similarly sought to promote the economic position of the *Bumiputera* (natives) and to contain the influence of the Chinese-owned enterprises (Higgott and Robison, 1985; Robison et al., 1985; Robison, 1986). Accordingly, multinational corporations have in fact been used by the state to balance and control powerful domestic (Chinese) business interests. The host governments rather than the foreign firms have tended to be the senior partners in this pact of domination.

Citing these successes does not deny that certain aspects of this ruling coalition, such as the "crony capitalism" of the Philippines under Ferdinand Marcos and the political patronage system controlled by the Indonesian military, are in accordance with the traditional dependency formulation of a coopted native elite, who serve as compradors for foreign firms typically interested in agricultural exports (sugar, coconut, and fruits for the Philippines) and mineral extraction (petroleum for Indonesia). These two cases, however, tend to be the exception rather than the rule. Generally, a nationalist elite, a politicized public, an increasingly competent and incorruptible bureaucracy, and a rising "learning curve" tend to gradually enhance the bargaining power of the host countries relative to the multinational corporations (Alam, 1989; Huang, 1989; Mardon, 1990; Moran, 1978).

As indicated above, dependency theorists tend to see multinational corporations as a means by which the core economies extract surplus from the periphery economies (Bornschier and Chase-Dunn, 1985). Even non-*dependentistas* (e.g., Bergsten et al., 1978; Gilpin, 1987; Krasner, 1978; Vernon, 1971) recognize that these companies may be used as points of political leverage by their home governments and that they may not consistently contribute to the welfare of their Third World hosts. Indeed, it was not so long ago that *The American Challenge*, written by Servan-Schreiber (1968), was popular reading in Western Europe. This best-seller warned that the corporate power and innovative capacity of U.S. companies threatened to take over the markets of the Western European countries and to undermine their political autonomy.

Although the international capital (investment as well as loans) market has expanded tremendously since the publication of Servan-Schreiber's book, the flow of this capital has become much more multilateral and less dominated by the United States. Pressured by the prospects of overseas protectionism and concerned with their precarious supplies of industrial resources, Japanese firms have in particular been expanding their foreign investment portfolio rapidly (Bobrow and Kudrle, 1987; Ozawa, 1979; Yoon, 1990).

Along with the other countries with a large bilateral trade surplus with the United States, Japan has begun large-scale investments to relocate some manufacturing operations to North America in anticipation of possible future trade barriers against its exports. Thus, the United States is increasingly becoming a major host country to others' foreign direct investments. The extent of this role reversal is perhaps most dramatic in the automobile industry, where Japanese firms have been projected to capture 45 percent of the U.S. market by the early 1990s (Reich, 1989). At the same time, U.S. firms have invested heavily in overseas production sites, such as Mexico and Brazil in Latin America (Jenkins, 1987), so that the automobile industry has increasingly become internationalized with local assembly of standard parts produced in different countries but based on common designs (the so-called "world car concept").

The newly industrializing countries have also recently produced their own large multinational corporations (Kumar, 1982). Hong Kong's large banks and South Korea's industrial conglomerates (the *chaebols*) are perhaps the best-known examples. They have, however, been joined recently by firms with lower capitalization, less expensive machinery, and greater reliance on overseas kinship ties in search of investment opportunities abroad. Faced with rising labor costs at home and threatened access to foreign markets (Aggarwal et al., 1987), the larger firms in Hong Kong, Singapore, Taiwan, and South Korea have begun a movement to relocate their more labor-intensive manufacturing operations in China, Thailand, Indonesia, and the Caribbean Basin. That Taiwan has recently become the largest investor in the Philippines is indicative of the emergence of Third World multinational corporations and the increasing multilaterization in foreign direct investment—tendencies that traditional dependency theories again would not have anticipated.

Dependency formulations, of course, also place a great deal of emphasis on the role of foreign debts in distorting and depressing the developmental potential of Third World countries. Of the Pacific Basin countries, Mexico, Peru, the Philippines, and South Korea have been among the largest debtor countries. During the mid-1980s, the former three countries were hit particularly hard by a combination of rising interest rates and falling demand for their traditional exports. In negotiating for debt rescheduling and additional bridge loans, they had to agree to some austerity measures by cutting back on imports and government subsidies.

In retrospect, however, the debtor governments have proved to be quite resilient in bargaining with their foreign bankers and the International Monetary Fund. Far from being powerless pawns under the spell of foreign creditors, they were able to obtain emergency credit on relatively favorable terms, to modify retrospectively the terms of austerity programs, and—for Peru—to declare a unilateral debt moratorium. Indeed, the sheer magnitude of the outstanding loans of the largest debtor countries (especially Mexico and Brazil) gives them substantial bargaining leverage with foreign creditors and the latter's home governments (Kahler, 1986; Stallings and Kaufman, 1989; Wellons, 1987; Wiarda, 1990, 1987). A formal declaration of default would mean the corporate demise of the bankers and would create strong ripple effects, seriously shaking financial confidence in these bankers' home countries. That the debtor governments were thus able to use the lenders' large "sunk investment" as a hostage in negotiating for further loans is again something not stressed in standard dependency formulations.

These formulations also appear to be quite unprepared for the evident changes in the evolving regional division of labor taking place in the Pacific Basin (see Balassa, 1981; Bradford and Branson, 1987; Caporaso, 1981). These changes indicate a gradual reversal in traditional commercial patterns that underlie the *dependentistas'* (as well as non-*dependentistas'*, such as Hirschman, 1945) concern with unequal terms of trade between the core and periphery economies and the consequent asymmetric political influence between the two sides. Although some Pacific Rim countries—such as Indonesia, the Philippines, Chile, and Peru—continue to rely heavily on the export of raw materials and agricultural produce (Goodsell, 1974; Hawes, 1987; Indorf and Mayerchak, 1989; Moran, 1974), other developing countries have become major exporters of manufactured goods.

Hong Kong, Singapore, Taiwan, South Korea, Thailand, China, and Mexico have all been able to establish a highly competitive export sector in consumer and industrial products, and have moved rather rapidly into making increasingly higher value-added and sophisticated goods for sale in the North American and European markets. In their bilateral trade with the United States, these countries have generally been able to compile a substantial surplus. Despite their asymmetric market reliance, the East Asian economies have resorted successfully to different qualitative measures in order to deflect or dampen U.S. attempts to restrict their exports quantitatively (Chan, 1987; Odell, 1985; Yoffie, 1983).

Indeed, if one is to measure dependency status by the extent of a country's trade deficit and foreign indebtedness, it is the United States among all Pacific Rim countries that has suffered the greatest downward mobility in its international position. Its trade balance has progressively deteriorated over recent years, and it has become the world's largest debtor country, with foreigners (mostly Japanese banks) supplying about half of its budgetary shortfalls. Just as importantly, the composition of U.S. exports is equally revealing about its changing comparative advantage in international trade. Grain, soybeans, cotton, tobacco, lumber, beef, oranges, and wine have assumed a greater importance in U.S. exports to East Asia. In effect, in a direct reversal of dependency expectations, the United States has come to rely increasingly on the sale of agricultural produce in exchange for manufactures from Japan, South Korea, Taiwan, and China.

This trade pattern applies as well to the primarily Caucasian, industrialized states of the Organization for Economic Cooperation and Development (OECD) in the region. Grain, petroleum, lumber, wool, and iron ore have been the major export items of Canada, Australia, and New Zealand. In return, they have become increasingly reliant on the manufactured exports and direct investment from the East Asian countries. Their sliding position in the international economy has been shared by the Soviet Union, whose largely unexplored natural resources (e.g., petroleum, lumber, and precious metals) in Siberia have become the main source of potential attraction for Japanese and Korean traders and investors (Whiting, 1981). A falling standard of living, lethargic economic production, and deteriorating terms of trade describe Moscow's economic plight. At the same time, the maladies of capitalist Australia—falling commodity prices, rising debt burden, and inefficient manufactures protected by state intervention—have become so severe that one of Canberra's own officials characterized it as a "Fledgling Banana Republic" (Higgott, 1987: 178).

In somewhat ironic contrast, the growing prosperity of the capitalist East Asian trading nations is actually apt to undermine a principal source of their export success. Both conventional statist and liberal theories assign considerable importance to competitive labor costs in this success. Whereas statist theorists tend to emphasize the political repression of organized labor and its exclusion from the "pact of domination" as a key determinant of these countries' developmental path (e.g., Deyo, 1989), liberal neoclassical theorists would emphasize a cheap and pliable work force as these countries' chief comparative advantage in international commerce (see Balassa, 1981; Bradford and Branson, 1987; Hofheinz and Calder, 1982; Linder, 1986).

Yet the very processes of rapid development have also raised wage scales and the cost of living in Hong Kong, Singapore, Taiwan, and South Korea, so that the work force is now neither docile nor inexpensive. Indeed, these economies are facing such a labor shortage, especially in the unskilled and semiskilled jobs, that they have increasingly resorted to the practice of importing foreign workers (the constant flow of Mainland refugees to Hong Kong, of course, has been continuously replenishing this British colony's labor supply). As these economies move further in the direction of developing high-tech manufacturing and service industries, labor costs are likely to reach levels comparable to the advanced industrial countries. Parenthetically, the trend of rising labor costs and shortage in these NICs has been accompanied by a process of increasing automation (e.g., the introduction of robotics in manufacturing) in the advanced industrial countries, thus further auguring a decline in the importance of industrial wages as a source of international comparative advantage.

The Pacific Basin, hence, appears to constitute a case of what Doran and his associates (1983) have called "dependency reversal." Many developing countries in the region have grown quite rapidly, moving from agricultural and natural resources to labor-intensive production to increasingly sophisticated manufacturing in large part because they were able to control, rather than being exploited by, foreign capital. Perhaps the most important explanation for this lies in what Raymond Vernon (1966) terms the "international product cycle." This theory argues that although many new manufactures require high-cost specialized production in the most advanced industrial centers, over time production becomes more standardized and labor intensive. This process allows developing countries to create a "comparative advantage" in industrialization at the low end of the product cycle and, eventually, to "learn by doing" and move up the product cycle to more sophisticated and higher value-added manufacturing. This precisely describes the postwar developmental success of first Japan, then the "gang of four" (Hong Kong, Singapore, South Korea, and Taiwan), and most recently the third wave of NICs (such as Thailand, Malaysia, and southern coastal China).

## Models of Pacific Basin Political Economies

Thus, recent developments in the Pacific Basin are quite pregnant with ironies. For example, although neoclassical economists exult over the workings of the international product cycle in the Pacific Basin, much more is at work than just the "magic of the marketplace." Just when the United States can point to the collapse of East European and Soviet communist regimes and to the major market reforms in China as a vindication of its doctrine of free enterprise and political freedom, the East Asian capitalist economies, with their much more statist practices, have seemingly turned the economic table on the United States by piling up huge trade surpluses. Whereas Washington has continued to pursue national power in the traditional manner of military security and territorial control (Choucri and North, 1975), its former pupils in East Asia have sought commercial competitiveness and industrial adjustment as an alternative avenue for upward status mobility in the international system, thus becoming "trading states" (Rosecrance, 1986). Indeed, Paul Kennedy (1987) argues that a heavy defense burden has often led to the economic decline of great powers in the modern era, a precept that clearly applies to the Soviet Union and probably to the United States as well. With respect to East Asia, the historical patterns are considerably more ambiguous. On the one hand, Japan's economic success has been attributed to its low defense burden, and Vietnam's economic plight to a "garrison state" mentality. On the other hand, heavy military expenditures and foreign threats have not precluded rapid economic growth in South Korea and Taiwan.

Concomitantly, precisely during the period when dependency theory was becoming particularly popular in Western academic circles, there has been a major push by the newly industrializing countries to close the economic distance separating themselves and the more advanced countries. The Matthew principle (the rich get richer, the poor poorer) decried by the *dependentistas* does not tell the whole story. In fact, the income gap between the NICs and the advanced OECD countries has narrowed considerably (Jackman, 1982). On the other hand, the gap between the NICs and the so-called Fourth World countries has become greater. This development, as well as the evolving patterns of trade and investment noted above, cannot be easily dismissed by adding almost as an afterthought a residual category called semiperiphery in the world economy.

The paradoxes and ironies that recent developments pose to conventional expectations can be further illustrated along the lines of four prototypes of political economy (Clark, 1989). The United States exemplifies the prototype combining a regulatory state, pluralistic society, capitalist economy, and commitment to a strong national defense. Because of the strong influence of laissez-faire philosophy and free enterprise ideology, Washington has generally been reluctant to initiate extensive economic intervention with the exception of a heavy defense burden that may well serve as a drag on the economy. Furthermore, because of the relative accessibility of the state to various competing social interest groups, the policy process tends to produce pork-barrel compromises or partisan gridlock (Lowi, 1979). Politicians as well as policies generally have short tenure due to constant electoral cycling (Miller, 1983). Popular preference as well as official proclivity decidedly favor consumption—private and public—at the expense of savings. Despite electoral rhetoric, there is a general reluctance to confront the trade-offs between guns and butter, employment and inflation, a balanced budget and higher taxes. Instead, the temptation is to try to "get a quart out of a pint pot" (Calleo, 1982). Ad hoc monetary manipulations in regard to interest and exchange rates are taken to put off more basic market adjustments and a strong commitment to fiscal restraint (Nau, 1990). Thus, short-term consumption comes at the expense of long-term growth.

In contrast to the United States, the Soviet Union and China, before their respective recent reforms, featured command economies with centralized planning. The emphasis was decidedly on the pursuit of import substitution and the development of heavy industries. Surplus was extracted from the agricultural sector to finance rapid industrialization, and consumer needs were neglected in favor of a high rate of savings and investment. The countries relied heavily on ideological fervor, mass mobilization, and political coercion; none of which was able in the end to overcome the inefficiencies and rigidities of their economies. Their massive defense expenditures, moreover, clearly hurt economic performance. Paradoxically, the recent turn toward market economics in both the Soviet Union and China has brought about severe adjustment trauma. Previously, their citizens had implicitly agreed to a social contract whereby they surrendered their political rights in exchange for the state's guarantee of a socioeconomic "safety net" in the form of subsidized housing, food, transportation, and medical care (Harding, 1987). With market liberalization, however, this safety net has increasingly been removed, leading to hoarding, black markets, rampant inflation, and severe shortage of daily necessities. The resulting popular discontent fueled massive political protests in both the Soviet Union and China (e.g., Tiananmen Square in 1989).

Mexico brings to mind a third prototype, which combines a corporatist state with a capitalist economy. The state is corporatist in the sense that it mediates among rather than dominates over several important blocs of social interests such as labor, business, and peasants (Collier, 1979; Malloy, 1987; Wiarda, 1981). In contrast to the newly industrializing East Asian economies, the corporatist Latin American countries (in addition to Mexico, Brazil and Argentina) are much larger and have historically placed more emphasis on import substitution (Evans, 1987; Gereffi and Wyman, 1990; Haggard, 1990). Moreover, the latter countries give a higher priority to consumption than to savings and investment. This consumption, however, has been characterized by a very skewed distribution of income (Fajnzylber, 1990). To buttress this inequity and to stifle the demands of organized labor, some corporatist states (e.g., Brazil, Argentina) have frequently resorted to authoritarian repression by military regimes.

The fourth and final prototype is the developmental state that features a strong commitment to rapid industrialization and export promotion. Japan offers the leading example, although this model has also been followed by Taiwan, South Korea, and Singapore (Johnson, 1982, 1981). Although professing a capitalist market ideology, the developmental state resorts to a variety of measures (e.g., interest subsidy, tax rebate, import license, currency control, and export quota) to promote specific industries. It sometimes owns and operates large public enterprises while encouraging technological upgrading, economies of scale, and orderly competition in the private sector (Amsden, 1989; Chan and Clark, 1992; Deyo, 1987; Haggard and Moon, 1989). Although excluding organized labor from the ruling political coalition, the developmental state has fostered paternalistic practices and "trickle down" economics that have produced rapid wage increases for workers and a highly egalitarian system of income distribution. In contrast to the Latin American corporatist model's emphasis on import substitution to meet internal demands, the East Asian developmentalist model has adopted a more outward-looking orientation in the pursuit of export expansion and international competitiveness. Moreover, in contrast to the U.S. model of electoral cycling and mass consumerism, the capitalist East Asia's developmental history has featured ruling elite continuity and high levels of savings to fuel continuous growth. It also presents an appealing contrast to the superpower emphasis on military security by emphasizing "comprehensive national security," which combines military concerns with economic well-being and political objectives. Thus, national development becomes the predominant goal (Chan, 1990).

## The Pacific Basin Political Economy

In sum, the recent experiences of Pacific Rim countries suggest a variety of policy choices between consumption and savings, economic growth and social equality, political stability and authoritarian politics, import substitution and export expansion, and strictly military and "comprehensive" definitions of national security. These differences notwithstanding, however, the Pacific Basin, just like the world as a whole, has become a more harmonious place. The decline of East-West tension and the turn to external economic relations by the socialist countries facilitate the development of a dense network of cross-cutting ties that should dampen and absorb possible future shocks to the system. These trends further contribute to the ongoing processes among the capitalist economies pointing to the globalization of production, the internationalization of capital markets, the interpenetration of national markets, and the spread of transnational coalitions in a variety of issue areas (see Moon, 1989, for a more pessimistic appraisal).

Moreover, as indicated earlier, the socialist economies have recently developed deeper and more numerous linkages with the capitalist ones, so that they have become increasingly integrated into the international political economy. Indeed, the general processes underlying this tendency toward globalization of production imply that many of the differences outlined above among the four prototypes of political economies are becoming more blurred. The modernization and democratization processes within the East Asian NICs have reduced the power and autonomy of their developmental states, whereas the regulatory states of the advanced industrial countries have taken on more corporatist and even some developmentalist functions. At the same time, the economic liberalization of the socialist countries has reintroduced private enterprise (albeit still at a rather small scale) and profit incentives, concomitantly reducing the role of central planning.

Although these processes are hardly sufficient to establish any convergence thesis among the countries of the Pacific Basin, the structure of their relations during the last decade or so has increasingly taken on the characteristics of complex interdependence (Keohane and Nye, 1989). In a system characterized by complex interdependence, military power recedes to the background, and matters such as monetary stability, commercial competition, technology transfer, and foreign investment rise to the top of the international agenda. In such a world, mutual partisan adjustment (Axelrod, 1984; Lindblom, 1965) replaces hegemonic stability (Kindleberger, 1973). Whereas both the extent and causes of the relative decline in U.S. power have been undergoing extensive debate (Kennedy, 1987; Nau, 1990; Prestowitz, 1988; Russett, 1985; Strange, 1987, Vogel, 1979), it seems that international regimes should be able to survive the demise of a hegemon (Keohane, 1984; Snidal, 1985) and that power transitions should not inevitably result in military clashes (Modelski, 1987; Organski and Kugler, 1980; Singer et al., 1972). Thus, although the arrival of a security community in the Pacific Basin (Deutsch et al., 1957; Merritt, 1966) seems still far off, the days of military confrontation and mercantilist rivalry are, we hope, behind us.

The following chapters attend to the policy contexts and options of different Pacific Rim countries, and they all try to place this discussion in the context of the interaction between international structure and domestic processes. They share a common concern in attempting to analyze the impact that international structures can have on domestic processes, and, conversely, the manner in which domestic processes can cumulatively transform international structures. A second unifying theme among these chapters is the interplay between change and continuity. In one way or another, they all ask how historical legacies, cultural inheritance, institutional norms, and policy precedents have tended to shape and direct previous and ongoing attempts to adapt to new circumstances and novel challenges. Third, they seek to understand and inform policy by probing how prudent statecraft, effort mobilization, learning by doing, and anticipatory adjustment may bring about successful adaptation and role graduation in the international political economy.

In Chapter 2, Steve Chan and Cal Clark pursue the themes of change and continuity by examining the international division of labor at the global as well as the regional level. They show that major changes can take place within a short time, so that some countries experience sharp upward mobility in this system whereas others undergo major downward mobility. Yet, this chapter also shows that the processes underlying and driving these changes are very much a part of the colonial and neocolonial legacies of countries. This coexistence of change and continuity is especially discernible in the divergent developmental paths taken by the various Pacific Rim countries— with some following the U.S. model of development and others imitating the Japanese model.

Replacing the cross-national focus of Chan and Clark, Tsuneo Akaha examines in Chapter 3 the role adjustment facing Japan's leaders as they prepare for a new age in international political economy. In particular, Japan is facing increasing pressure to move beyond its subordinate role in an alliance with the United States and its emphasis on economic relations in foreign policy, ironically because its growing economic stature inevitably involves it in a much broader range of political matters. Consequently, its agenda has now expanded to (1) improving relations with the successor states to the USSR, the PRC, and North Korea, with whom it has previously had tense relations; (2) managing the increased economic frictions with the United States, its former patron and protector; (3) assuming a larger role in international diplomacy; and (4) integrating political and economic objectives in its rapidly expanding interactions (e.g., trade, investment, and aid) with the Third World. Thus, economic success has created diplomatic problems for Japan, although their solution will require innovative diplomacy and leave Tokyo with a larger and more balanced role in global affairs.

Following Akaha's analysis of Japan, James Hsiung addresses in Chapter 4 similar issues from the perspective of Chinese leaders, who have to adjust their policies in a world of declining military confrontation and rising economic competition. However, the essential problem for the PRC seems to be the opposite of the one facing Japan. Whereas China proved fairly adept at playing the game of multilateral diplomacy for most of the 1980s (even after the Tiananmen Square affair), it now must reform its domestic economic and political systems in order to achieve its chief policy objectives for the 1990s. These policy objectives have remained constant, even though Beijing's international environment has undergone major changes in the recent past. They are to develop a modern and unified China without causing internal instability and external opposition. Accordingly, the challenges of international balance of power and those of domestic modernization and national unification with Hong Kong and Taiwan tend to affect one another. How successful the Chinese leaders are in revamping their country's socioeconomic and political structure will have a profound effect on their efforts to seek the reintegration of Hong Kong and Taiwan into a "Greater China," and to play a new mediating role between Japan and the United States in the Pacific region.

The cases of Japan and China are followed by Chapter 5, in which Gerald Fry analyzes the latest Asian NIC, Thailand. This country's political economy has been characterized by both rapid change and persistent continuity. Whereas on the surface Bangkok's politics can be quite volatile and prone to military coups, the Thai polity has shown substantial stability due to factors such as royal legitimacy, bureaucratic rule, and the cultural proclivity toward "soft ball" politics. Concomitantly, although the Thai economy has grown rapidly in the recent years, it still faces some persistent problems such as considerable regional and sectoral income inequities, continuing ecological degradation, and hyper urban sprawl. Indeed, the latter problems have been exacerbated by rapid economic growth. Fry's analysis offers reasons for this mixed record of policy performance. It sets the Thai experience in the context of the developmental histories of its regional peers as well as prevalent Western theorizing on political economy. In particular, although Thailand's experience is generally consistent with "modernization theory," it also shows the need to go beyond this approach's normal emphasis upon neoclassical economics and cultural modernization by considering the roles of human capital development, the distribution of agricultural land, and traditional political norms.

In Chapter 6, Danny Lam and Ian Lee introduce us to the three capitalist economies with Chinese populations or traditions—namely, Taiwan, Hong Kong, and Singapore. They investigate the reasons behind the commercial adaptability and entrepreneurial dynamism of these Chinese NICs. They argue against the prevalent view that a developmental state has been the guiding force behind these economies' rapid growth, and suggest instead that the small- and medium-size family-operated enterprises have been the most dynamic sector. These enterprises have stressed flexible manufacturing, a strategy that the authors have described as "guerrilla capitalism." This Chinese approach of decentralized adaptation offers a sharp contrast to the typical Western orientation of Fordism that emphasizes mass production of standard manufactures in order to capture the economies of scale. It gives these small NICs the wherewithal to adjust to rapid changes in the international market conditions.

Whereas Lam and Lee examine the interactions between traditional sociocultural institutions and commercial practices, Chi Huang in Chapter 7 probes the linkage between political regimes and state policies. Specifically, he asks whether leadership changes matter in terms of the government's spending tendencies. Pursuing a sophisticated design of "most-similar systems analysis," Huang searches for evidence of fiscal changes in the wake of the violent leadership transition after the assassination of Park Chung Hee in South Korea and the peaceful one after the death of Chiang Kai-shek in Taiwan. The results of his interrupted time series analysis are somewhat inconclusive, and thus do not offer clear evidence for accepting the hypothesis that peaceful leadership turnovers tend to be followed by gradual fiscal increases, whereas violent and abrupt regime changes are more likely to result in major and sudden adjustment in the government's spending decisions. Thus, regime alterations may or may not be followed by fiscal changes that are independent of the unfolding secular trends. Huang concludes by suggesting the incorporation of further variables in future research on this topic, which should especially take into account the influence of the international environment and the differentiation between elite-oriented and mass-oriented government spending.

Just as the state should not be treated as a *deux ex machina* in explaining policy outcomes, we should also not overlook its relevance when appropriate. Continuing the comparative focus of the previous chapters, Russell Mardon and Won Paik contrast the developmental contexts and prospects of South Korea and Thailand in Chapter 8. They conceptualize the "manufacturing miracles" of East Asia as occupying different positions in the international product cycle (Japan, the four Little Dragons, and the emerging third wave of NICs in descending order of technological sophistication and value added). Long-term viability and dynamism are determined by efforts to upgrade an economy from one niche to another. However, there is an ongoing debate over whether laissez-faire economics or state leadership is the key factor engendering this capability for economic transformation.

The historical experiences of the two countries analyzed in Chapter 8 tend to represent the statist and liberal approaches to development. South Korea has pursued a statist policy of "sovereignty en garde," whereby it requires foreign investors to submit to a variety of terms as a condition for being allowed into its economy. These terms include agreements on export quotas, joint ventures, technology transfer, personnel training, and eventually divestiture of foreign ownership in favor of local producers. In contrast to South Korea, Thailand has a much softer state, a less efficient bureaucracy, a weaker indigenous entrepreneurial class, and a much more prevalent influence exercised by foreign investors. It has basically adopted an open door policy to foreign direct investment, which has been primarily attracted by Thailand's low labor costs. The foreign companies, however, have not been required to help the development of indigenous producers. Ownership and management control accordingly have remained in the hands of foreigners, and little technology transfer has taken place. Mardon and Paik, therefore, conclude that Thailand's policy does not prepare it very well to climb the ladder of the international product cycle. Indeed, when Thailand's labor costs become more expensive, investors are likely to relocate their manufacturing plants to other offshore platforms, leaving the country without a strong entrepreneurial and technological base to sustain its recent growth. By comparison, the active intervention by Seoul on behalf of indigenous firms has contributed to the development of such a foundation, thus giving South Korea a major advantage in continuing its ascent into the more capital- and knowledge-intensive stages of the international product cycle. In sum, then, Chapter 8 argues that a state's acts of commission and omission can have a major impact on shaping and promoting industrialization.

Following Mardon and Paik, Kit Machado offers in Chapter 9 a sector-specific study of Malaysia's automobile industry, using it to compare the postulates of statist and dependency theory. He traces the development of this important industry as it evolves under the joint influence of Kuala Lumpur's program of indigenous industrialization and the Japanese automobile firms' strategies to regionalize and globalize their production and investment.

Machado compellingly demonstrates the dynamic interaction between the domestic and foreign forces that underlie Malaysia's efforts to assemble and expand a native industry to manufacture motor vehicles. The commitment by that country's top leadership to launch such an industry merged with the giant Japanese corporations' desire to overcome their potentially deteriorating trade positions caused by yen appreciation, escalating labor costs, and rising foreign protectionism. To some extent, Malaysia's pursuit of a foreign partner to develop the local assembly and production of auto parts was successful. It was able to raise the local content of the Saga to 60 percent, thus entitling this model for concessionary treatment under the General System of Preferences in exporting to the United Kingdom. Yet this relative success in graduating to a higher value-added level in the international division of labor has come at the expense of deepening Malaysia's dependency on Japanese capital and technology, worsening its terms of bilateral trade, and entailing a transfer of managerial responsibility of its auto industry from native Malaysians to Japanese nationals. Indeed, it appears that the Japanese firms have leveraged their local partnerships to gain greater corporate control, to further extend their commercial penetration of the local and regional ASEAN (Association of Southeast Asian Nations) markets, and to exploit the economies of scale by regionalizing their parts production. Thus, Machado argues that bargaining structure and outcome in this particular case continue to be asymmetrically in favor of the Japanese transnational firms, and offers us a further example of how external influences can shape indigenous development.

Finally, in Chapter 10 Clark and Chan summarize the convergent and divergent developmental patterns among the Asian Pacific political economies. They try to identify the key factors that have shaped the historical trajectories of these political economies, and the possible policy lessons and implications to be drawn from past experiences. In particular, structural flexibility, policy adaptability, and conducive historical circumstances seem to have enabled some of the East Asian capitalist countries to achieve rapid economic growth with substantial political stability. These more successful countries, moreover, have been especially adept in bridging the various contending policy lores prevalent in the West and in developing their own mix of heterodox policy packages that cut across conventional ideological lines. Such eclecticism has been an important source of their policy strength and adaptability.

The international structure in the Pacific Basin, therefore, has changed in several fundamental ways within the past decade. First, in the strategic realm the bipolar division into Cold War camps has ended, and there are even growing interactions and negotiations between the halves of the two nations divided by the Cold War—China and Korea. Second, in the economic sphere the global division-of-labor and the old hierarchy of development have shifted considerably. Third, as a consequence of these two structural changes, economic competition among former allies in the "capitalist camp" is becoming much more intense.

These structural changes have presented challenges to the domestic political economies of the nations in the now evolving Pacific Basin; and these challenges have set off an ongoing interaction between domestic processes and international structures. As Akaha and Hsiung argue, these broad shifts in the international environment seemingly necessitate considerable reorientations in the policies of Japan and China, the two large Asian nations at the center of the Pacific Basin. Major structural adjustments are also called for in the United States and, to an even greater extent, in the Soviet Union. The smaller Pacific Rim nations, of course, face significantly stronger pressures for adaptation, while having fewer capabilities to manipulate the international system. For example, Huang's sophisticated statistical analysis showed that, despite the very different natures of their political histories and regime changes, Korea and Taiwan responded fairly similarly to the two oil crises of the 1970s in terms of downsizing their governments. These results certainly suggest the importance of external structural imperatives.

Most of the chapters, however, suggest the importance of domestic factors and processes in shaping how individual countries react to these substantial shifts in the economics and politics in the Pacific Basin. Chan and Clark demonstrate that different patterns of economic activity exist within the region that have been shaped by the U.S. and Japanese colonial (and neocolonial) models and heritage. According to Fry, Thailand's economic success has depended upon its culture and political traditions, which have produced stability and appropriate economic policies without a descent into "hard" authoritarianism. Lam and Lee, furthermore, argue that Chinese culture has created an innovative economy of flexible production and guerrilla capitalism in the Chinese NICs (and, to a lesser extent, in southern coastal China). As a result, small-scale Chinese firms throughout the region have been able to upgrade production far more than most analysts thought possible (e.g., from textiles to low-tech electronics assembly to high-tech computers), thereby promoting the continued international competitiveness of their nations.

Beyond showing the complex interaction of international structure and domestic processes, these findings and arguments are suggestive about the relative importance of three other broad themes in political economy—change versus continuity in the Pacific Basin, external versus internal forces in influencing economic and social outcomes, and the market versus the state in explaining economic performance. For each of these debates, the chapters here imply that extreme commitment to either position is simply not warranted. Despite considerable change in the region, many continuities can be discerned as well; the response to common external forces by these countries is clearly conditioned by their domestic cultures and political economies; and both state and market are evidently important because it is easy to debunk simplistic theories based on one or the other. Thus, we must move beyond unicausal references to market, state, and external dependence to more sophisticated and nuanced combinations of these factors in order to understand the evolving Pacific Basin.

## References

Aggarwal, V. K., R. O. Keohane, and D. B. Yoffie. 1987. "The Dynamics of Negotiated Protectionism." *American Political Science Review* 81: 345–366.

Alam, M. S. 1989. *Governments and Markets in Economic Development Strategies: Lessons from Korea, Taiwan, and Japan*. New York: Praeger.

Amin, S. 1974. *Accumulation on a World Scale: A Critique of the Theory of Underdevelopment*. New York: Monthly Review Press.

Amsden, A. H. 1989. *Asia's Next Giant: South Korea and Late Industrialization*. New York: Oxford University Press.

Amsden, A. H. 1985. "The State and Taiwan's Economic Development." In P. B. Evans, D. Rueschemyer, and T. Skocpol (eds.), *Bringing the State Back In*, pp. 78–104. New York: Cambridge University Press.

Amsden, A. H. 1979. "Taiwan's Economic History: A Case of Etatism and a Challenge to Dependency Theory." *Modern China* 5: 341–379.

Axelrod, R. 1984. *The Evolution of Cooperation*. New York: Basic Books.

Balassa, B. 1981. *The Newly Industrializing Countries in the World Economy*. New York: Pergamon.

Barrett, R. E., and M. K. Whyte. 1982. "Dependency Theory and Taiwan: Analysis of a Deviant Case." *American Journal of Sociology* 87: 1064–1089.

Becker, D. G. 1983. *The New Bourgeoisie and the Limits of Dependency: Mining, Class, and Power in "Revolutionary" Peru*. Princeton, N.J.: Princeton University Press.

Bennett, D. C. and K. E. Sharpe. 1985. *Transnational Corporations Versus the State: The Political Economy of the Mexican Auto Industry*. Princeton, N.J.: Princeton University Press.

Bergsten, C. F., T. Horst, and T. H. Moran. 1978. *American Multinationals and American Interests*. Washington, D.C.: Brookings Institution.

Biersteker, T. J. 1987. *Multinationals, the State, and Control of the Nigerian Economy*. Princeton, N.J.: Princeton University Press.

Bobrow, D. B., and R. T. Kudrle. 1987. "How Middle Powers Can Manage Resource Weakness: Japan and Energy." *World Politics* 39: 536–565.

Bornschier, V., and C. Chase-Dunn. 1985. *Transnational Corporations and Underdevelopment*. New York: Praeger.

Bradford, C. I., Jr., and W. H. Branson (eds.). 1987. *Trade and Structural Change in Pacific Asia*. Chicago: University of Chicago Press.

Bradshaw, Y., and Z. Tshandu. 1990. "Foreign Capital Penetration, State Intervention, and Development of Sub-Saharan Africa." *International Studies Quarterly* 34: 229–251.

Calleo, D. 1982. *The Imperious Economy*. Cambridge, Mass.: Harvard

University Press.

Caporaso, J. A. 1981. "Industrialization in the Periphery: The Evolving Global Division of Labor." *International Studies Quarterly* 25: 347–384.

Cardoso, F. H., and E. Faletto. 1979. *Dependency and Development in Latin America*. Berkeley: University of California Press.

Chan, S. 1990. *East Asian Dynamism: Growth, Order, and Security in the Pacific Region*. 1990. Boulder, Colo.: Westview.

Chan, S. 1987. "The Mouse That Roared: Taiwan's Management of Trade Relations with the U.S." *Comparative Political Studies* 20: 251–292.

Chan, S., and C. Clark. 1992. *Flexibility, Foresight, and Fortuna in Taiwan's Development: Navigating Between Scylla and Charybdis*. London: Routledge.

Chan, S., C. Clark, and D. R. Davis. 1990. "State Entrepreneurship, Foreign Investment, Export Expansion, and Economic Growth: Granger Causality in Taiwan's Development." *Journal of Conflict Resolution* 34: 102–129.

Chase-Dunn, C. 1989. *Global Formation: Structures of the World Economy*. New York: Basil Blackwell.

Choucri, N., and R. C. North. 1975. *Nations in Conflict: National Growth and International Violence*. San Francisco: Freeman.

Clark, C. 1989. *Taiwan's Development: Implications for Contending Political Economy Paradigms*. New York: Greenwood.

Collier, D. (ed.). 1979. *The New Authoritarianism in Latin America*. Princeton, N.J.: Princeton University Press.

Deutsch, K. W., S. A. Burrell, R. A. Kann, M. Lee, Jr., M. Lichtenman, R. E. Lindgren, F. L. Loewenheim, and R. W. Van Wagenen. 1957. *Political Community and the North Atlantic Area: International Organization in the Light of Historical Experience*. New York: Greenwood.

Deyo, F. C. 1989. *Beneath the Miracle: Labor Subordination in the New Asian Industrialism*. Berkeley: University of California Press.

Deyo, F. C. (ed.). 1987. *The Political Economy of the New Asian Industrialism*. Ithaca, N.Y.: Cornell University Press.

Deyo, F. C. 1981. *Dependent Development and Industrial Order: An Asian Case Study*. New York: Praeger.

Doran, C. F. 1977. *Myth, Oil, and Politics: Introduction to the Political Economy of Petroleum*. New York: Free Press.

Doran, C. F., G. Modelski, and C. Clark. 1983. *North/South Relations: Studies of Dependency Reversal*. New York: Praeger.

Encarnation, D. J. 1989. *Dislodging Multinationals: India's Strategy in Comparative Perspective*. Ithaca, N.Y.: Cornell University Press.

Evans, P. B. 1987. "Class, State, and Dependence in East Asia: Lessons for Latin Americanists." In F. C. Deyo (ed.), *The Political Economy of the New Asian Industrialism*, pp. 203–226. Ithaca, N.Y.: Cornell University Press.

Evans, P. B. 1979. *Dependent Development: The Alliance of Multinational, State, and Local Capital in Brazil*. Princeton, N.J.: Princeton University Press.

Evans, P. B., D. Rueschemyer, and T. Skocpol (eds.). 1985. *Bringing the State Back In*. New York: Cambridge University Press.

Fajnzylber, F. 1990. "The United States and Japan As Models of Industrialization." In G. Gereffi and D. Wyman (eds.), *Manufacturing Miracles: Paths of Industrialization in Latin America and East Asia*, pp. 323–352. Princeton, N.J.: Princeton University Press.

Frank, A. G. 1969. *Capitalism and Underdevelopment in Latin America*. New York: Monthly Review Press.

Friedman, D. 1988. *The Misunderstood Miracle: Industrial Management and*

*Political Change in Japan.* Ithaca, N.Y.: Cornell University Press.

Gereffi, G., 1982. *The Pharmaceutical Industry and Dependency in the Third World.* Princeton, N.J.: Princeton University Press.

Gereffi, G., and D. Wyman (eds.). 1990. *Manufacturing Miracles: Paths of Industrialization in Latin America and East Asia.* Princeton, N.J.: Princeton University Press.

Gerschenkron, A. 1966. *Economic Backwardness in Historical Perspective.* Cambridge, Mass.: Harvard University Press.

Gilpin, R. 1987. *The Political Economy of International Relations.* Princeton, N.J.: Princeton University Press.

Gilpin, R. 1981. *War and Change in World Politics.* New York: Cambridge University Press.

Gold, T. B. 1986. *State and Society in the Taiwan Miracle.* Armonk, N.Y.: Sharpe.

Goodsell, C. T. 1974. *American Corporations and Peruvian Politics.* Cambridge, Mass.: Harvard University Press.

Grieco, J. M. 1984. *Between Dependency and Autonomy: India's Experience with the International Computer Industry.* Berkeley: University of California Press.

Haggard, S. 1990. *Pathways from the Periphery: The Politics of Growth in the Newly Industrializing Countries.* Ithaca, N.Y.: Cornell University Press.

Haggard, S., and C. I. Moon (eds.). 1989. *Pacific Dynamics: The International Politics of Industrial Change.* Boulder, Colo.: Westview.

Haggard, S., and C. I. Moon. 1983. "The South Korean State in the International Economy: Liberal, Dependent or Mercantile?" In J. G. Ruggie (ed.), *The Antinomies of Interdependence: National Welfare and the International Division of Labor,* pp. 131–189. New York: Columbia University Press.

Harding, H. 1987. *China's Second Revolution: Reform after Mao.* Washington, D.C.: Brookings Institution.

Hawes, G. 1987. *The Philippine State and the Marcos Regime: The Politics of Export.* Ithaca, N.Y.: Cornell University Press.

Higgott, R. 1987. "Australia: Economic Crises and the Politics of Regional Economic Adjustment." In R. Robison, K. Hewison, and R. Higgott (eds.), *Southeast Asia in the 1980s: The Politics of Economic Crisis,* pp. 177–217. Sydney: Allen & Unwin.

Higgott, R., and R. Robison (eds.). 1985. *Southeast Asia: Essays in the Political Economy of Structural Change.* London: Routledge and Kegan Paul.

Hill, H. 1988. *Foreign Investment and Industrialization in Indonesia.* New York: Oxford University Press.

Hirschman, A. O. 1945. *National Power and the Structure of Foreign Trade: Studies in International Political Economy.* Berkeley: University of California Press.

Hofheinz, R., Jr., and K. E. Calder. 1982. *The Eastasia Edge.* New York: Basic Books.

Huang, C. 1989. "The State and Foreign Investment: The Cases of Taiwan and Singapore." *Comparative Political Studies* 22: 93–121.

Hufbauer, G. C. 1990. "Background Paper." In *The Foreign Trade Debate: Reports of the Twentieth Century Fund Task Force on the Future of American Trade Policy,* pp. 37–226. New York: Priority Press.

Indorf, H. H., and P. M. Mayerchak. 1989. *Linkage or Bondage: U.S. Economic Relations with the ASEAN Region.* New York: Greenwood.

Inglehart, R. 1990. *Cultural Shift in Advanced Industrial Society.* Princeton, N.J.: Princeton University Press.

Jackman, R. W. 1982. "Dependence on Foreign Investment and Economic Growth in the Third World." *World Politics* 34: 175–196.

Jenkins, R. 1987. *Transnational Corporations and the Latin American Automobile Industry*. Pittsburgh: University of Pittsburgh Press.

Johnson, C. 1982. *MITI and the Japanese Miracle: The Growth of Industrial Policy, 1925–1975*. Stanford, Calif.: Stanford University Press.

Johnson, C. 1981. "Introduction—The Taiwan Model." In J. C. Hsiung (ed.), *Contemporary Republic of China: The Taiwan Experience, 1950-1980*, pp. 9–18. New York: Praeger.

Jones, L. P., and I. Sakong. 1980. *Government, Business, and Entrepreneurship in Economic Development: The Korean Case*. Cambridge, Mass.: Harvard University Press.

Kahler, M. 1986. *The Politics of International Debt*. Ithaca, N.Y.: Cornell University Press.

Kennedy, P. M. 1987. *The Rise and Fall of the Great Powers: Economic Change and Military Conflict from 1500 to 2000*. New York: Random House.

Keohane, R. O. 1984. *After Hegemony: Cooperation and Discord in the World Political Economy*. Princeton, N.J.: Princeton University Press.

Keohane, R. O. 1980. "The Theory of Hegemonic Stability and Changes in International Economic Regimes," In O. R. Holsti, R. M. Siverson, and A. George (eds.), *Change in the International System*, pp. 131–162. Boulder, Colo.: Westview.

Keohane, R. O., and J. S. Nye, Jr. 1989. *Power and Interdependence*. Glenview, Ill.: Scotts Foresman.

Kindleberger, C. P. 1981. "Dominance and Leadership in the International Economy: Exploitation, Public Goods, and Free Rides." *International Studies Quarterly* 25: 242–254.

Kindleberger, C. P. 1973. *The World in Depression, 1929–1939*. Berkeley: University of California Press.

Krasner, S. D. 1978. *Defending the National Interest: Raw Materials Investment and U.S. Foreign Policy*. Princeton, N.J.: Princeton University Press.

Kumar, K. 1982. "Third World Multinationals: A Growing Force in International Relations." *International Studies Quarterly* 26: 397–424.

Lam, D. K. K. 1988. "Guerilla Capitalism: Export Oriented Firms and the Economic Miracle in Taiwan (1973–1987)." Paper presented at the annual meeting of the American Association for Chinese Studies, Palo Alto, Stanford University.

Leys, C. 1974. *Underdevelopment in Kenya: The Political Economy of Neo-Colonialism, 1964–1971*. Berkeley: University of California Press.

Lindblom, C. E. 1965. *The Intelligence of Democracy: Decision Making Through Mutual Adjustment*. New York: Free Press.

Linder, S. 1986. *The Pacific Century: Economic and Political Consequences of Asian-Pacific Dynamism*. Stanford, Calif.: Stanford University Press.

Lowi, T. J. 1979. *The End of Liberalism*. New York: Norton.

Malloy, J. M. (ed.). 1987. *Authoritarianism and Corporatism in Latin America*. Pittsburgh: University of Pittsburgh Press.

Mardon, R. 1990. "The State and Effective Control of Foreign Capital: The Case of South Korea." *World Politics* 43: 111–138.

Merritt, R. 1966. *Symbols of American Community*. New Haven, Conn.: Yale University Press.

Miller, N. R. 1983. "Pluralism and Social Choice." *American Political Science Review* 77: 734–747.

Mirza, H. 1986. *Multinationals and the Growth of the Singapore Economy.* New York: St. Martin's.

Modelski, G. 1987. *Long Cycles in World Politics.* Seattle: University of Washington Press.

Moon, C. I. 1990. "Beyond Statism: Rethinking the Political Economy of Growth in South Korea." *International Studies Notes* 15: 24–27.

Moon, C. I. 1989. "Conclusion: A Dissenting View on the Pacific Future." In S. Haggard and C. I. Moon (eds.), *Pacific Dynamics: The International Politics of Industrial Change,* pp. 359–374. Boulder, Colo.: Westview.

Moon, C. I. 1988. "The Demise of a Developmentalist State? Neoconservative Reforms and Political Consequences in South Korea." *Journal of Developing Societies* 4: 67–84.

Moran, T. H. 1978. "Multinational Corporations and Dependency: A Dialogue for *Dependentistas* and Non-*Dependentistas.*" *International Organization* 32: 79–100.

Moran, T. H. 1974. *Multinational Corporations and the Politics of Dependence: Copper in Chile.* Princeton, N.J.: Princeton University Press.

Morawetz, D. 1981. *Why the Emperor's New Clothes Are Not Made in Colombia? A Case Study in Latin American and East Asian Manufactured Exports.* New York: Oxford University Press.

Moulder, F. V. 1977. *Japan, China and the Modern World Economy: Toward a Reinterpretation of East Asian Development ca. 1600 to ca. 1918.* London: Cambridge University Press.

Myrdal, G. 1968. *Asian Drama: An Inquiry into the Poverty of Nations.* New York: Pantheon.

Nau, H. R. 1990. *The Myth of America's Decline: Leading the World Economy into the 1990s.* New York: Oxford University Press.

Newfarmer, R. S. 1980. *Transnational Conglomerates and the Economies of Dependent Development.* Greenwich, Conn.: JAI Press.

Nye, J. S., Jr. 1990. *Bound to Lead: The Changing Nature of American Power.* New York: Basic Books.

Odell, J. S. 1985. "The Outcomes of International Trade Conflicts: The U.S. and South Korea, 1960–1981." *International Studies Quarterly* 29: 263–286.

Okimoto, D. I. 1989. *Between MITI and the Market: Japanese Industrial Policy for High Technology.* Stanford, Calif.: Stanford University Press.

Olson, M., Jr. 1982. *The Rise and Decline of Nations: Economic Growth, Stagflation, and Social Rigidities.* New Haven, Conn.: Yale University Press.

Olson, M., Jr. 1963. "Rapid Growth as a Destabilizing Force." *Journal of Economic History* 23: 529–552.

Organski, A. F. K., and J. Kugler. 1980. *The War Ledger.* Chicago: University of Chicago Press.

Ozawa, T. 1979. *Multinationalism: Japanese Style.* Princeton, N.J.: Princeton University Press.

Phillips, K. 1990. *The Politics of Rich and Poor: Wealth and the American Electorate in the Reagan Aftermath.* New York: Random House.

Prestowitz, C., Jr. 1988. *Trading Places: How We Allowed Japan to Take the Lead.* New York: Basic Books.

Rabushka, A. 1979. *Hong Kong: A Study in Economic Freedom.* Chicago: University of Chicago Press.

Reich, S. 1989. "Roads to Follow: Regulating Direct Foreign Investment." *International Organization* 43: 543–584.

Robison, R. 1986. *Indonesia: The Rise of Capital.* Sydney: Allen & Unwin.

Robison, R., K. Hewison, and R. Higgott (eds.). 1985. *Southeast Asia in the 1980s: The Politics of Economic Crisis.* Sydney: Allen & Unwin.

Rodan, G. 1989. *The Political Economy of Singapore's Industrialization: National State and International Capital.* New York: St. Martin's.

Rosecrance, R. N. 1986. *The Rise of the Trading State: Commerce and Conquest in the Modern World.* New York: Basic Books.

Russett, B. M. 1985. "The Mysterious Case of Vanishing Hegemony: Or, Is Mark Twain Really Dead?" *International Organization* 39: 207–232.

Servan-Schreiber, J. J. 1968. *The American Challenge.* New York: Atheneum.

Singer, J. D., S. Bremer, and J. Stuckey. 1972. "Capability Distribution, Uncertainty, and Major Power War, 1820–1965." In B. M. Russett (ed.), *Peace, War, and Numbers,* pp. 19–48. Beverly Hills, Calif.: Sage.

Snidal, D. 1985. "The Limits of Hegemonic Stability Theory." *International Organization* 37: 579–614.

Stallings, B., and R. Kaufman (eds.). 1989. *Debt and Democracy in Latin America.* Boulder, Colo.: Westview.

Stepan, A. 1978. *The State and Society: Peru in Comparative Perspective.* Princeton, N.J.: Princeton University Press.

Strange, S. 1987. "The Persistent Myth of Lost Hegemony." *International Organization* 41: 551–574.

Tugwell, F. 1975. *The Politics of Oil in Venezuela.* Stanford, Calif.: Stanford University Press.

Tyson, L. D. 1990. "Managed Trade: Making the Best of Second Best." In R. Z. Lawrence and C. L. Schultze (eds.), *An American Trade Strategy: Options for the 1990s,* pp. 142–185. Washington, D.C.: Brookings Institution.

Vernon, R. 1971. *Sovereignty at Bay: The Multinational Spread of U.S. Enterprises.* New York: Basic Books.

Vernon, R. 1966. "International Investment and International Trade in the Product Cycle." *Quarterly Journal of Economics* 80: 190–207.

Vogel, E. F. 1979. *Japan As Number One.* New York: Harper & Row.

Wade, R. 1990. *Governing the Market: Economic Theory and the Role of Government in East Asian Industrialization.* Princeton, N.J.: Princeton University Press.

Wade, R. 1988. "State Intervention in 'Outward-Looking' Development: Neoclassical Theory and Taiwanese Practice." In G. White (ed.), *Development States in East Asia,* pp. 30–67. London: Macmillan.

Wallerstein, I. 1974. *The Modern World-System: Capitalist Agriculture and the Origins of the European World-Economy in the Sixteenth Century.* New York: Academic Press.

Wellons, P. A. 1987. *Passing the Buck: Banks, Governments and Third World Debt.* Boston: Harvard Business School.

Whiting, A. S. 1981. *Siberian Development and East Asia: Threat or Promise?* Stanford, Calif.: Stanford University Press.

Wiarda, H. J. 1990. "The Politics of Third World Debt." *PS* 21: 411–418.

Wiarda, H. J. 1987. *Latin America at the Crossroads: Debt, Development, and the Future.* Boulder, Colo.: Westview.

Wiarda, H. J. 1981. *Corporatism and National Development in Latin America.* Boulder, Colo.: Westview.

Yoon, Y. K. 1990. "The Political Economy of Transition: Japanese Foreign Direct Investment in the 1980s." *World Politics* 43: 1–27.

Yoffie, D. B. 1983. *Power and Protectionism: Strategies of the Newly Industrializing Countries.* New York: Columbia University Press.

# 2

# The Rise of the East Asian NICs: Confucian Capitalism, Status Mobility, and Developmental Legacy

## Steve Chan & Cal Clark

The structure of the global economy has changed considerably over the past several decades. Perhaps most important, the economic position of the "core" or advanced industrial societies has been strongly challenged by the rise of newly industrializing countries (NICs) from the Third World "periphery." Instances of industrialization can be found in various parts of the Third World, such as Argentina, Brazil, and India, but the most dynamic and successful NICs thus far have clearly been in East Asia. Several recent studies (e.g., Balassa, 1988; Gereffi and Wyman, 1989; Haggard, 1990) have argued that the political institutions, social coalitions, and resource endowments of the East Asian NICs differed substantially from the conditions in Latin America and, thereby, created a different and more successful development strategy.

This chapter examines the role of the East Asian NICs in the global economy. It asks whether there has been any major recent change in the international division of labor, whether the external constraints pinpointed by dependency theory may work in ways that have not been generally recognized, and whether the East Asian NICs constitute a special case of "Confucian capitalism." The first section discusses how the rise of the NICs has affected perspectives on the political economy of development; the second uses cluster analysis to depict the structure of the world economy in 1981 and 1988; the third focuses upon the similarities and differences among the Pacific Basin political economies; and the fourth is a brief conclusion.

To anticipate, we argue two points pertinent to the ongoing debate about the political economy of development. First, we contend that the international division of labor should be treated as a dynamic rather than static concept, and one that is subject to substantial transformation within a short interval. Thus, contrary to the classical dependency formulation, status mobility and role graduation are possible for the so-called periphery countries. Second, and in conformity with the dependency perspective, we contend that the development efforts and choices of these late industrializers have been seriously constrained by the legacies of heavy foreign economic, political, and social penetration. The history of this penetration has had a profound and enduring influence on these countries' respective class formations, political coalitions, and patterns of economic production, consumption, and distribution, which in turn have shaped their development strategies. We demonstrate the general validity of these arguments through cluster analysis of developmental patterns at the global level as well as among the Pacific Rim countries. Therefore, our analysis shows that important changes and continuities can coexist in the politics and economics of development.

## The Rise of the NICs and the Political Economy of Development

During the past two and half decades, a number of developing countries have undergone comparatively rapid and sustained economic growth and industrial modernization. As a result, some of these NICs, such as Singapore, Hong Kong, and Taiwan, have now achieved per capita income levels that would entitle them to be considered "high-income economies" by the World Bank's standards. The physical quality of life index (PQLI, comprised of the three indicators of average life expectancy, adult literacy, and infant mortality) shows that these countries have already achieved the norm among the OECD (Organization of Economic Cooperation and Development) members.

Although lagging behind on per capita income and/or PQLI, several other NICs have made greater progress toward industrial "deepening" in their effort to launch second-stage import substitution aimed at the development of an indigenous capability for producing various capital and intermediate goods. Brazil, Mexico, and South Korea have been relatively successful in their push to establish domestic heavy and chemical industries—albeit at the cost of heavy foreign indebtedness. In view of the rising tide of foreign protectionism and their own changing comparative advantage, these countries (as well as those NICs mentioned earlier) have increasingly tried to raise the capital and technology content of their manufactured exports in order to maintain and improve their trade competitiveness.

Poised behind these "first-wave NICs" are later comers such as Malaysia, Portugal, Thailand, Sri Lanka, and even China. They are eager to court foreign direct investment and to leverage their low labor costs to carve out an export niche overseas. Already, they have scored impressive export gains in light manufactures (e.g., textiles, footwear, and electrical appliances), in which the first-generation NICs have experienced declining comparative advantage.

The superior economic performance of the East Asian NICs has led scholars and policymakers to search for an "East Asian development model" (e.g., Balassa, 1988; Berger and Hsiao, 1988; Hofheinz and Calder, 1982; Johnson, 1981; Kuznets, 1988). Rapid development in East Asia has evidently exhibited a number of similar economic, social, and political features. Economic strategy has generally emphasized expanding exports and finding niches of comparative advantage in the global economy, rather than using protectionism to pursue import substitution or the reliance upon internal markets. In terms of sectoral phasing, most of the countries have moved upward along the international product cycle from light to heavy to high-technology industries over fairly brief time spans, indicating that their comparative advantages are far from static. The East Asian societies have been marked by comparatively equal distributions of income, opportunities for upward mobility, strong proclivities for entrepreneurship, and a high emphasis on education to promote the creation of human capital. Politically, the state has taken a leading role in structuring the economy and in targeting leading sectors (Hong Kong excepted); most of the countries have been marked by a high level of political stability that is remarkable in the developing world; and authoritarian governments of varying hues and rationales have predominated (political life in even democratic Japan and Singapore is dominated by one continuously ruling party). These economic, social, and political characteristics, in addition, are undergirded by the region's Confucian culture, whose values promote respect for authority, merit-based mobility, family entrepreneurship, and, in Japan, "groupist" dynamics that seem well suited for large-scale corporations and bureaucracies (Berger and Hsiao, 1988; Chan, 1990; Cheng and Haggard, 1987; Cumings, 1984; Deyo, 1987; Fei, 1986; Gold, 1986; Haggard and Moon, 1989; Hofheinz and Calder, 1982; Johnson, 1982; Linder, 1986; Lockwood, 1965; Pye, 1985; Vogel, 1979).

The emergence of the East Asian and other NICs has coincided with the relative economic decline of the industrial leaders. The economic ailments of the United States—including declining productivity, persistent fiscal deficit, and mounting trade imbalance—have been well publicized. The United States shares with Britain the process of deindustrialization, whereby manufactured goods are increasingly imported from abroad rather than produced at home. In order to pay for these imports, the United States has become insistent that its trade partners buy more oranges, wheat, beef, and tobacco in return. Such a role reversal would not have been expected by orthodox dependency theorists (Amin, 1974; Frank, 1969; Galtung, 1971). In the classical formulation of this perspective, the international political economy is based on a sharp and hierarchical division between the "topdogs" and "underdogs." The topdogs—

or the core countries—are supposed to specialize in the more lucrative manufacturing activities. Conversely, the underdogs—or the periphery countries—are supposed to be condemned to the role of suppliers of foodstuff and raw materials for the core. This differentiation between the developed and underdeveloped nations drawn by the classical dependency formulation has become increasingly blurred by the rise of the NICs. The rapid industrial ascendance of the latter countries shows that economic stagnation is not the inevitable fate for the Third World countries and that status mobility and "role graduation" are possible. In response, several scholars working within the dependency tradition (e.g., Cardoso, 1973; Evans, 1979; Gereffi, 1983) constructed models of "dependent development," which showed how industrialization was possible in the periphery, even though this process was highly dependent upon the core economies and was distorted in terms of its economic and social consequences.

If the classical dependency views of a rather static and dichotomized world system are subject to criticism, other aspects of this theoretical tradition continue to offer useful insights about the nature and evolution of the international division of labor (Caporaso, 1981; Higgott and Robison, 1985). This can be seen in the debate over the East Asian development model, which is rather ironic because dependency theory per se is not normally associated with either side.

In light of the recent economic successes of the East Asian NICs, two competing explanations in particular have received much scholarly and policy attention. On the one hand, adherents to the neoclassical approach to economic development emphasize the "magic of the marketplace" (Balassa, 1981; Linder, 1986). They deduce from the "East Asian miracles" the importance of "getting prices right," which is often equated with a policy of export-oriented industrialization (as opposed to a policy of import-substitution industrialization). On the other hand, proponents of governmental leadership in late-industrializing efforts argue that the East Asian miracles have been due to the strong and steady guiding hand of their respective developmental states (Alam, 1989; Amsden, 1989; Gold, 1986; Johnson, 1982; Jones and Sakong, 1980; Wade, 1990; White, 1988). Official attempts to overcome market imperfections and, significantly, also to deliberately distort market conditions in some desired directions (e.g., with respect to credit allocation, foreign exchange rate, and labor cost) are seen to be critical in these NICs' successful pursuit and creation of dynamic comparative advantage in the international product cycle.

In contrast to the *dependentistas*, both the neoclassical and statist analysts tend to give more weight to domestic than foreign factors in late industrialization. Moreover, to the extent that international exchanges play an important part in such industrialization, countries are taken to be autonomous units following their natural (for the neoclassicalists) or created (for the statists) advantages. The extent to which prior foreign influences and external networking constitute critical initial conditions and persistent constraints that shape the subsequent nature of these exchanges is often not analyzed sufficiently. The extent to which current development strategies, consumption patterns, and class and other institutional alignments are influenced by and embedded in the histories of external trade, cultural hegemony (or subjugation), institutional development, and elite assimilation or cooptation also is not sufficiently addressed. In these regards, the dependency perspective is still useful in reminding us that the legacies of foreign economic, political, and ideological ties tend to have powerful and enduring influences on individual Third World countries' current development choices and patterns.

Our perspective, therefore, argues for the coexistence of elements of change and continuity in the international political economy. On the one hand, this system is characterized by dynamic comparative advantages, changing product cycles, and an evolving division of labor. Status mobility and even role reversal are possible if not easy in this system. The prevalence of references to the "Dutch disease" and the "British disease" in the literature indicates that commercial competitiveness and industrial leadership are hardly static concepts to be achieved once and for all. Conversely, recent popular books featuring titles such as *Japan As Number One: Lessons for America* (Vogel, 1979); *Trading Places: How We Allowed Japan to Take the Lead* (Prestowitz, 1988); *Asia's Next Giant: South Korea and Late Industrialization* (Amsden, 1989); and *The Eastasia Edge* (Hofheinz and Calder, 1982) certainly bring the point home that economic laggards are not necessarily forever locked into a position of inferiority, and that it is possible for them to catch up.

The possibility for such status adjustment, however, has to be understood in the context of opportunities as well as constraints created by the continuities in a developing country's neocolonial relations with its core associate(s). Positively, such continuities offer the chance for coattail growth, learning by imitation, and orderly "graduation" to successive stages of industrial deepening and maturation. Negatively, these ties engender enduring ideological "baggage," entrenched socioeconomic interests, and precarious "pacts of domination" that reduce the officials' policy space and often preclude the adoption of certain avenues of national development because of the opposition from powerful distributional coalitions (Olson, 1982).

We demonstrate the analytic utility of these arguments by resorting to two sets of cluster analysis of the relevant economic indicators of individual countries. This statistical technique allows us to group together items (in this case, countries) based on the similarity of their scores on a set of defining characteristics. We first undertake a snapshot of the global division of labor at the beginning of the decade of the 1980s (1981), and then another one toward its end (1988). This procedure enables us to determine whether the NICs, especially the East Asian ones, occupied a distinct niche in the international division of labor, and whether there is evidence of continued mobility in the global economy during this decade. Then a second round of cluster analysis of just the Pacific countries at the end of the 1980s is used to test a recent argument about the different development strategies among the NICs.

## The Structure of the
## International Political Economy in the 1980s

Our empirical indicators are those commonly nominated in the literature (e.g., Balassa, 1981; Bradford and Branson, 1987; Gereffi and Wyman, 1989; Naya, 1987), and are especially selected to identify the emergence of NICs. These countries are characterized by their middle-income levels in global ranking, rapidly expanding gross domestic product (GDP), and a comparatively high rate of investment necessary to sustain this growth. Although these countries have placed varying emphases on export expansion versus import substitution as a development strategy (Gereffi and Wyman, 1990), their export portfolios have tended to follow the dynamic logic of the international product cycle. We therefore also examine the respective shares of primary commodities, minerals and fuels, textiles, and machinery and transport equipment in each country's total exports in order to indicate the source of its international competitiveness.

Except for Taiwan (CEPD, 1989), all the pertinent data have been derived from the World Bank (1990, 1989, 1983). Naturally, the sample of countries has been limited to those with available data for the indicators just mentioned. Variations in data availability account for the discrepancies in the spatial coverage between 1981 and 1988. After some experimentation, we settled for organizing the countries into six clusters for both the beginning and the end of the 1980s because this distribution of the data seems to provide the most efficient and valid picture of the international economic hierarchy. The results of the cluster analysis are presented in Table 2.1.

The patterns in Table 2.1 are suggestive of the incorporation of individual countries in the international division of labor and their respective positions in the global political economy. A comparison of the two temporal observations (in 1981 and 1988, the latter being the most recent time period with available data) in turn helps to establish the extent of dynamic adjustment that has taken place in the international division of labor within a rather short interval. In their broad outlines the empirical patterns in Table

2.1 conform to our general expectations of change and continuity, but the assignment of individual countries in specific categories is sometimes quite unexpected.

At the beginning of the 1980s, the world was divided, in essence, into two large groups of developed and developing nations. Seven other Third World nations comprised four residual categories, one of them clearly representing a unique configuration of Confucian capitalism. In just eight years, this structure of international economies changed very significantly. First, both of the large groups of developed and developing countries were significantly reduced in size as they became more similar or cohesive in their economic characteristics. Second, the small 1980 group of three Confucian capitalist states became subsumed within a much broader group of NICs. Third, the size of some of the other residual groups expanded slightly as well.

A major group in 1981 is comprised mostly of the members of the OECD, whose joint characteristics were high per capita income, moderate rates of GDP growth, and generally diversified trade portfolios. We were somewhat surprised by the assignment of several middle-income countries to this cluster of mature industrial economies. Among these surprises were Singapore, Mexico, Yugoslavia, and especially Yemen (Arab Republic). An examination of the data profiles of these countries reveals two areas of commonality with their more advanced OECD associates: substantial rates of capital investment and, even more remarkably, rather high shares of machines and transport equipment in their export composition.

By far the largest group of countries identified by the 1981 data point to a cluster of developing countries that had comparatively low income and that tended to specialize in the export of agricultural commodities or industrial minerals. Beyond these commonalities, the countries in this group are quite heterogeneous. We find several middle-income Latin American countries, such as Argentina and Brazil, as well as a number of low-income but large Asian economies, such as China and India, even though both of these subsets possessed rather extensive socioeconomic infrastructure and industrial capabilities. They shared membership in this cluster with the smaller and much less industrialized African countries. One notable and somewhat unexpected country placement in this category is New Zealand. Our analysis found that despite its fairly high per capita income, its low GDP growth rate and emphasis on agricultural exports made this country structurally more similar to the Third World developing countries than the OECD members with which it is typically associated.

Another group revealed by the 1981 data clearly identifies three East Asian NICs—South Korea, Taiwan, and Hong Kong—as a distinct cluster.

They were characterized by extraordinarily high rates of GDP growth as well as domestic investment (and reinvestment) rates to sustain this growth. Moreover, they showed a high level of manufacturing content in their exports, both at the "low" end of textiles and at the "high" end of machines and transport equipment. This cluster provides empirical support for arguing the existence of an East Asian model of economic development.

---

Table 2.1    Global Division of Labor: 1981 and 1988

---

| 1981 | 1988 |
|------|------|
| Developing Countries | Developing Countries |
| Argentina | Argentina |
| Bolivia | Australia |
| Brazil | Benin |
| Burkina Faso | Burkina Faso |
| Cameroon | Burundi |
| Central African Republic | Central African Republic |
| Chile | Colombia |
| China | Costa Rica |
| Colombia | Dominican Republic |
| Congo | Ecuador |
| Costa Rica | El Salvador |
| Dominican Republic | Ethiopia |
| Ecuador | Ghana |
| Egypt | Guatemala |
| El Salvador | Honduras |
| Ethiopia | Ivory Coast |
| Greece | Kenya |
| Guatemala | Madagascar |
| Honduras | Malawi |
| India | Mali |
| Indonesia | Mauritania |
| Ivory Coast | Mozambique |
| Jamaica | New Zealand |
| Kenya | Paraguay |
| Liberia | Rwanda |
| Libya | Senegal |
| Madagascar | Somalia |
| Malawi | Sudan |
| Malaysia | Tanzania |
| Morocco | Uganda |
| Nepal | Uruguay |
| New Zealand | Zimbabwe |
| Nicaragua | |

Table 2.1 *(continued)*

| 1981 | 1988 |
|---|---|

Nigeria
Panama
Papua New Guinea
Paraguay
Peru
Philippines
Portugal
Senegal
South Africa
Sri Lanka
Sudan
Syria
Tanzania
Thailand
Togo
Trinidad and Tobago
Tunisia
Turkey
Uruguay
Venezuela

Textile Exporters
Bangladesh
Pakistan

Developed Countries
Australia
Austria
Belgium
Canada
Denmark
Finland
France
Germany, West
Hungary
Ireland
Israel
Italy
Japan
Mexico
Netherlands
Norway
Singapore
Spain
Sweden

Textile Exporters
Bangladesh
Haiti
Mauritius
Pakistan

Mineral Exporters
Algeria
Bolivia
Cameroon
Chile
Congo
Egypt
Gabon
Indonesia
Jordan
Kuwait
Niger
Nigeria
Norway
Papua New Guinea
Peru
Saudi Arabia
Syria
Togo
Trinidad and Tobago
United Arab Emirates
Venezuela
Yemen Arab Republic
Zambia
Zaire

Stagnant Socialism
Laos
Poland

NICs
Brazil
China
Greece
Hong Kong
Hungary
India
Ireland
Israel

Table 2.1    Global Division of Labor: 1981 and 1988

| 1981 | 1988 |
|------|------|
| Switzerland | Jamaica |
| United Kingdom | Korea, South |
| United States | Malaysia |
| Yemen, Arab Republic | Mexico |
| Yugoslavia | Morocco |
| | Nepal |
| East Asian NICs | Philippines |
| Hong Kong | Portugal |
| Korea, South | Singapore |
| Taiwan | South Africa |
| | Spain |
| Oil Exporters 1 | Sri Lanka |
| Saudi Arabia | Taiwan |
| | Thailand |
| Oil Exporters 2 | Tunisia |
| Kuwait | Turkey |
| | Yugoslavia |
| | |
| | Developed Countries |
| | Austria |
| | Belgium |
| | Canada |
| | Denmark |
| | Finland |
| | France |
| | Germany, West |
| | Italy |
| | Japan |
| | Netherlands |
| | Sweden |
| | Switzerland |
| | United Kingdom |
| | United States |

A fourth cluster identified for 1981 has only two members: Bangladesh and Pakistan. The distinguishing features of these two South Asian countries were their low income levels and the comparatively high concentration of textiles in their export portfolios. Lacking either cash crops or strategic minerals to sell to the rest of the world, these countries have focused on this light manufacturing requiring relatively high labor input and low technology and capital input. Textiles production has traditionally constituted an integral part of the first stage (or the "easy" phase) of import substitution, as well as having played an important role in contributing to the initial export push of previous waves of NICs (including Japan, the first non-Western NIC).

Finally, the 1981 data identify Saudi Arabia and Kuwait as two special and, indeed, unique cases without comparable counterparts. The major differences between these two oil exporters appear to be that whereas Kuwait had a much higher per capita income than Saudi Arabia, it experienced substantially lower GDP growth during 1970–1981.

Parallel to the clusters derived from the 1981 data, Table 2.1 presents the data patterns uncovered for 1988 using the same indicators. One constellation suggested by the 1988 data identifies the advanced industrial economies, which share the common characteristics of high per capita income, moderate GDP growth rates, and comparatively high shares of manufactured exports. Between 1981 and 1988, this club had become more exclusive, as it was limited to nations normally considered mature industrial societies.

The principal group of developing countries is considerably smaller than it was at the beginning of the decade, as a significant number of its members moved to join the ranks of the NICs as described below. Perhaps the most remarkable finding regarding this cluster is the addition in its membership of Australia. The economic structure of this country as well as that of Argentina and New Zealand had become rather similar to the typical profile of Third World countries with low economic growth and heavy reliance on primary commodities in foreign exchange.

In 1986, Australia's treasurer reportedly described his country as a "Fledgling Banana Republic" (Higgott, 1987: 178). Although injudicious, this characterization was not without factual support in regard to the unfolding process of the "Latin Americanization" of that country as it faced mounting economic challenges due to falling commodity prices, rising debt burden, and inefficient and uncompetitive industries. Canberra's attention had increasingly been diverted from growth-creation concerns to balance-of-payments headaches. In a typical syndrome described by the dependency perspective, the country found itself having to sell more primary products and borrow more external loans in order to pay for its imports. To compound its predicament in an ironic reversal of "core-periphery" trade relations, Australia found itself competing increasingly with the commodity exports from the European Economic Community and the United States, who had been urging Japan and the East Asian NICs to import more wheat, beef, wool, and coal in order to balance their respective bilateral trade deficits. Finally, although the Australians had hoped that foreign direct investment would give their economy a boost, such investment failed to materialize in sufficient quantity.

Moreover, multinational corporations generally bypassed Australia's manufacturing sector, and directed their investment overwhelmingly to mineral extraction instead—a situation that would again alarm dependency theorists.

Therefore, the deleterious patterns of economic stagnation, declining terms of trade, and rising foreign capital domination described in classical dependency formulations continue to be valid for describing the development predicaments of some countries, even though we may not customarily associate these countries with the Third World. Australia offers a prime case in point. Its experiences, as well as those of Argentina, constitute graphic examples of downward mobility in the evolving international division of labor. With their European settlers and abundant natural resources, both countries were at one time deemed by experts to be the odds-on favorites for rapid economic development among the late industrializing countries. Their actual performances have fallen far short of these great expectations.

Unlike in 1981, a second major cluster of developing nations emerges in 1988, consisting of the more dynamic late industrializing countries. Clearly the ranks of the high-growth NICs with substantial manufacturing sectors had expanded greatly since the early 1980s, when, according to our data, it appeared to be a rather restricted East Asian phenomenon. By 1988, this group included a number of countries that had apparently "graduated" from the rather heterogeneous group of less developed countries in 1981. In addition to the countries already mentioned, Brazil, Greece, India, Jamaica, Malaysia, Morocco, Sri Lanka, Thailand, Tunisia, and Turkey had joined this group, distinguished by its rapid economic expansion, large capital investment, and high manufacturing content in export trade. Perhaps more fittingly than their 1981 placement in the category of advanced industrial economies, Mexico, Singapore, and Spain were reassigned to this group of NICs according to the 1988 data. Interestingly, several of the more successful socialist economies— namely, China, Hungary, and Yugoslavia—were associated with this group. The dramatic increase in the number of these NICs within a rather short interval offers persuasive evidence of the rapid changes taking place in the international division of labor.

Three smaller groups of developing countries can also be discerned. First, the cluster of countries with a high percentage of textile exports expanded in 1988 to include Haiti and Mauritius. As the pertinent indicator refers to the share of textiles in their total exports rather than the absolute value of their textile exports, these low-income countries were still rather minor players in this field. Nevertheless, the arrival of these more recent entrants would only lead to a more crowded field in this traditional export area for NICs. Second, another distinct group identified for 1988 consists of the traditional Third World exporters of minerals and fuels. The members of the Organization of Petroleum Exporting Countries are especially prominent in this group. Although these countries had experienced rapid economic growth during the 1970s, by the late 1980s they were faced with increasing economic strains due to the decline in oil prices. Thus, for example, the average annual rate of GDP change during 1980–1988 was − 3.3 percent for Saudi Arabia, − 1.1 percent for Kuwait, − 4.5 percent for the United Arab Emirates, − 0.2 percent for Gabon, and 0.9 percent for Venezuela. Parenthetically, given the increasing importance of North Sea oil for its economy, Norway had become a member of this resource-exporting group. Finally, in a group by themselves, there were Laos and Poland, two socialist countries that faced serious problems of economic stagnation in the late 1980s.

The structure of the international economy, therefore, changed significantly even in a rather short time span. The observed changes have mixed implications, though, both concerning the classical dependency viewpoint of a fixed international hierarchy and concerning Confucian capitalism as a distinct pathway from the periphery. On the one hand, the tremendous increase in the number of NICs in just seven years demonstrates much greater upward mobility than the conventional dependency theory was wont to recognize; on the other hand, the international structure also seemed to be evolving toward a greater differentiation between several "have" and "have not" groups throughout the 1980s. At the beginning of the 1980s, the Confucian capitalism of three NICs formed a unique pattern of national economic activities. However, many other developing countries seemed to have learned this pattern by the end of the decade; and Confucian Japan did not stand out among the most advanced industrial economies at either time point.

## Developmental Legacies
## Among the Pacific Rim Countries

The data patterns presented thus far support the view of a dynamic global political economy with considerable upward as well as downward status mobility for individual countries. This mobility and the developmental courses underlying it, however, have been significantly constrained by the historical forces of imperialism and colonialism. In an essay contrasting the industrialization paths of Latin America and East Asia, Fajnzylber (1990) argues that these paths have reflected the experiences and examples presented by their respective regional hegemons, namely, the United States and Japan.

Due to its own historical conditions, the U.S. model of development emphasizes consumption instead of savings, production for domestic rather than foreign markets, economic freedom as opposed to social integration, and short-term gratification at the expense of long-term liabilities (e.g., deficit financing, inflation, and resource exports in order to pay for current consumption). Thus, most U.S. firms have been inward-looking, being usually content to sell to a large and secured domestic market. Both the mass ethos and the federal tax system clearly favor consumption rather investment. The doctrines of free enterprise and private accumulation further exacerbate this tendency, with issues of social equity and income distribution assuming distinctly secondary importance. At the same time, this ideology restrains "big government" and champions instead the virtues of unhampered market forces.

Given its historical conditions of resource scarcity and a small domestic market, Japan developed an alternative model of development that stresses long-term industrial planning, high capital investment, "conquest" of external markets, and a cultural ethos encouraging austere consumption and social integration. Moreover, the idea that the government should intervene in the marketplace in order to promote some common good receives much greater support and legitimacy than in the United States.

Fajnzylber (1990) contends that whereas Latin America has sought to reproduce the "American way of life," East Asia has emulated the Japanese model of development. The respective incorporation of these two regions in the U.S. and Japanese spheres of formal or informal colonial influence has led to particular patterns of domestic consumption, production, wealth distribution, and interest alignment, which in turn severely limited the strategic choices available to the peripheral countries in these regions to pursue subsequent development. In Latin America, these historical legacies as well as the ongoing dense networks of interactions with the United States have meant the persistence of the U.S. model as reflected by (1) biases toward production for domestic consumers; (2) high levels of consumption especially by the urban upper class; and (3) heavy reliance on traditional agricultural or mineral exports in order to finance the import of consumer luxuries. These tendencies, in turn, explain the Latin American countries' general preference for import-substitution industrialization, their high foreign debt burden and chronic fiscal crises, their failure to graduate from commodity exports, and their system of unequal income distribution. In contrast, these same inferences would suggest that the East Asian NICs are more adept in pursuing overseas business, more bent on practicing fiscal conservatism, more resistant to "exuberant" consumption, and more inclined to place a high premium on social integration.

We undertake a preliminary test of the validity of these expectations for the Pacific Rim capitalist economies (the Latin American countries being excluded from the sample). We are interested in this group because it includes some of the most dynamic economies in the recent past as well as others whose performance has not been nearly as satisfactory. Given their former colonial status and long-standing dense interactions, we would expect South

Korea and Taiwan to follow the Japanese model of development, with its emphasis on a strong developmental state, outward economic orientation, dynamic pursuit of international product cycle in manufacturing, relatively austere patterns of mass consumption, and high level of social integration as manifested by a comparatively equitable system of income distribution.

Conversely, for the same reasons of historical ties and institutional legacies, we expect the Philippines to follow the U.S. model of development. It is the most "Latin American" of the Asian countries (Evans, 1987; Hawes, 1987: 31, 38–39) due to its Catholic culture, its traditional *latifundia* economy, its "soft" and fragmented state, the political dominance of its agro-export oligarchy (especially the "sugar bloc"), and the economic penetration of foreign business interests (especially by U.S. investors who were guaranteed the same economic freedoms as native citizens as a condition for Washington's granting political independence to the Philippines). Moreover, the Philippines exhibits the same Latin American syndrome of economic stagnation, financial corruption, "crony capitalism" (rent-seeking based on patronage), ostentatious consumption by the elite, wide income gaps between the rich and the poor, and mounting external debts coupled with deteriorating terms of trade.

Extrapolating from the logic of Fajnzylber (1990), we suppose that the other Pacific Rim countries would adopt intermediate positions between the U.S. and Japanese models. The political economies of Hong Kong and Singapore should be more similar to those of Taiwan and South Korea than to those of the Southeast Asian countries. They should therefore be located closer to the Japanese model. On the other hand, the socioeconomic structures of Australia, New Zealand, and Canada have a great deal in common—such as their reliance on the export of primary products, moderate levels of economic growth, mass consumption of high value-added products, and less egalitarian systems of income distribution—when compared to the East Asian economies. They should therefore be located closer to the U.S. model. Finally, we hypothesize that Malaysia, Thailand, and Indonesia should show important departures from both the U.S. and Japanese models.

These expectations are checked via a cluster analysis of the political economies of the countries just mentioned. We deliberately excluded gross national product (GNP) per capita in this analysis because the level of a country's economic development or affluence is not our immediate concern. We are interested instead in the similarities and differences in the structural conditions of the Pacific Rim political economies. This analysis includes the following variables: (1) the share of agricultural and mineral products in a country's total exports in 1988, (2) the average annual rate of its GDP growth during 1980–1988, (3) the average annual rate of its exports during 1980–1988, (4) its gross domestic savings as a percentage of GDP in 1988, (5) the ratio of income shares between the wealthiest and poorest 20 percent of its population, and (6) the share of its total household consumption devoted to "transport and communication" (World Bank, 1990, 1989).

The last variable is intended to capture a society's tendency toward exuberant consumption. The cost of operating and maintaining personal motor vehicles usually constitutes a substantial portion of this expenditure item. The relative size of this cost, in turn, offers an approximate measure of luxury consumption, especially in Third World countries. South Korea provides an example of the sharp incongruity that may exist in the production and consumption of personalized transportation: although that country has emerged as a world competitor in automobile production, its per capita ownership of automobiles was only one-tenth to one-fifteenth of that of Latin American countries of comparable economic size (Fajnzylber, 1990: 338).

The results of this second round of cluster analysis are reported in Table 2.2, which tracks the countries' group memberships for each of the seven iterations in the analysis. Thus, it shows how the countries line up if they are broken into two clusters, three clusters, and so on until seven clusters. The patterns thus revealed again support our expectations in broad outlines, even though there are occasional deviations by individual cases.

Table 2.2    Models of Development in the Pacific Region

| | Number of Clusters | | | | | |
|---|---|---|---|---|---|---|
| | 7 | 6 | 5 | 4 | 3 | 2 |
| Japan | 1 | 1 | 1 | 1 | 1 | 1 |
| Korea, South | 2 | 2 | 2 | 1 | 1 | 1 |
| Taiwan | 2 | 2 | 2 | 1 | 1 | 1 |
| Hong Kong | 2 | 2 | 2 | 1 | 1 | 1 |
| Singapore | 3 | 3 | 3 | 2 | 2 | 2 |
| Malaysia | 3 | 3 | 3 | 2 | 2 | 2 |
| Australia | 4 | 4 | 3 | 2 | 2 | 2 |
| New Zealand | 4 | 4 | 3 | 2 | 2 | 2 |
| Canada | 4 | 4 | 3 | 2 | 2 | 2 |
| Thailand | 4 | 4 | 3 | 2 | 2 | 2 |
| United States | 5 | 5 | 4 | 3 | 2 | 2 |
| Philippines | 6 | 5 | 4 | 3 | 2 | 2 |
| Indonesia | 7 | 6 | 5 | 4 | 3 | 2 |

Most notably, if the Pacific Rim countries are forced into two clusters, we clearly see alignment patterns along the U.S. and Japanese models of development. Japan, South Korea, Taiwan, and Hong Kong form one distinct constellation, whereas the rest of the countries are associated in an opposite group. When we allow the countries to be sorted into three and four clusters, Indonesia emerges as a rather distinct class by itself and, as hypothesized, the United States and the Philippines coalesce to present yet another pattern. Further disaggregation of the group compositions lead to Japan breaking away to form its own category at step 5; Australia, New Zealand, Canada, and (somewhat surprisingly) Thailand presenting a common subset at step 6; and Singapore and Malaysia merging into yet another category at step 7.

These results generally support the existence of two distinct models of development. These models represent not only the ideological hegemony of the United States and Japan in propagating developmental paradigms, but also the concrete historical impact of their colonial and neocolonial legacies in shaping the production, consumption, and distribution patterns in their respective follower nations. South Korea, Taiwan, and Hong Kong have developed along the Japanese lines, whereas the Philippines, in particular, has been influenced by the U.S. model. Although these cases thus conform to our expectations, the results in Table 2.2 also indicate several other areas where these expectations need further elaboration.

Contrary to our initial hunches, the political economy of Singapore appeared to have less in common with the East Asian NICs than with its Southeast Asian neighbors, especially Malaysia. Although this finding may be somewhat surprising in view of the common suggestion that the economic structures of Singapore and Hong Kong are rather similar due to their traditional function as regional entrepôts, their developmental histories suggest that they are more "kissing cousins" than "twins" (Krause, 1988). Moreover, despite suggestions about the efficacy of Chinese culture for promoting entrepreneurship and competitive small-scale business (e.g., Fei, 1986; Pye, 1985), Singapore has, after all, a multiethnic society and, because of its geographic location, has had much closer cultural and economic contact with its Southeast Asian neighbors (especially Malaysia) than with Hong Kong, Taiwan, and China.

Indeed, Singapore and Malaysia were once united in a federation. Both have also been the most successful countries in their region in recruiting foreign direct investment and in pursuing a policy of export-oriented industrialization. They had, for example, developed into major export platforms for electronics and semiconductors. In regard to their export emphasis, manufacturing growth, and high rates of domestic capital formation, Singapore and—to a lesser extent—Malaysia differed from the other Southeast Asian countries and resembled more the political economies of South Korea, Taiwan, and Hong Kong. However, in contrast to the East Asian NICs, Singapore and Malaysia also featured rather high levels of exuberant consumption and rather skewed distribution of national income—the two characteristics that tended to identify them with their ASEAN (Association of Southeast Asian Nations) neighbors. Thus, despite Singapore's large Chinese community and Malaysia's avowed Look East Policy in designing its development strategy, these differences continued to distinguish them from the East Asian NICs.

Indonesia's structural conditions also turned out to differ more from those of the Philippines and, indeed, from all the other Pacific Rim countries than we expected. As a low-income oil-exporting country pursuing import-substitution, the military-dominated government in Djakarta was sufficiently distinct to emerge as a separate category by itself. Among all the countries in our sample, the fusion of state, local, and foreign capital was the greatest in Indonesia, where the pursuit of economic nationalism and state capitalism seemed also to resemble most the Brazilian model described by Evans (1987). Through their control of a myriad of state concessions, monopolies, licenses, and subsidies, the Indonesian generals, politicians, and bureaucrats sought to sustain and expand their personal as well as bureaucratic power, patronage, and revenues (Robison, 1986).

Finally, a comparatively skewed pattern of income distribution, heavy emphasis on agro-exports, substantial U.S.-style consumption habits, and moderate rates of savings and export expansion resulted in Thailand's structural conditions being more like those in Australia, New Zealand, and Canada than those faced by its Southeast Asian neighbors. In comparison with these neighbors, Bangkok's development strategy has also been built more on the basis of domestic capital and has avoided taking on heavy foreign debts (Hewison, 1987: 53).

The clusters of national economies in the Pacific Basin, therefore, conform fairly closely to the contours of Fajnzylber's (1990) arguments about the structural consequences of colonialism and neocolonialism. Thus, although Japanese colonialism was certainly not popular in Taiwan nor especially in Korea, it created structural legacies—such as governmental institutions and social coalitions facilitating the creation of a developmental state (Cumings, 1984; Haggard, 1990)—that evidently contributed to the area's postwar dynamism. In contrast, the United States and its former colony, the Philippines, as well as the former British dependencies (Canada, Australia, and New Zealand) have a significantly different (and during the 1980s clearly less successful) type of political economy. By itself, this suggests the distinctiveness of Confucian capitalism presented by the Chinese, Japanese, and Korean societies. However, the fact that Britain's two Chinese colonies, Hong Kong and Singapore, split in their respective adherence to the Japanese and U.S. models shows that neither colonial legacy nor cultural tradition provides a complete explanation of developmental trajectory.

## Status Mobility and Developmental Legacy

We started this paper by arguing that the international division of labor should be treated as a dynamic rather than static concept. Accordingly, status mobility and role graduation are possible and, indeed, should be expected. Contrary to the view expressed by the classical dependency formulation, the periphery countries are not necessarily locked into a permanent position of economic inferiority. It is possible for the economic laggards to launch rapid development through effort mobilization, strategic choice, disciplined collaboration, learning by doing, and emulation of successful role models (Amsden, 1989; Bobrow and Chan, 1987; Clark, 1989; Dore, 1990; Kahn, 1984; Morawetz, 1981; Yoffie, 1983).

Building upon the conclusion that upward status mobility was possible, the leading role of the East Asian capitalist nations among the NICs led to an argument for a model of Confucian capitalism based upon such legacies of the Chinese culture as respect for authority that underlies strong developmental states, family-based entrepreneurship, and the high value placed on education and savings (Hofheinz and Calder, 1982; Kahn, 1984; Prestowitz, 1988; Pye, 1985; Vogel, 1979). Our two types of cluster analysis provided some support for this argument. Most of the smaller Confucian capitalist states (Singapore excepted) are following a Japanese style of development, and at the beginning of the 1980s a very distinctive group of high-performance East Asian NICs existed. However, a significant number of other developing countries were able to replicate this pattern by the end of the decade, thereby casting serious doubts upon cultural determinism and suggesting that broad economic organizational features, as well as production technology, can be diffused fairly rapidly in the contemporary world.

At the same time, however, our findings imply that these efforts, choices, and learning are necessarily constrained for the developing countries by virtue of their status as late industrializers. Their officials and people are not really free agents able to choose optimal policy mixes from the menu offered by the neoclassical or statist paradigms. Their countries do not exist as isolated units. On the contrary, their domestic economic and political institutions are to a significant extent the products of their dense historical and ongoing interactions with their respective formal or informal "metropole." This internal (as well as the external) context limits, perpetuates, and indeed, "drives" particular national paths to development (Cardoso and Faletto, 1979; Cumings, 1984; Evans, 1979; Indorf and

Mayerchak, 1989; Moulder, 1977). In this important sense, the dependency theorists have pointed to the pervasive and persistent penetration of the peripheral societies by powerful foreign economic, political, and cultural influences. For this reason, development in the periphery is apt to be much less autonomous and much more exogenously determined than the neoclassical and statist analysts tend to assume.

## References

Alam, M. S. 1989. *Governments and Markets in Economic Development Strategies: Lessons from Korea, Taiwan, and Japan.* New York: Praeger.
Amin, S. 1974. *Accumulation on a World Scale: A Critique of the Theory of Underdevelopment.* New York: Monthly Review Press.
Amsden, A. H. 1989. *Asia's Next Giant: South Korea and Late Industrialization.* New York: Oxford University Press.
Balassa, B. 1988. "The Lessons of East Asian Development: An Overview." *Economic Development and Cultural Change* 36: S273–S292.
Balassa, B. 1981. *The Newly Industrializing Countries in the World Economy.* New York: Pergamon.
Berger, P., and H. H. M. Hsiao (eds.). 1988. *In Search of an East Asian Development Model.* New Brunswick, N.J.: Transaction Books.
Bobrow, D. B., and S. Chan. 1987. "Understanding Anomalous Successes: Japan, Taiwan, and South Korea." In C. F. Hermann, C. W. Kegley, Jr., and J. N. Rosenau (eds.), *New Directions in the Comparative Study of Foreign Policy,* pp. 111–130. Boston: Allen & Unwin.
Bradford, C. I., Jr., and W. H. Branson (eds.). 1987. *Trade and Structural Change in Pacific Asia.* Chicago: University of Chicago Press.
Caporaso, J. A. 1981. "Industrialization in the Periphery: The Evolving Global Division of Labor." *International Studies Quarterly* 25: 347–384.
Cardoso, F. H. 1973. "Associated Dependent Development: Theoretical and Practical Implications." In A. Stepan (ed.), *Authoritarian Brazil: Origins, Policy, and Future,* pp. 149–172. New Haven, Conn.: Yale University Press.
Cardoso, F., and E. Faletto. 1979. *Dependency and Development in Latin America.* Berkeley, Calif.: University of California Press.
Chan, S. 1990. *East Asian Dynamism: Growth, Order, and Security in the Pacific Region.* Boulder, Colo.: Westview.
Cheng, T. J., and S. Haggard. 1987. *Newly Industrializing Asia in Transition.* Berkeley, Calif.: Institute of International Studies, University of California.
Clark, C. 1989. *Taiwan's Development: Implications for Contending Political Economy Paradigms.* New York: Greenwood.
CEPD (Council for Economic Planning and Development). 1989. *Taiwan Statistical Data Book.* Taipei: author.
Cumings, B. 1984. "The Origins and Development of the Northeast Asian Political Economy: Industrial Sectors, Product Cycle, and Political Consequences." *International Organization* 38: 1–40.
Deyo, F. C. (ed.). 1987. *The Political Economy of the New Asian Industrialism.* Ithaca, N.Y.: Cornell University Press.
Dore, R. 1990. "Reflections on Culture and Social Change." In G. Gereffi and D. Wyman (eds.), *Manufacturing Miracles: Paths of Industrialization in Latin*

*America and East Asia*, pp. 353–367. Princeton, N.J.: Princeton University Press.

Evans, P. B. 1987. "Class, State, and Dependence in East Asia: Lessons for Latin Americanists." In F. C. Deyo (ed.), *The Political Economy of the New Asian Dynamism*, pp. 203–226. Ithaca, N.Y.: Cornell University Press.

Evans, P. B. 1979. *Dependent Development: The Alliance of Multinational, State, and Local Capital in Brazil*. Princeton, N.J.: Princeton University Press.

Fajnzylber, F. 1990. "The United States and Japan as Models of Industrialization." In G. Gereffi and D. Wyman (eds.), *Manufacturing Miracles: Paths of Industrialization in Latin America and East Asia*, pp. 323–352. Princeton, N.J.: Princeton University Press.

Fei, J. C. H. 1986. "Economic Development and Traditional Chinese Cultural Values." *Journal of Chinese Studies* 3: 109–124.

Frank, A. G. 1969. *Capitalism and Underdevelopment in Latin America*. New York: Monthly Review Press.

Galtung, J. 1971. "A Structural Theory of Imperialism." *Journal of Peace Research* 8: 81–117.

Gereffi, G. 1983. *The Pharmaceutical Industry and Dependency in the Third World*. Princeton, N.J.: Princeton University Press.

Gereffi, G., and D. Wyman (eds). 1990. *Manufacturing Miracles: Paths of Industrialization in Latin America and East Asia*. Princeton, N.J.: Princeton University Press.

Gereffi, G., and D. Wyman. 1989. "Determinants of Developing Strategies in Latin America and East Asia." In S. Haggard and C. I. Moon (eds.), *Pacific Dynamics: The International Politics of Industrial Change*, pp. 23–52 Boulder, Colo.: Westview.

Gold, T. B. 1986. *State and Society in the Taiwan Miracle*. Armonk, N.Y.: Sharpe.

Haggard, S. 1990. *Pathways from the Periphery: The Politics of Growth in the Newly Industrializing Countries*. Ithaca, N.Y.: Cornell University Press.

Haggard, S., and C. I. Moon (eds.). 1989. *Pacific Dynamics: The International Politics of Industrial Change*. Boulder, Colo.: Westview.

Hawes, G. 1987. *The Philippine State and the Marcos Regime: The Politics of Export*. Ithaca, N.Y.: Cornell University Press.

Hewison, K. 1987. "National Interests and Economic Downturn: Thailand." In R. Robison, K. Hewison, and R. Higgott (eds.), *Southeast Asia in the 1980s: The Politics of Economic Crisis*, pp. 52–79. Sydney: Allen & Unwin.

Higgott, R. 1987. "Australia: Economic Crises and the Politics of Regional Economic Adjustment." In R. Robison, K. Hewison, and R. Higgott (eds.), *Southeast Asia in the 1980s: The Politics of Economic Crisis*, pp. 177–217. Sydney: Allen & Unwin.

Higgott, R., and R. Robison (eds.). 1985. *Southeast Asia: Essays in the Political Economy of Structural Change*. London: Routledge & Kegan Paul.

Hofheinz, R., and K. E. Calder. 1982. *The Eastasia Edge*. New York: Basic Books.

Indorf, H. H., and P. M. Mayerchak. 1989. *Linkage or Bondage: U.S. Economic Relations with the ASEAN Region*. New York: Greenwood.

Johnson, C. 1982. *MITI and the Japanese Miracle: The Growth of Industrial Policy, 1925–1975*. Stanford, Calif.: Stanford University Press.

Johnson, C. 1981. "Introduction—The Taiwan Model." In J. C. Hsiung (ed.), *Contemporary Republic of China: The Taiwan Experience, 1950–1980*, pp. 9–18. New York: Praeger.

Jones, L., and I. Sakong. 1980. *Government, Business, and Entrepreneurship in*

*Economic Development: The Korean Case*. Cambridge, Mass.: Harvard University Press.

Kahn, H. 1984. "The Confucian Ethic and Economic Growth." In M. A. Seligson (ed.), *The Gap Between the Rich and Poor*, pp. 78–80. Boulder, Colo.: Westview.

Krause, L. B. 1988. "Hong Kong and Singapore: Twins or Kissing Cousins?" *Economic Development and Cultural Change* 36: S45–S66.

Kuznets, P. W. 1988. "An East Asian Model of Economic Development: Japan, Taiwan, and South Korea." *Economic Development and Cultural Change* 36: S11–S43.

Linder, S. B. 1986. *The Pacific Century*. Stanford, Calif.: Stanford University Press.

Lockwood, W. W. (ed.). 1965. *The State and Economic Enterprises in Japan*. Princeton, N.J.: Princeton University Press.

Morawetz, D. 1981. *Why the Emperor's New Clothes Are Not Made in Colombia? A Case Study in Latin American and East Asian Manufactured Exports*. New York: Oxford University Press.

Moulder, F. V. 1977. *Japan, China, and the Modern World Economy: Toward a Reinterpretation of East Asian Development, ca. 1600 to ca. 1918*. London: Cambridge University Press.

Naya, S. 1987. "Asian and Pacific Developing Countries: Performance and Issues." In W. C. Kim and P. K. Y. Young (eds.), *The Pacific Challenge in International Business*, pp. 19–61. Ann Arbor, Mich.: UMI Research Press.

Olson, M., Jr. 1982. *The Rise and Decline of Nations: Economic Growth, Stagflation, and Social Rigidities*. New Haven, Conn.: Yale University Press.

Prestowitz, C., Jr. 1988. *Trading Places: How We Allowed Japan to Take the Lead*. New York: Basic Books.

Pye, L. W., with M. W. Pye. 1985. *Asian Power and Politics: The Cultural Dimensions of Authority*. Cambridge, Mass.: Harvard University Press.

Robison, R. 1986. *Indonesia: The Rise of Capital*. Sydney: Allen & Unwin.

Vogel, E. F. 1979. *Japan As Number One: Lessons for America*. Cambridge, Mass.: Harvard University Press.

Wade, R. 1990. *Governing the Market: Economic Theory and the Role of Government in East Asian Industrialization*. Princeton, N.J.: Princeton University Press.

White, G. (ed.). 1988. *Developmental States in East Asia*. New York: St. Martin's.

World Bank. 1990, 1989, 1983. *World Development Report*. Washington, D.C.: Oxford University Press.

Yoffie, D. B. 1983. *Power and Protectionism: Strategies of the Newly Industrializing Countries*. New York: Columbia University Press.

# 3

# Japan's Post–Cold War Challenges and Opportunities in Asia Pacific

*Tsuneo Akaha*

The long-awaited effects of the thaw in the East-West Cold War have finally reached the shores of Asia Pacific. The Soviet Union and the Republic of Korea (South Korea) have established diplomatic relations. China and South Korea have exchanged trade offices and appear committed to the expansion of bilateral commercial ties. Japan and China have managed to restore their cautious but friendly relations, which had been disrupted by the June 1989 Tiananmen incident. However, improvement in Soviet-Japanese relations has been extremely limited despite the April 1991 summit in Tokyo between Prime Minister Toshiki Kaifu and President Mikhail Gorbachev, the first top Soviet leader ever to visit Japan. Moreover, Tokyo and Pyongyang have gone through several rounds of talks since 1990 without much progress toward the establishment of diplomatic relations. Finally, Japan's relations with its closest ally, the United States, are under growing pressure and scrutiny as the two biggest economic powers of the world try to manage their relations better in the post–Cold War world.

## Postwar Japanese Foreign Policy: Key Dimensions

The postwar Japanese foreign policy was conducted along four key dimensions. First, Japan defined its close alliance with the United States as the cornerstone of its foreign policy. This meant, most fundamentally, that Tokyo wanted to maintain its security treaty with Washington at almost any cost, domestically and externally. Within the U.S. ideological orbit, Tokyo's postwar foreign policy basically followed Washington's lead, as in the case of the delayed normalization of diplomatic ties with the People's Republic of China and the largely hostile relations with the Soviet Union interspersed by periods of limited, uneasy détente with the communist giants. Second, the

49

coincidence of U.S. hegemonic interests and the U.S.-focused Japanese policy allowed Tokyo to pursue a minimalist security policy, limiting its defense capabilities to those required for strictly defensive purposes and avoiding major political commitments or military entanglements overseas. Third, within the U.S.-dominated international political economy, Tokyo pursued a foreign policy dedicated almost exclusively to the growth of Japanese economy. As a result, Japan achieved miraculous economic growth, its GNP leaping from a mere $24.6 billion in 1955 to a whopping $2,833.7 billion in 1989. Fourth, Tokyo's foreign policy pursuits were focused on Japan's immediate environment, the Pacific Basin, conducting more than 70 percent of its global trade within the region throughout the postwar period. North America, Northeast Asia, and Southeast Asia constituted the areas of Japanese foreign policy preoccupation, with Europe, Africa, and Latin America only occasionally attracting attention in Tokyo. Even the Middle East, from which Japan imported more than 76 percent of its oil supply as early as 1955 (70.8 percent in 1989), did not attract much foreign policy attention in Tokyo until the first oil crisis of 1973.

## Recent Changes in Japanese Foreign Policy

In the wake of Japan's rise to the status of the world's second most powerful economy and against the background of the relative decline of U.S. hegemony since the 1970s, Japanese foreign policy has come under mounting pressure along all four dimensions outlined above (Akaha, 1990). First, Tokyo's Washington-focused foreign policy has come under increasing criticism in Japan, and Washington has similarly come under mounting domestic pressure to review its alliance relations with Tokyo. Washington's incessant pressure on Tokyo over the issues of defense burden-sharing and bilateral trade imbalance are seen in Japan as a misguided policy based on the U.S. leadership's failure to understand the root causes of its domestic economic difficulties and declining influence in world politics. In the eyes of most Japanese, the burgeoning trade and budget deficits of the United States are both a consequence of U.S. industry's failure to adapt to the increasingly competitive global marketplace and a result of Washington's failure to develop an effective industrial policy. Echoing Paul Kennedy's (1987) analysis, many Japanese also believe that Washington has failed to control its military spending and scale down its security commitments to reflect its declining ability to finance policies at home and abroad. From their vantage point, the most urgent task for the United States is not to bash its ally of almost forty years but to "put its own house in order." From the U.S. point of view, Japan should disavow its "free-rider" status and shoulder a defense burden commensurate with its enhanced economic power. It is generally believed in the United States that many of the U.S. economic ills faced today result from Japanese companies' relentless export drive and Tokyo's failure to open the nation's well-protected market to foreign imports. The resultant mismatch of mutual expectations and the politicization of the bilateral relations across the Pacific have shaken the two sides' confidence in managing the bilateral alliance (Akaha, 1991a).

Second, in part due to the U.S. pressure just mentioned and in part because of the conservative swing in the balance of political power in Japan since the 1970s, Tokyo has managed to boost its defense capabilities substantially. Japan today has the third largest defense budget in the world, and its armed forces are equipped with some of the world's most sophisticated weapons (Drifte, 1990). The Japanese Self-Defence Forces (SDF) are well on their way to being able to defend not only Japan's land territories but also its sea lines of communication (SLOCs) to a distance of 1,000 nautical miles from its shores. The increasing Soviet military presence in East Asia during the 1960s, 1970s, and most of the 1980s has also been an important factor in Japanese arms buildup. The quantitative and, more recently, qualitative improvements in the Soviet Far Eastern and Pacific forces have strengthened the position of right-wing elements in Japan who favor expanded defense capabilities and intensification of U.S.-Japanese security cooperation. However, the perennial sense of resource vulnerability among the Japanese and the relative success of Tokyo's economics-first foreign policy in earlier decades have led Tokyo to adopt a "comprehensive security policy," according to which the nation limits its military capabilities to strictly defensive ones and relies on nonmilitary means for the protection of its largely economic interests beyond its defense perimeters (Akaha, 1991b).

Third, the oil crises of 1973 and 1979, the protracted Iran-Iraq war, the deterioration of Indochinese politics, and the continuing political crisis in the Philippines all have challenged Tokyo's economics-focused foreign policy. Tokyo's response to these developments has been to attempt to translate its growing economic power into political influence. In the Arab-Israeli conflict, Tokyo has adopted a pro-Arab position at the risk of alienating Israel, and Japanese companies have joined the Arab boycott of Israel. During the first Gulf conflict, Tokyo maintained diplomatic and commercial ties with both Iran and Iraq and attempted to serve as an intermediary between them. In Southeast Asia, Tokyo has extended the largest part of its official development assistance (ODA) to the Philippines and other ASEAN (Association of Southeast Asian Nations) countries in order to shore up their domestic economies. Tokyo has also actively supported ASEAN policy in favor of a comprehensive political settlement of the Cambodian conflict.

Tokyo has, moreover, begun to interject explicitly political and strategic considerations into its foreign policy. This is most apparent in Japanese ODA, which is increasing its strategic character (Yasutomo, 1986). Tokyo has extended economic assistance to countries as distant as Pakistan, Turkey, Egypt, Kenya, Zimbabwe, Jamaica, Sudan, Poland, Hungary, Panama, and Nicaragua—countries with which Japan traditionally has had only limited economic ties. It is no coincidence that these countries are considered strategically important by the United States. Tokyo and Washington have consulted closely on ODA policy. More recently, Tokyo has decided to base its ODA decisions in part on such political factors as the defense spending and arms export policy and democratization efforts in the countries receiving or wishing to receive Japanese assistance. Although the effect of such policy remains to be seen, there is no question that the Japanese ODA program, which was the largest in the world in 1989 (the second largest in 1990, after the U.S. program), has become an instrument of foreign policy in Tokyo.

Tokyo's decision to expand its ODA both in amount and in geographical scope is based on several considerations. First, foreign policymakers recognize that Japan as an economic superpower must make a major contribution to the development of the world economy. Second, they believe Japan's position as the world's leading creditor nation ($261.7 billion in external credits in 1988) and the nation with the largest surplus ($95 billion in trade surplus in 1988) puts it in a favorable position to play a major role in the provision of economic assistance to developing countries. Third, foreign policy planners understand that with its high external dependence on natural resources, Japan's economy is closely linked to the stable progress of developing countries. Fourth, there is a national consensus that Japan is constitutionally prohibited and politically restrained from playing a direct military role abroad and that ODA is one of the few ways in which it can contribute to international peace and security. Finally, foreign policymakers in Tokyo believe that Japan should share with developing countries its experience as the first non-Western nation to achieve dramatic economic development in less than a century (Foreign Ministry, 1989: 15–16).

Tokyo's increasingly globalist perspective is articulated in its International Cooperation Initiative. First announced by Prime Minister Noboru Takeshita in 1988 and actively followed by his successors, Sosuke Uno and Toshiki Kaifu, the initiative calls on Japan to strengthen its contribution to international peace, to expand its ODA, and to promote international cultural exchange. A major component of the new policy is to expand Japanese contributions to the United Nations and its peacekeeping and humanitarian activities. For example, in 1989 Japan became the third largest financial contributor to UN peacekeeping operations behind the United States and the Soviet Union. Japanese financial (and in some cases, personnel) contributions have gone to the Good Offices Mission in Afghanistan and Pakistan (UN-GOMAP), the Iran-Iraq Military Observer Group (UNIIMOG), the Interim Force in Lebanon (UNIFIL), the Disengagement Observer Force (UNDOF), the UN Peace Keeping Force in Cyprus (UNFICYP), the

Transition Assistance Group in Namibia (UNTAG), the UN Observer Group in Central America (ONUCA), and the UN Observer Mission in Nicaragua (ONUVEN). Japan's contributions to UN refugee and reconstruction programs, amounting to $259 million in 1990, have also gone beyond the area of Asia Pacific, its traditional foreign policy focus. The UN High Commissioner for Refugees (UNHCR) and the UN Relief and Works Agency (UNRWA) for Palestine refugees in the Near East have been the major recipients of Japanese financial support (Akaha, 1991b: 328-329).

## Changing Asia Pacific Alliance and Alignment

The changes in Japanese foreign policy reviewed above have taken place in the context of several major trends at the global and regional levels. Most importantly, the deteriorating domestic condition and the weakening international position of the superpowers have resulted in global tension reduction of proportions unprecedented in postwar history. This has had and continues to have far-reaching consequences for the pattern of security alliance and political alignment at the regional level. The effect of the end of the global Cold War was most immediately felt in Europe where the superpower conflict had created the most clear-cut regional division, ideologically and geographically.

In contrast, the thaw in the Cold War has been slow in coming in Asia. There are basically two reasons for this. First, in dismantling the global and regional institutions of Cold War rivalry, the Soviet Union and the United States have placed their priorities primarily on Europe, with Asia having to wait longer for global "peace dividends." Second, the heterogeneous background and character of Asia Pacific disputes has allowed neither a simultaneous reduction of bilateral or multilateral tensions nor a uniformly positive response among the regional powers to the global trends. As the following discussion points out, this complicates Japan's foreign and security policy options.

## Japan-Soviet Relations

The first pronouncement of the Soviet post–Cold War policy toward Asia came in Mikhail Gorbachev's Vladivostok speech in 1986 and his Krasnoyarsk speech in 1988. Calling the Soviet Union an Asia Pacific power, the Soviet leader expressed Moscow's desire to develop cooperative relations with its Asian neighbors and called for arms control in the region. However, it was not Japan but China with which Gorbachev wanted to achieve rapprochement first. Nor could Tokyo respond favorably to

Gorbachev's call for the establishment of a comprehensive regional security framework and for arms control and confidence building measures (CBMs). To Japan (and to the United States) Gorbachev's proposals were extremely vague, clearly one-sided, and evidently suspect. It is true that the Sino-Soviet rapprochement resulted in some favorable developments, the most notable being the substantial Soviet force reduction in Asia. However, the quantitative reductions in the Soviet Far Eastern and Pacific forces have been compensated for by qualitative improvements (Boeicho, 1990: 44–59).

Until very recently, the Soviets have underestimated the importance of economic power in international politics and therefore undervalued Japan as an international factor. By the time Gorbachev realized the potential value of Japanese economic resources to his policy of perestroika, his domestic power base had eroded so much that he could not successfully extend his policy of new political thinking to relations with Tokyo. More precisely, when he visited Tokyo in April 1991, he was in no position to offer meaningful concessions to Japan on the territorial dispute between the two countries over what the Japanese call the "Northern Territories," or the Habomai group, Shikotan, Kunashiri, and Etorofu islands to the northeast of Japan. President of the Russian Federation Boris Yeltsin, caught in a fierce power struggle with Gorbachev, lost no time in warning the Soviet president that he would do irreparable damage to Soviet national interests if Moscow should acquiesce to Tokyo's demand for the simultaneous return of the disputed islands to Japan. The Soviet leader fell short of meeting Kaifu's minimum goal in the summit, to secure Gorbachev's acknowledgment of Japan's latent sovereignty over the disputed islands. However, the communiqué issued at the conclusion of the Tokyo summit explicitly recognized the existence of the territorial dispute and even mentioned the islands by name.

Economic relations between the two countries did expand from the late 1960s to the early 1980s, primarily due to the large resource development projects in Siberia and the Soviet Far East for which the Japanese government provided large credits and loans (Ogawa, 1986, 1983; Smith, 1987). However, the Soviet invasion of Afghanistan in 1979 and the resulting deterioration in East-West relations sent the bilateral economic relations on a downward spiral after 1982. The structural change in the Japanese economy following the oil crises in the 1970s also substantially reduced its energy dependence. This, along with the oil glut in the 1980s, reduced the complementarity between the Soviet and Japanese economies. As a result, Japanese-Soviet trade today represents only slightly more than one percent of Japan's global trade. Japanese business leaders are mindful of their economy's resource vulnerability and have certainly not lost sight of the long-term prospects of energy, timber, and fisheries development in Siberia and the Soviet Far East (Ogawa and Komaki, 1991; Ogawa and Murakami, 1991). However, they were troubled by the uncertainties surrounding the relationship between the Soviet Union and Russian Federation governments and between them and local authorities, by the lack of progress toward a market economy, and by the ambiguous legal status of joint ventures and other types of foreign investment in the Soviet Union.[1] Japanese concerns about their neighbors' political and economic future have continued even after the disappearance of the Soviet Union and the emergence of the Commonwealth of Independent States in December 1991.

At the London Summit in 1991, a disagreement emerged between Germany and France on the one hand, and the United States, Britain, and Japan on the other. Concerned with the destabilizing effect of Soviet disintegration on its European neighbors, Bonn and Paris argued in favor of Western assistance to the faltering Soviet economy. However, Washington, London, and Tokyo remained reluctant to move beyond the technical assistance then under way. Subsequently, however, U.S. President George Bush appeared to move closer to the German-French position, although not explicitly so stating. At the Bush-Gorbachev summit in Moscow in July 1991, for example, Bush stated twice that the Soviet-Japanese territorial dispute was one of the remaining obstacles to the full reconciliation between the East and the West, and nudged the Soviet leader to concede on this issue. Bush realizes that the transformation of the economy of the former Soviet Union into a market economy is of fundamental importance to the integration of the new Commonwealth into the world economy and to the construction of a new world order. He recognizes that Western economic aid is essential to the success of economic reform in the Commonwealth. However, Washington is not in a position to extend such economic aid to Moscow and must look to Japan for large assistance. Bush knows that Moscow must move first to remove the thorns of the Russian-Japanese territorial dispute before Tokyo will extend a helping hand.

Tokyo would want to avoid international isolation should the other leading industrial countries decide to extend economic assistance to the Commonwealth of Independent States, but at the same time it would want sufficient concessions from Moscow before it would join the other Western countries. One cannot be optimistic that Yeltsin will be prepared to make major concessions soon. The rising nationalism and the increasingly important role of public opinion in his republic are two new hurdles the Russian president will have to clear if he is to find a solution that is acceptable to Tokyo. To encourage Yeltsin to move in this direction, Tokyo would have to extend some economic aid and private companies would have to put some investments in Russia's Far Eastern region, including the Northern Territories, and produce visible benefits of improved Russian/Commonwealth–Japanese relations. This would be an uncertain prospect, to say the least.

The failed coup attempt in Moscow in August 1991 did not make decisions in Tokyo any easier. On the one hand, Tokyo welcomed the downfall of the hardliners in Moscow, but, on the other hand, it deepened its concern about the rising Russian nationalism accompanying Yeltsin's rise to an unequaled position of power in the then-disintegrating Soviet Union and now in the new Commonwealth. Moreover, it will be some time before the radical economic reform plan that Yeltsin implemented in January 1992 will show its effects on the country's crisis-ridden economy.

## Relations with North and South Korea

The most dramatic sign of the thaw in the Cold War in East Asia so far has been the establishment of diplomatic ties between the Soviet Union and South Korea in October 1990. Chinese–South Korean relations have also improved, with the two countries establishing trade offices in each other's capitals in the winter of 1990. These developments have stunned North Korea. Whether the apparent international isolation of Pyongyang would lead Kim Il Sung's regime, which commands more than one million troops, toward some unpredictable act of desperation or force it instead to seek new and improved foreign relations is a question that largely remains unanswered. The future of post-Kim North Korea is even more uncertain.

The Korean situation presents both challenges and opportunities to Japan. The fast pace of Soviet–South Korean rapprochement surprised Tokyo, but it was a welcome development. Japan soon began talks with North Korea to establish diplomatic relations between the two countries, most importantly to prevent further isolation of Pyongyang (Kitazume, 1990: 4). Even though North Korea has long viewed Japan as little more than a willing servant of U.S. interests in the region and therefore an obstacle to its unification strategy (Roy, 1988), evidently Pyongyang wants to establish diplomatic relations with Tokyo as quickly as possible. North Korea would want to counter the recent diplomatic feats of its southern rival. As well, Pyongyang wants to tap Japanese economic resources to save its devastatingly backward economy. North Korea's trade with Japan amounted to $502 million in 1989, only one-sixtieth of the South Korean–Japanese trade (Masaki, 1990: 3). Fortunately, Moscow and Beijing both welcome Tokyo's attempt to establish diplomatic ties with Pyongyang. Even though there is a growing Japanese sentiment in favor of expanded economic ties with North Korea, Tokyo is very cautious so as not to hurt the interests of Washington or Seoul.

Washington has been deeply concerned about Pyongyang's refusal to commit itself formally and unequivocally to the full safeguards inspections by the International Atomic Energy Agency (IAEA) of the nuclear facilities in North Korea. The nuclear issue has become more urgent with improved

South Korean relations with the Soviet Union and China. Moscow's leverage over Pyongyang has diminished and leaves virtually no one in a strong position to put diplomatic pressure on North Korea (Spector, 1990). Washington wants Tokyo to use whatever leverage the latter may have in its diplomatic talks with Pyongyang. Tokyo has made this one of the central issues in its negotiation with Pyongyang and consults closely with Washington. Another potential concern of the United States has been the North Korean insistence on a nuclear-free Korean peninsula, which would require the withdrawal of U.S. nuclear weapons from South Korea. Pyongyang has linked this demand to the issue of international nuclear inspections in North Korea.

Recent developments have reduced but not totally eliminated Japan's concerns about North Korea's nuclear development and about North Korea–South Korea relations. Amidst intelligence reports suggesting that North Korea was as little as a year away from completing a crude atomic weapon, Washington announced in early November 1991 that it was halting its long-scheduled troop reduction in South Korea until Pyongyang accepted IAEA safeguards inspections and stopped its nuclear fuel reprocessing program. Tokyo followed suit by declaring that it would not establish diplomatic relations with Pyongyang until the latter dismantled its center for reprocessing nuclear fuel and also agreed to international inspection. On November 26, 1991, Pyongyang announced that it was prepared to permit international inspection of its secret nuclear installations if the United States also allowed inspections to guarantee that it was removing all nuclear weapons from South Korea. The United States and South Korea responded with a decision in December to allow the North Koreans to inspect any civil or military sites in South Korea in return for reciprocal rights in the North and an agreement that neither Seoul nor Pyongyang would produce weapons-grade plutonium. Seoul also declared that the United States no longer had any nuclear weapons on Korean soil.

This international pressure was instrumental in the North–South Korean conclusion on December 13 of a treaty of reconciliation and nonaggression, which renounced armed force against each other. On December 26, Seoul revealed Pyongyang's pledge to sign and carry out an agreement permitting international inspections of its nuclear facilities "at an early date." Finally, on December 31, North and South Korea reached full agreement to make the Korean peninsula nuclear-free. More specifically, the accord banned construction of facilities capable of reprocessing nuclear waste and enriching uranium. Although details of the agreement were yet to be worked out, the accord was welcomed in Washington and Tokyo.

Tokyo's cautious approach to Pyongyang has been well conceived, taking into consideration both the common interests of all the parties concerned and the limits to Tokyo's ability to influence Korean affairs.

There are now enhanced opportunities for Japan to contribute to the implementation of the security and confidence-building measures that are developing on the peninsula. The most urgent task for Tokyo is to normalize its relations with Pyongyang and assist North Korea, but to do so without harming its relations with Seoul, a point well understood by the Japanese public.[2]

Tokyo and Seoul agree that they should expand a dialogue with North Korea and work to prevent the international isolation of Pyongyang (Wanner, 1990). Besides the consequences of Tokyo-Pyongyang diplomatic talks for the nuclear and nonaggression issues, Seoul has been very watchful concerning the issue of Japanese compensation for North Korea. The "Pyongyang communiqué," issued by Kim Il Sung, former Japanese Deputy Prime Minister Shin Kanemaru, and Socialist party Vice Chairman Makoto Tanabe in September 1990, indicated a Japanese willingness to make financial restitutions to North Korea for the suffering that Japan had caused to the North prior to World War II and for the "losses suffered by the Korean people in the 45 years following the end of the war" (Cutter, 1990: 1, 4). Because South Korea had not received any compensation from Japan for any "postwar losses," Seoul demanded clarification of Tokyo's position on this issue. Kanemaru visited President Roh in Seoul in October 1990 and reportedly explained that the postwar losses amounted to interest on the amount Japan should have paid North Korea when it paid $500 million ($300 in grants and $200 in loans) in compensation to South Korea in 1965 (Masaki, 1990: 3). In the Tokyo-Pyongyang negotiations for the establishment of diplomatic relations, the Japanese government has repeatedly rejected the North Korean demand for postwar damages but has stated it will be prepared to extend economic aid to North Korea. Even if Tokyo agreed to pay compensation for North Korea's prewar losses only, the question would still remain as to whether such payment should precede or follow the establishment of diplomatic relations. The timing of the latter remains a highly problematic issue, linked as it will be to the progress in the unification talks between Seoul and Pyongyang.

Another concern of South Korea is to make sure that Japanese economic aid to North Korea will not be used in Pyongyang's military buildup (Saito, 1990: 10). Lastly, Seoul has also been troubled by the Pyongyang communiqué's reference to "one Korea." North Korea had previously rejected any proposal that would have the effect of recognizing two Koreas. Seoul had argued the North's "one Korea" formula was designed to block Seoul's membership in the United Nations (Weissman, 1990: 3). This problem was eliminated, however, when both North Korea and South Korea were admitted into the United Nations in September 1991. Thus, yet another obstacle to Japanese–North Korean rapprochement has disappeared.

## *Improving Relations with China*

Japan's relations with China have been affected surprisingly little by the recent global trends, with the bilateral ties developing more according to a logic of their own. Up until June 1989, China had been largely successful in pursuing its two most important foreign policy objectives: being secure from external military threat and creating favorable conditions for economic development. However, in the wake of the crackdown on the democratic movement at Tiananmen Square in June 1989, Chinese foreign policy experienced a major setback. Japan joined the Western sanctions against China by suspending a $5.9 billion aid program, which was due to start in fiscal year 1990, and barring all high-level contacts. However, after Beijing took several steps in response to the Western criticisms of its human rights, Tokyo sought to restore normal relations with Beijing. At the Houston summit in July 1990, Prime Minister Kaifu sought the other leaders' understanding toward Japan's "special relationship" with China and soon thereafter announced planned resumption of untied yen loans. In September, Tokyo also lifted the ban on high-level diplomatic contacts with Beijing, encouraged by China's normalization of relations with Indonesia and Singapore in August. By the summer of 1991 Japanese-Chinese relations had returned to the pre-Tiananmen level. Prime Minister Kaifu visited Beijing in August, marking the first visit by the leader of a major industrialized democracy since June 1989.

The official Chinese view of regional trends is generally in accord with Tokyo's strategy to promote economic interdependence and political stability in Asia Pacific through enhanced economic ties. China's exports to Japan have grown from $5,652 million in 1986 to $12,054 million in 1990, although its imports from Japan have declined from $9,856 million to $6,130 million during the same period. The $21,910 million two-way trade contrasts sharply with Japanese-Soviet trade, which amounted to a mere $5,914 million in 1990. Beijing knows that its long-term economic needs dictate a pragmatic foreign policy, including stable and expanding relations with Japan.

There are a number of issues, however, that could dampen the relations between Japan and China. One such issue is the dispute over the Senkaku (Tiaoyu) Islands in the East China Sea, which are claimed by Tokyo, Beijing, and Taipei. Although Japan and China appear to want to put the issue on the back burner for now, the dispute could flare up again as a consequence of China's development of a blue-water navy. Beijing also appears to be concerned about Japan's growing military power. A Chinese official, for example, has been quoted as saying that the Chinese military was pressing for additional funds in the new five-year plan, partly on the ground that China must counter Japan (Kristoff, 1990: A7). Chinese general concerns about Japan's potential military power turned into more specific apprehensions when Tokyo decided to dispatch minesweepers to the Gulf after the UN Security Council declared the end of the Gulf War.[3] Finally, Japanese and Western commercial groups operating in China find it difficult to assess the political risk of doing business in China. There are reports of a continuing struggle over who should succeed Deng Xiaoping. Moreover, many government entities and industrial enterprises are experiencing severe financial shortages and debt problems due to tighter credit under Beijing's austerity policy instituted in the fall of 1988 to combat rampant inflation (WuDunn, 1990). By and large, however, Japanese-Chinese relations are as good today as they have ever been.

## Strained Japan-U.S. Relations

The mounting economic difficulties in the United States have forced Washington to seek ways to reduce the economic burden of its global strategy. It has cut its defense spending, sought nuclear and conventional arms control agreements with Moscow, and reduced the U.S. military presence overseas. The United States has put increasing pressure on Japan and other members of the Western alliance to increase their share of the common defense. Tokyo has responded cautiously but affirmatively.

Since the end of the 1980s, coinciding with the end of the global Cold War and the diminution of the perceived Soviet threat to the West, some in the United States and Japan have called for a major review of the U.S.-Japanese security alliance. Some have maintained that the overall political interests of the two countries require the broadening of the scope of bilateral cooperation to include not only bilateral security issues but also closer cooperation and coordination over regional and global political, security, and economic problems (Makin and Hellman, 1989). Others have warned that the two countries might drift apart unless the existing security arrangements are revised into a more balanced one with reciprocal defense obligations and more equal burden sharing (Pyle, 1989). And still others have maintained that the overall political interests of Tokyo and Washington are so closely intertwined, particularly in view of the degree of bilateral economic interdependence, that the two sides are unlikely to change the existing alliance structure for the foreseeable future (Zagoria, 1991: 57–58).

The Gulf crisis resulting from Iraq's invasion of Kuwait in August 1990 was the first serious challenge to the U.S.-Japanese security alliance in the post–Cold War period. Tokyo's seemingly grudging contributions to the U.S.-led military action against Iraq did serious damage to the image of Japan as an alliance partner. At the same time, Washington's apparently rash and virtually unilateral decision to send military forces to the Gulf and its uncontrolled criticisms of Tokyo's more constrained behavior during the crisis generated a great deal of resentment among the increasingly self-confident Japanese. Prior to the crisis, the U.S. public was divided fairly evenly in its view of Japan as an ally. By May 1991, according to a *Nikkei* poll, however, 43.7 percent of the U.S. population found Japan to be less reliable than before the Gulf War, and only 21.9 percent found Japan to be a more reliable ally than before the war (Wanner, 1991: 4–6).

As the Cold War was beginning to wind down in Asia Pacific in the spring of 1990, very few Japanese imagined that within a year they would be contributing $9 billion to a multinational military mission halfway around the world, that the Maritime SDF ships would be sweeping mines in the Gulf, or that the Philippines, Malaysia, and Singapore would allow a Japanese fleet of minesweepers to call at their ports on its way to the Middle East. Nor would they have predicted that in little more than a year a majority of them would be in favor of Japanese participation in UN-sanctioned peacekeeping operations. However, the tactical bungling by Prime Minister Kaifu and his successor, Kiichi Miyazawa, and the opposition-controlled House of Councillors have so far prevented parliamentary approval of legislation to establish a Japanese military corps to perform such a role. In the next several years, Tokyo will come under greater U.S. pressure to contribute to international peace and security in a more timely and visible manner than it did during the Gulf crisis.

On the economic front, despite some signs of improvement in bilateral trade, U.S.-Japanese relations remain strained. Japan's bilateral trade surplus dropped from $56 billion in 1987 to $41 billion in 1990. By the late 1980s, Japanese economic growth had become more driven by domestic demand expansion than by export pressure. In mid-1991, the trade gap began to grow again, however, as Japanese demand for imports fell. Moreover, the dramatic increase in Japanese direct investments in the United States in recent years (from $10 billion in 1986 to $26 billion in 1989) has created a specter of a Japanese "economic invasion" of the United States. The continuing economic woes in the United States are likely to sustain protectionist momentum and feed the Japan-bashing fever in Congress, particularly as the 1992 presidential election nears. There will be ample opportunity for U.S. politicians to exploit the growing public perception that the economic power of Japan is a greater threat to the United States than the military power of the disappearing Soviet Union and that by the turn of the century Japan will be a greater economic power than the United States.

## Deepening Relations with Southeast Asia

The credibility and legitimacy of political leadership depend increasingly on economic performance. This has several broad implications for Asia Pacific and for Japan. First, Asia Pacific leaders will continue to see regional stability and cooperation as a prerequisite for the successful pursuit of their domestic economic agenda. Second, Japan's Asia Pacific neighbors will continue to seek economic assistance from Tokyo. Third, Tokyo will come under increasing pressure to open its domestic markets to the products, including manufactures, from most other Asia Pacific countries, which will likely continue their export-driven economic development strategy.

Tokyo's minimalist security policy and economically oriented and Asian-focused foreign policy seem to have been vindicated by deepening relations between Japan and ASEAN countries. Since the announcement of the Fukuda Doctrine in 1977, Tokyo has aggressively cultivated friendly ties with ASEAN members. As a result, Japan today is the most or the second most important trade partner for all ASEAN countries. What are the likely future trends?

As protectionism in the industrialized world continues to grow, Japan's expanding domestic markets begin to have political significance. The presence of Japanese direct investments in ASEAN countries, particularly in the manufacturing sector, is also bound to grow. Through transnational activities of Japanese corporations, the horizontal as well as vertical integration of Japanese and ASEAN industries will accelerate. However, an overbearing Japanese presence in the region may generate some anti-Japanese sentiments, particularly if the well-educated and articulate middle class in the region should experience a sudden downturn in their economic well-being, such as can be caused by an abrupt rise in the inflation rate. Tokyo also needs to avoid the impression that it is forming a regional economic bloc under its domination, to the exclusion of extraregional powers.

The region's externally oriented economies are increasingly affected by global economic developments, such as the ongoing Uruguay Round of GATT (General Agreement on Tariffs and Trade) negotiations, regional economic groupings (such as the European Community [EC] and the North American Free Trade Area [NAFTA]), trends in interest rates, demand for savings, capital formation, and foreign investments. Moreover, some Southeast Asian nations are concerned that the Asia Pacific Economic Cooperation (APEC) forum, established in 1989 with active Japanese support, may undermine the degree of influence the ASEAN forum has accorded them vis-à-vis Japan. Interest is also growing among the countries facing the Sea of Japan to bring their economies into closer association. Although many obstacles remain to the establishment of what some (Ogawa and Komaki, 1991) call a "Japan Sea-rim Economic Zone," support for the idea is likely to grow among the coastal regions of Japan, North and South Korea, Russia, and China as their political relations improve. The development of a potentially competitive regional grouping in Northeast Asia is bound to raise some concern among the Southeast Asian countries. In all these developments, Japan must keep in close consultation with ASEAN nations.

On the political front, Japan has generally viewed national and regional economic development as essential to the political stability of Southeast Asia. The regional powers also see domestic resilience as the most important aspect of their national security. These complementary views between Japan and ASEAN countries are likely to continue. Moreover, Japan has consistently supported ASEAN's policy in favor of a comprehensive political settlement of the Cambodian conflict, and it will continue to support and contribute to the UN-administered postwar settlement in Indochina. Japan's cooperation with China and the United States on this issue is also likely to continue. Of some concern to ASEAN countries, however, is the likelihood that some of Japan's ODA and investments in the region may be diverted to Vietnam after the Cambodian conflict comes to an end. ASEAN leaders remember that within two years of the end of the Vietnam War, Japan became the most important trade partner of the unified Vietnam. Again, this calls for close consultation between Japan and ASEAN countries.

## Conclusions

Japan's post–Cold War policy will be built largely on its fairly successful foreign policy during the Cold War. Its close alliance with the United States is not likely to end for quite some time, but some strains are clearly observable in the political, security, and economic relations between the two countries, and they require more effective consultation between Tokyo and Washington. As the bilateral relations across the Pacific increase their impact on global and regional developments, Tokyo and Washington must help each other in bridging the gap between the former's traditionally passive and minimalist foreign policy and its increasingly globalist perspectives as well as between the latter's globalist strategies and its increasingly constrained resources. Above all else, Tokyo and Washington must improve their communication to avoid the kind of mismatch of expectations that did much damage to their relations during the recent Gulf crisis.

Although Japan's successful record in maintaining its economic security will likely prevent a sudden shift in its security policy to a heavier emphasis on military security, post–Cold War crises such as the Gulf War will push Japanese policies in competing and conflicting directions. Tokyo must express more loudly and more clearly what philosophy will inform and guide its foreign and security policies so as not to give rise to false hopes or ill-founded concerns among its neighbors.

Finally, the international community expects greater sharing of Japan's economic wealth. The internationalization of Japan must proceed both internally and externally. Japan must expand the international community's access to its domestic workings and it must share more of its wealth and experience with the world. Japan indeed faces daunting post–Cold War challenges as well as expanded opportunities to contribute to the construction of a new world order.

## Notes

1. This information comes from interviews with representatives of small and large businesses in Niigata and Tokyo in summer 1991.
2. A *Nihon Keizai Shimbun* (1990: 7) survey in October 1990 revealed that 51.9 percent of the respondents agreed that in principle normalization was a good thing but that Tokyo should take full account of its relations with Seoul before proceeding. Another 19.7 percent wanted to see early normalization of diplomatic relations between Tokyo and Pyongyang, and 18.9 percent thought it was premature to establish formal ties with North Korea.
3. This information comes from interviews with several Chinese political scientists in Beijing in summer 1991.

## References

Akaha, T. 1991a. "Trade Friction, Security Cooperation, and the Soviet Presence in Asia." In T. D. Mason and A. M. Turay (eds.), *U.S.-Japan Trade Friction: Its Impact on Security Cooperation in the Pacific Basin*, pp. 113–157. London: Macmillan.
Akaha, T. 1991b. "Japan's Comprehensive Security Policy: A New East Asian Environment." *Asian Survey* 31: 324–340.
Akaha, T. 1990. "Japan's Security Policy after U.S. Hegemony." In K. Newland (ed.), *The International Relations of Japan*, pp. 147–173. London: Macmillan.
Boeicho. 1990. *Boei hakusho [Defense Whitepaper]*. Tokyo: Okurasho insatsukyoku.
Cutter, H. 1990. "North Korea Warms to Japan." *Japan Times Weekly International Edition*, October 8–14.
Drifte, R. 1990. *Japan's Rise to International Responsibilities: The Case of Arms Control*. London: Athlone.
Foreign Ministry. 1989. *Japan's ODA Annual Report, 1989*. Tokyo: author.
Kennedy, P. 1987. *The Rise and Fall of the Great Powers: Economic Change and Military Conflict from 1500 to 2000*. New York: Random House.
Kitazume, T. 1990. "Japan May Benefit by Seoul-Moscow Pact." *Japan Times Weekly International Edition*, October 8–14.
Kristoff, N. D. 1990. "China, Reassessing Its Foes, Views Japan Warily." *New York Times*, October 23.
Makin, J. H., and D.C. Hellman. 1989. *Sharing World Leadership? A New Era for America and Japan*. Washington, D.C.: American Enterprise Institute.
Masaki, H. 1990. "Expectations Mount for Kanemaru Trip to N. Korea." *The Japan Times Weekly International Edition*, September 24–30.

*Nihon Keizai Shimbun.* 1990.

Ogawa, K. 1986. "Nisso keizai kankei no genjo to tenbo" [The Present Situation and Prospects of Japan-Soviet Economic Relations]. In *Soren keizai kenkyuu nichibei shimpojumu hokokusho* [Report on Japan-U.S. Symposium on Soviet Economic Studies], pp. 17–23. Tokyo: Soren to'o boekikai.

Ogawa, K. 1983. *Soren no taigai boeki to Nihon* [Soviet External Trade and Japan]. Tokyo: Jiji tsushinsha.

Ogawa, K., and T. Komaki. 1991. *Kan nihonkai keizaiken* [Japan Sea-rim Economic Zone]. Tokyo: Nihon keizai shimbun.

Ogawa, K., and T. Murakami. 1991. *Mezameru soren kyokuto: Nihon no hatasu yakuwari* [Awakening Soviet Far East: The Role Japan Should Play]. Tokyo: Nihon keizai hyoronsha.

Pyle, K. 1989. "The Burden of Japanese History and the Politics of Burden Sharing." In J. H. Makin and D. C. Hellman (eds.), *Sharing World Leadership? A New Era for America and Japan,* pp. 41–77. New York: American Enterprise Institute.

Roy, D. 1988. "North Korea's Relations with Japan: The Legacy of War." *Asian Survey* 28: 1280–1293.

Saito, T. 1990. "North Korea Releases Japanese Seamen in Move to Advance Relations." *JEI Report* 40B.

Smith, G. B. 1987. "Recent Trends in Japanese-Soviet Trade." *Acta Slavica Iaponica* 5: 111–123.

Spector, L. S. 1990. "Nonproliferation Challenges in the 1990s." Paper presented at the Monterey Institute of International Studies, Monterey, Calif.

Wanner, B. 1991. "American and Japanese Attitudes on Bilateral Relations: A Crisis in the Making?" *JEI Report* 31A.

Wanner, B. 1990. "Roh Diplomacy Could Precipitate Key Changes in Regional Relations." *JEI Report* 22B: 6–7.

Weissman, S. R. 1990. "Japan and North Korea Set Talks on Ties." *New York Times,* September 29.

WuDunn, S. 1990. "Pessimism on Chinese Trade." *New York Times,* June 4.

Yasutomo, D. 1986. *The Manner of Giving: Strategic Aid and Japanese Foreign Policy.* Lexington, Mass: Lexington Books.

Zagoria, D. S. 1991. "Major Power Relations in East Asia," In R.A. Scalapino and G. I. Chufrin (eds.), *Asia in the 1990s: American and Soviet Perspectives,* pp. 49–59. Berkeley, Calif.: Institute of East Asian Studies, University of California.

# 4

# China in the Twenty-First Century Global Balance: Challenge and Policy Response

## James C. Hsiung

In this chapter, I shall attempt two ambitious tasks: (1) to ascertain what challenge is likely to confront the People's Republic of China in the global and regional balance of the twenty-first century, and (2) to speculate on what is likely to be the PRC's policy response.

The discussion will begin with an examination of the global balance of power in the decades ahead. We shall then proceed to address the configuration of forces in Asia Pacific and, finally, to zero in on the PRC's likely response. There is no doubt that the new world order will, in large measure, be defined by the circumstances attendant to the end of the Cold War, which in itself represents the culmination of global developments since the end of World War II.

### The Post–Cold War Order Defined

To the best of my knowledge, nobody has yet systematically defined the emergent post–Cold War world order, which, in all probability, is to continue beyond the last decade of the present century. Clearly, the following three phenomena have to be considered for a working definition of the new world order:

1. The United States and the Soviet Union no longer face each other in a perpetual ideologically motivated confrontation, as they did for four decades after 1945.

2. Each of the two opposing alliance structures, as represented by NATO and the Warsaw Treaty Organization Pact (WTO), lost its erstwhile rationale as a vehicle of struggle against the other bloc. In fact, the "Charter

of Paris," signed on November 19, 1990, by thirty-four participants, including both superpowers, Canada, and all countries in Europe
except Albania, officially called an end to the Cold War, or "the era of
division and confrontation." The WTO was formally disbanded seven
months later.

   3. The international economic structure and the Third World are no
longer extended battlegrounds—or, to be more exact, the domains from
which the West endeavored to keep out the "Soviet bloc." For the first
signs of this dual change, one needs only to look at two important events
in 1990. One was the extension of "observer" status to the Soviet Union
by GATT (General Agreement on Tariffs and Trade); the other was the
U.S.-Soviet alignment in support of the UN Security Council resolutions
on the Gulf crisis following Iraq's invasion of Kuwait in the summer
of 1990. The PRC also joined the U.S. bandwagon in condemning
Saddam Hussein's aggression. At the height of the Cold War era,
Iraq's credentials as an unrelentingly anti-West and anti-Israel Third
World country would have won unquestioned Chinese backing. Times
had changed.

   The new world order ushered in by the end of the Cold War,
indeed, distinguishes itself by three major characteristics. First, the bipolarity that dominated the world system for more than four decades came to
an end, yielding to a new multipolarity.[1] In Europe alone, the continent
saw the return of a fluid, multiple balance of power, possibly among
seven local principal actors. Measured by the size of their respective
military forces alone, they are, in descending order, the Soviet Union,
France, Germany (united), Britain, Poland, Czechoslovakia, and Hungary.
On the global scale, it is safe to say that the United States, the only
remaining superpower, will find company with at least six other
major powers—the Soviet Union, Japan, the PRC, Germany, Britain,
and France—in what Samuel P. Huntington (1991) calls a "uni-
multipolarity."

   In the four and a half decades since the end of World War II,
nuclear bipolarity has guaranteed what John Lewis Gaddis (1986) calls
Europe's "long peace." In contrast, multipolarity augurs less well for
systemic stability for a number of reasons. With the increase in polarity,
the number of dyads and alliance permutations also increases. Power
distribution across the system will become more uneven, making balance
of power more tenuous. In game-theoretic language, there is less trans-
parency of defections by states, and the cost of sanctions also goes up as
the $n$ in the $n$–person game expands. All this makes deterrence
difficult. Empirically, the world from 1816 through 1946 was
multipolar; it also experienced numerous major wars, including the

two world wars.

The second major characteristic of the post–Cold War world order is the decline in the salience of strategic nuclear weapons. The world is in a transition from nuclear to conventional deterrence at the central (global) level. In the Cold War era, the strategic pillar of mutual assured destruction (MAD) made conquest difficult and expansion futile by either camp. The futility of expansion accounted for robust deterrence. Moreover, nuclear deterrence was robust for at least two other reasons: (1) due to the futility of overkill, it was possible for the superpowers to reach a weapons parity and, thus, equilibrium, bringing stability to the system; and (2) ever fearful of the massive destructive might of nuclear weapons, each superpower had a powerful incentive to constrain its followers, lest a reverse proxy war break out unwittingly (Jervis et al., 1985: 193ff.).

The return of conventional deterrence, however, spells instability for international relations, mainly because of an irrepressible power imbalance problem. As there is no similar overkill restraint with conventional weapons, endless arms races will create endless power imbalances. Proliferation of biochemical weapons and ballistic missiles will further complicate the situation. Deterrence, which has to depend on threat making, will be difficult, as threat making will not work well in conditions of power imbalance because, if directed against the inferior party, the threats will heighten its resolve to redress the balance. For example, following the second Moroccan crisis in 1911, Germany decided to catch up with Britain militarily, in response to Lloyd George's unyielding posture (Langer 1950: 758). If, on the other hand, threats are directed against the superior party, they will only encourage it to strike first before the balance is reversed. Thus, Germany decided to strike first in 1914, in order to arrest the incipient inferiority of the Dual Alliance, Germany and Austro-Hungary, vis-à-vis the military might of the Triple Entente, paving the way for World War I (Sarbrosky, 1989).

Empirically, the world of the nineteenth century was a typical period of conventional deterrence. If the study of Alan Alexandroff (1981: 67) is any indication, conventional deterrence succeeded no better than 37 percent of the time in deterring wars. A consequence from the return of multipolarity and conventional deterrence is greater instability. For one thing, it may result from the rise of "local bullies" at the regional level. The Saddam Hussein episode was but one example of such a local bully syndrome.

The third, and final, characteristic of the post–Cold War world order is that economic security (see Dell, 1987: 14–51; Kennedy, 1987: 446) will rival, and even eclipse, military security in importance. Because of both the end of the Cold War and the internal troubles besetting the Soviet Union, the military threat once ominously posed by the Soviets is fast receding. In 1988, U.S. government strategists were already forecasting that by the year 2010 the Soviet Union will lose its status as the world's third largest

economic power, after the United States and Japan. China will fill in as the
world's number three economic power, according to the same assessments
(USCLTIS, 1988). After 1990, with the growing disintegration of the Soviet
Union, these early gloomy forecasts seem even more plausible. As economic
security intrudes into our consciousness, geoeconomics will weigh more
heavily in global strategic thinking during the twenty-first century, as
geopolitics used to.

In the post–Cold War era, self-defense by national weapons will
substitute for that crucial public good known as nuclear deterrence that a
hegemon was able to offer to its allies. Unlike before, global security will
not be the only international public good a hegemon can or is expected to
provide to allies in the post–Cold War era ahead. The provision of stable
international monetary, financial, and trading conditions will be—even more
than before—another necessary qualification of world leadership. In contrast
to the age of what Keohane and Nye (1977) have called "complex
interdependence," the post–Cold War age of overriding economic security will
make this demand on hegemonic leadership even more imperative (Makin,
1989: 10–18).


## Asia Pacific

In terms of geoeconomics, the West European single-market integration
(EC92), which will come into effect at the end of 1992, may produce dire
consequences. Already it is sending tremors to all other regions, including
Asia Pacific. Non-Europeon nations, therefore, have to brace for a future of
unprecedented competition bordering on economic warfare. In response, the
U.S./Canadian free trade zone, which is to be extended to Mexico and
possibly the Caribbean, sets in motion a reactive regional integration effort
for North America. Following a conference in Australia in late 1989, an Asia
Pacific regional organization—Asia Pacific Economic Cooperation
(APEC)—was constructed in response to the EC92 challenge.

With the collapse of communism in Eastern Europe and the onset of an
emergent market economy in its wake, it is very possible that the West
European supertrading bloc will eventually spill over into Eastern Europe.
An eventual linkup with the republics of the former Soviet Union is within
the realm of possibility. Faced with the added pressures for economic reforms
at home, the Soviet Union is likely to redirect its attention westward to
Europe, adopting a "Europe first" strategy and abandoning its various
interests in Asia (Pollack, 1990: 726).

The United States, on the other hand, is most likely in these
circumstances to turn more toward Asia Pacific in search of a counterbalance
to West Europe. The stakes are high. The West European community has a

combined population of 323 million and a GNP of more than $4.6 trillion. It accounts for 20 percent of world trade (Eurostat, 1982; U.S. Department of State, 1988), and as a region its trade with the United States is second only to U.S. trade with Asia Pacific (U.S. Department of Commerce, 1990).[2] Despite European Community assurances that its single-market integration will not result in a "Fortress Europe," there is a risk, nonetheless, that intra-European deals will be made and a Eurocentric regime installed at the expense of outside trading partners.

From the U.S. standpoint, an alliance between the North American and Asia Pacific regional blocs will be the best strategy for coping with the threat from the EC after 1992. That eventuality, of course, depends on the ability of the United States to retain leadership in both blocs. As it leans more and more toward Asia Pacific, however, the United States may face an unusual, even bizarre, situation in which the fading military threat of a long-time adversary (the Soviet Union) is dwarfed and replaced by the potent economic threat posed by a long-time partner (Japan). In 1985, the United States became a debtor nation for the first time since 1914, and it has now become the world's largest debtor nation. It has had to borrow $100 to $120 billion annually, much of it from Japan. Until such time as the borrowing ends, Japan is in effect subsidizing U.S. hegemony (Gilpin, 1987: 336–340).

Looking to the future, the United States is faced with Japanese threats in three ways: (1) U.S. national security could be affected if the Japanese lead in a variety of militarily important technologies continues to expand; (2) the growth of Japanese economic power threatens U.S. economic well-being; and (3) the increase in Japan's economic might means a corresponding increase in its influence in the world and a relative decline in U.S. influence (Huntington, 1991: 10).

From Beijing's standpoint, there are at least four scenarios for Asia Pacific: a U.S./Japan duopoly; a Russian breakthrough; a regime dominated by the PRC; and a collaborative multilateral order. Of these, the first three are either undesirable or unlikely. Only the last scenario is preferable and possible; Beijing could do its share toward its realization. A realistic strategy for the PRC would be to develop nonantagonistic relations with all the region's principal actors and to promote a collaborative framework for their mutual relations (Pollack, 1990: 723ff.). In the section below, I shall expand on what is the most likely policy response from China, along these lines, to the kind of global and regional balance discussed above.

## A Rational PRC Policy Response

The word "rational" used in this discussion of China's policy response is defined by reference to its dominant strategy in view of its purported goals and optimal outcome(s), given the conditions of the objective environment. In order to promote a collaborative multilateral framework, it will not be enough for the PRC to focus on military capability, as the post–Cold War order will be postnuclear. Beijing will have to adopt a strategy that will accentuate diplomatic adroitness and economic potential as well. A rational long-term strategy would consist of three components: (1) to play an honest broker in the intensifying rivalry between the United States and Japan; (2) to upgrade China's economic strength through revamping its (communist) socioeconomic and political system at home and by enhancing its economic linkage with the global and regional economic structures outside; and (3) to pursue a "Greater China" scenario, which comes down to seeking the extension of national unification to Taiwan after the projected 1997 retrocession of Hong Kong. I shall elaborate on each of these three points below.

*Playing honest broker.* During the 1990s, Beijing can look favorably upon three developments with far-reaching effects. The first two have been alluded to above: the receding Soviet military threat, and its probable replacement by the Japanese threat to U.S. economic security. The third development is the Gulf crisis of 1990–1991, which has taught many an important lesson for the future. For one, the crisis has underlined the vulnerability of an economy, such as that of Japan, that is too heavily dependent upon external supplies of vital resources. As a result, Japan has learned to appreciate, even more than before, the value of a closer sourcing of the strategic resources needed by its economy. Thus, while all other nations had their eyes on the Gulf conflict, Japan since the fall of 1990 has begun to improve its ties with the PRC (*Japan Times Weekly*, 1990).

From the Iraqi episode, both Japan and the United States learned that in the post–Cold War world, although the fixation of superpower conflict is gone, states have to worry about intraregional threats coming from a "local bully." The desire not to isolate China and force it to become a local bully has been driven home equally in Washington and Tokyo, in their respective reevaluations of their China policy in the wake of the Iraqi aggression. For the United States, furthermore, Chinese cooperation proved important in UN Security Council votes on sanctions against Iraq.

Thus, in the post–Cold War context, China's power chips have in effect grown vis-à-vis the region's principal players, Washington and Tokyo included. That being the case, Beijing will be in a better position to play an honest broker. Japanese per capita GNP by 1988 had outstripped that of the United States by a ratio of $21,020 to $19,840. Japanese growth rates, at 6.5 percent during 1965–1980 and 3.9 percent during 1980–1988, overshadowed those of the United States, at 2.7 percent and 3.3 percent during the same periods. Japan's economic weight is further buttressed by an expanding military might as measured by the steady growth—at 5 percent annually since the mid-1980s—of its defense spending. For five consecutive years, these defense expenditures breached the long-held ceiling of 1 percent of Japan's GNP (Chen, 1990; IBRD, 1990). Just as Chinese resources proved attractive to Japan, China's status as the world's third largest military power and, hence, its potential as a regional counterweight to Japan is, at least psychologically, of value to the United States. Thus, the PRC has the potential to play a "pivotal" role in the future U.S./Japan/PRC triad, very similar to the role it played in the U.S./Soviet/PRC triad during the early 1980s (Hsiung, 1985a: 107–131). The rest is up to Chinese diplomatic skills.

*Domestic reforms.* The PRC sees the surrounding Asia Pacific region not simply as an economic entity, but as a vehicle for Japanese, U. S., and even Soviet strategic ambitions in Asia. China's scenario for the future does seem to project the nation as a major political and economic actor with key interests in the region. That projected role also requires that it prepare itself accordingly (Howe, 1990: 680; Tao, 1984: 2; Yuan, 1984: 2–5).

This view accords with the reality that, in the forthcoming politics of economic warfare, China can no longer bury its head in the sand, pleading "self-reliance" as Mao Zedong used to exhort. The second component of PRC policy response to the challenge of the future global and regional balance, therefore, is to upgrade China's economic capability, through internal restructuring and by becoming more a part of the Asia Pacific economic community. Otherwise, China might degenerate into an economic "colony" (Huan, 1985).

But the PRC has to prove itself to be an economically adequate and reckonable member of the regional community. This will not be easy. Admittedly, the Commission on Long-Term Integrated Strategy, during the Reagan presidency, did offer an unabashedly rosy assessment that by the year 2010 the PRC "may have the world's second or third largest economy . . . [and] may well become a superpower" (USCLTIS, 1988: 6). Private economists such as Staffan B. Linder (1986) likewise projected an economically much stronger China by the twenty-first century. Linder foresees China's GDP to equal that of the United States and Europe by the year 2000, provided that the reforms begun in 1978 will continue unabated and that the annual growth rate is kept at 4 percent.

Nevertheless, all such forecasts predated the Tiananmen debacle of 1989, even though I have not seen any retraction of these rosy forecasts in the wake of that episode. Of late, Japanese businessmen see the PRC as second only to Thailand as a future location for investment, and second only to South Korea as a regional economic competitor by the year 2000 (Howe, 1990: 692). Regardless of one's position on the Tiananmen upheavals, they were a clear indication that something had gone awry in the post-1978 reforms. Elsewhere, I have developed the thesis of China's "paradox of partial reform" (Hsiung, 1990). Here, let me say merely that the outbreak of the 1989 massive unrest bespeaks of the extent of discontent, arising from a widespread sense of relative deprivation unleashed by the PRC's partial reform. Relative deprivation, in short, derived from inequities in income distribution as new economic measures, such as market reforms, brought windfalls to some but not all of the population, victimizing, above all, the intellectuals. More importantly, the outbursts of discontent, in and by themselves, also pointed up the dire need for more complete reforms that required nothing less than a wholesale overhaul of the entire socioeconomic and political system.

Without a thorough reform, as the intensity of the unrest attests, there is no hope for the PRC to keep up with the march of time, as its neighbors will surpass it in relative economic strength. As military sinews count less and less in the future, the race between nations will increasingly shift to the economic sphere. Beijing will have to address the anomalies that had culminated in the 1989 upheavals. An effective remedial program has to reflect two tenets: (1) the economic reforms must be supported by concomitant, even prior, political and social change; and (2) every reform measure must be well orchestrated and coordinated with all other measures (Hsiung, 1990).

The Beijing leadership faces manifold challenges. First, for rational maximization, the symbiotic economic structure, in which both a command sector and a market sector have coexisted since 1985, must be drastically altered by accentuating the role of the market. In doing so, full private ownership rights must be restored, so that the bankruptcy law on the books can have real meaning (otherwise the state will be stuck with bankrupt state-owned enterprises). The second challenge has to do with whether the regime has the courage and determination to institute the rule of law, to supplant the habitual rule by policy. Third, there is the more fundamental question of whether the Chinese Communist party (CCP) is willing to give up its monopoly of political power after four decades. The answer to this question holds the key to two others: multiparty governance and electoral democracy.

Another task, perhaps even more fundamental than those mentioned above, is social change, which can come about only through a better educated population. Equal attention will have to be paid to "informal education" and basic moral and civic discipline to rid the nation of the strident militancy and insolence among the young that so often erupts into violence and serious crimes. The most challenging task, in this respect, will be that of erasing the lingering effects of the "Red Guard mentality" about which so many in China complain.[3] The regime will have to admit that the zealous Maoist destruction of the Confucian Chinese culture is at the root of the younger generation's loss of civic discipline and moral character. The family, whose role was repressed by the Maoists for fear that it might rival party authority, will have to be brought back to the center stage of Chinese society.

Only with a sweeping reform of the whole system, as outlined here, will the PRC be able to improve the quality of its population and remain as a serious player in a postnuclear and multipolar world. At a minimum, China will have to bring itself up to a respectable level of economic development before it will be able to play a meaningful role in Asia Pacific as a regional power (Gelber, 1990).

Beijing's leadership, looking to the twenty-first century, seems fully aware of the imperative of building up the nation as a modern, economically respectable power. The "three steps forward" strategy approved by the CCP in 1978 was once again reaffirmed at the Seventh Plenum of the Thirteenth Central Committee (CC) meeting in December 1990 (*Renmin Ribao*, 1991a). The strategy targeted as the first step is the doubling, by 1990, of China's GNP from the 1980 base. The second step is to double the 1990 GNP by the year 2000, making China a "decently well-to-do" (*xiaokang*) country. The third step is to make China a "basically modernized country" by the middle of the twenty-first century (*Renmin Ribao*, 1991b).

During the 1990s—or the second step of the long-range plan—according to the communiqué issued by the recent CC plenum, China will endeavor to (1) maintain an annual growth of 6 percent; (2) upgrade general education, push for progress in science and technology, and streamline the economic system and management techniques, paving the way for sustained growth well into the twenty-first century; and (3) adopt the "responsibility system" widely in productive enterprises and so on (*Renmin Ribao*, 1991a). More interesting is the transparent language used to suggest elevating the role of the market while still paying lip service to socialist planning. Equally important are the explicitly stated goals of "upgrading the socialist spiritual ethos" and "perfecting the socialist rule of law [sic]" (*Renmin Ribao*, 1991a). Perhaps not surprisingly, the CCP document speaks of continuing to build China's coastal areas and, more particularly, to develop an "externally oriented" (literally, "turning outward") economy. The last reference seems to suggest a deliberate intent to dovetail the Chinese economy with the global, or regional, economy.

It is as though the kind of lessons we said should be learned from the Tiananmen unrest were actually taken to heart by the CCP Central Committee in its deliberations at the Seventh Plenum. Quite appropriately, the same CCP document speaks of China's needs of: (1) "striding into the twenty-first century with our heads held high" as a result of "[our] economic revival and social progress"; and (2) "standing up firmly in the Orient" without fear but with vibrant vitality. To the extent that the strategy, as reaffirmed by the Central Committee, purports to support China's needs and goals in the twenty-first century, it represents a rational policy response within the frame of reference we laid out above. It is in this light that China's more recently expressed need for "a peaceful international environment" is to be understood (Jiang, 1991: 15).

*Chinese reunification.*    The third measure in the PRC's policy response to the challenge of the post–Cold War, postnuclear, and interdependent world would be, in part, supplemental to the second measure above. The ultimate test of an economically vibrant China, come tomorrow, is whether or not the nation then can carry weight in at least the regional economic context. Christopher Howe (1990: 689) has suggested a linkage between China's interests in Asia Pacific and the rationale for a "Greater China" scenario. Much can be said about this scenario.

Deng Xiaoping's (1984) reunification formula, known as "one country, two systems," was first enunciated in 1984 at about the same time as negotiations were being held with Britain on the return of Hong Kong in 1997. When the final accords were announced, they embodied Deng's model and committed the PRC to respecting Hong Kong's existing "social and economic systems," which will "remain unchanged for fifty years." In the agreements, the words "capitalist system" were explicitly used in reference to Hong Kong's present system.[4] Commentators were quick to point out that the guaranteed PRC tolerance of Hong Kong's capitalistic system after 1997 was meant for Taiwan, to which Beijing wanted to offer assurances for unification (Hsiung, 1985b). The PRC's coastal development and great circulation strategies, designed to give the coastal provinces' economies an external orientation, were also initiated at the same time (Howe, 1990: 688; Wang, 1986). There may be more than meets the eye in the timing of these seemingly unrelated events.

The missing rationale became more explicit only after Tiananmen and the collapse of East European communism. In China today, Hong Kong is discussed in connection with its possible role as a catalyst in the PRC's own modernization and, at least, as a source of information and capital. It is also portrayed as a "bridge" for bringing Taiwan into a bloc with a "common front," which will be effective in economic competition especially against Japan and the United States (Feng, 1989; Howe, 1990: 690; Jing, 1989).

Beijing's bid for unification with Taiwan, in the past, was always considered by outside analysts mainly in political, nationalistic terms. However, looking to the twenty-first century there are reasons to view it in a new perspective. In the first place, as geoeconomics gains in importance, the PRC will be looking upon the Taiwan question increasingly in economic terms (*Renmin Ribao*, 1991a: ch. 5, sec. 65). The synergetic effects from the amalgamation of the Mainland's vast resources and market potential with Taiwan's booming economy and entrepreneurial dynamism, of course, defy precise estimation. But, at the macro (as opposed to per capita) level, the GNP ratio between Mainland China and Taiwan is 3-to-1 ($376.5 billion to $126 billion, using 1988 figures).[5] If the net effect can be graphically symbolized by GNP alone, a reunited China will mean an immediate GNP boost by a third, by merely combining the two figures.

In the second place, the "U.S. factor" was, at least in Beijing's eyes, a great obstacle to Chinese unification in the past. In the post-Tiananmen phase, when PRC-U.S. relations were sent down a bumpy slope, Beijing has less reason to be concerned about Washington's possible objections. The end of the Cold War, plus the concomitant normalization of Sino-Soviet relations, makes the U.S. connection less valuable to the PRC. The U.S. factor, therefore, will consequently be less relevant for the China unification question. On the other hand, in the event the anticipated U.S.-Japan rivalry materializes, Washington may even welcome the union of the two Chinese sides. Otherwise, Taiwan, as it exists in its present form, might well be lassoed into the Japanese economic orbit, not necessarily the interest of the United States. A China united under U.S. chaperonage, on the other hand, is most likely to remain in the U.S. camp when the chips are down.

With the reunited China in tow, the United States will be able to play an unchallenged leadership role in APEC. In that event, cross-nation sectoral complementarity within APEC will offer solutions to the farm and "deindustrialization" problems of the United States (Linder, 1986: ch. 4). It will also help to contain the adversarial dimensions of the U.S.-Japan relationship. Under a working joint U.S./Japan condominium, APEC will only gain in strength and will be in a position to offer, for all its members, an effective counterweight to the overbearing European Community (Hsiung, 1989: 42).

By the twenty-first century, Taiwan may also show more positive interest in a united China. In a world of economic warfare, the island will be at a disadvantage scrambling for Earth's depleting natural resources in competition with other resource-dependent economies and members of closed trading blocs, such as West Europe and North America. Unification with the Mainland will offer Taiwan access to badly needed resources and a vast potential market. Moreover, this unity move will be all the more palatable should it come after the Mainland's systemwide restructuring, such as the one discussed above.

All these eventualities simply illustrate that the Greater China scenario is not as unrealistic as it might sound at first. Already there are distinct signs of progress in Taiwan toward the direction of unification. Since 1987, when the floodgates were opened, two million people from Taiwan have visited the Mainland, including many on business scouting trips. By the end of 1990, indirect trade (via Hong Kong) had topped $4 billion. Taiwan investments in some 2,000 projects on the Mainland aggregated $1.6 billion (Silk, 1990;

Wang, 1991). A National Unification Commission (NUC), directly under the supervision of the president, sprang into existence in early 1991. To help implement its policy directives is a new cabinet-level action arm known as the Mainland Affairs Foundation Council. In addition, a semi-official Straits Exchange Foundation was set up to run errands for the Council on a "contractual" basis. It sent its first delegation on an exploratory mission to Beijing, where it met with officials of the Taiwan Relations Office under the State Council in April–May 1991. More importantly, a National Unification Program, which was billed as "historic," was adopted, after much debate, by the NUC in March as the ultimate directive guiding Taiwan's approach to its relations with the Mainland (*Central Daily News,* 1991a; Shen, 1991).

On May 1, 1991, the Nationalist government in Taipei officially ended its hostility toward the communist regime on the Mainland by ending the so-called period of "Mobilization for the Suppression of Communist Rebellion," after more than forty years. Taiwan conditioned its further opening to the Mainland on Beijing's internal democratization, renouncing the use of force in dealing with Taiwan, and agreeing not to isolate Taiwan diplomatically. Although it remains to be seen where all these developments will lead, one thing is clear: contacts between the two sides of the Taiwan Strait are no longer illegal. The official policy of "no contact," formulated by the late President Chiang Ching-kuo, is now being rolled back. In a way, the government in Taipei is being pushed into relaxing its previous position by the pressures built up among the citizenry, many of whom either want to do business with the Mainland or just want to undo the barriers that have segregated the two sides since 1949.[6]

Already, one salutary bonus (for Taiwan) accruing from Taiwan's policy change toward the Mainland had become clear, as soon as early May 1991, when Japan was reported (by the influential *Asahi Shimbun*) to be contemplating upgrading its present "unofficial" relations with the island to the quasidiplomatic level. Japan had downgraded its relations with Taiwan in 1972, when it switched diplomatic recognition to Beijing. According to analysts in Taipei, Japan may feel secure that the PRC would not react nastily to its upgraded relations with Taiwan, now that the latter's relations with Beijing have shed the previous straightjacket.[7] Similar bonuses of this sort, such as in Taiwan-Philippine relations, will offer fortuitous but reassuring vindication for Taipei's policy change toward the Chinese Mainland.

## Conclusions

We have seen that, given the post–Cold War conditions and the projected global balance in the twenty-first century, the PRC has to learn to prepare itself for a world of intense economic competition. Because military might will weigh less on the scales of power among nations, Beijing has to adopt a strategy that will accentuate diplomatic adroitness and economic prowess. In order to elevate itself as a serious economic power, as we discussed, it has a lot of housecleaning to do; and it has to integrate its economy more fully with the external—more particularly the Asia Pacific regional—economy. With some luck, China may be in a position to play a useful mediating role in the mounting rivalry between Japan and the United States, each jostling for leadership in APEC.

If the Greater China scenario bears fruit, it would result in the rise of a new, economically vibrant actor (the united China) on the world stage. In the final analysis, China's future lies in its success in, first, revamping its own socioeconomic and political system and, second, in its bid to unite with Taiwan, following the return of Hong Kong in 1997 (hence, the Greater China Scenario). In a roundabout way, the three outcomes are actually intertwined: The PRC's systemwide restructuring and its delivery on the "fifty years no change" promise to the retroceded Hong Kong will, inevitably, have a bearing on the eventuality of unification with Taiwan. On the other hand, the prospect of Taiwan unification makes it imperative for the Mainland regime to revamp itself and make its "one country, two systems" commitment stick for Hong Kong.

We have seen how geoeconomic calculations call for such a rational strategy. In game-theoretic language, what we have laid out above is the dominant strategy for Beijing, as it serves the purpose of an optimal outcome, in anticipation of the conditions that will probably prevail in the decades ahead. But, in a real sense, the dominant strategy also conjures up the specter of a Prisoners' Dilemma. The overriding needs of internal self-revamping and of not reneging on the "one country, two systems" commitment in respect to Hong Kong may very well paint Beijing into a corner. The latter commitment may severely constrain the PRC's discretion until the year 2047. Furthermore, the endgame of self-revamping might eventually necessitate, and effectuate, the self-immolation of communism in China. The question of how Beijing is going to extricate itself from this apparent paradox is not within the realm of this writing. Foreseeing this potential self-entrapment, nonetheless, Beijing's leaders might just opt to abandon or drastically alter the rationally deduced dominant strategy spelled out in these pages. However, that option would be at the cost of forgoing not only the likelihood of unification with Taiwan, but the very prospect of being a serious contender in the twenty-first century balance of power, even at the regional level.

## Notes

1. John Mearsheimer (1990: 7) defines a "pole" as a state that has a reasonable prospect of defending itself against the leading state in the system by its own efforts But I am using the term "multipolarity" more loosely to mean multiple balance of power free from the bipolar constraints the world has known since the late 1940s.

2. U.S. trade with Asia Pacific (Japan, South Korea, Taiwan, Hong Kong, and Singapore) is the largest share of total U.S. trade. It totaled $223.93 billion in 1988, which was $35.42 billion more than U.S. trade with Western Europe (including OECD states), or $47.09 billion more than U.S. trade with the European Economic Community for the same year. (Figures compiled from U.S. Department of Commerce, 1990: 808f., table 1406.)

3. "Red Guard mentality" is a catchall phrase to denote blind negation of tradition, raucous and bellicose conduct, lack of minimal self-discipline, defiance of any authority, and other unruly traits, which still prevail among many Chinese youths. This was brought to my attention during my sabbatical in China in 1989.

4. Sino-British Joint Declaration (September 26, 1984), Art. 3, Para. 5; and Annex 1: Elaboration by the People's Republic of China on Its Basic Policies. Texts in the *New York Times* (1984).

5. The 3-to-1 ratio is based on figures given in IISS (1990: 148 and 177). The U.S. Department of Commerce (1990), however, gives the PRC's GNP as $470.07 billion, as against Taiwan's $101.3 billion, for the year 1987. The ratio, according to these figures, is 4.7-to-1, instead.

6. Sixty percent of those polled expressed support for the repeal, as from May 1, 1991, of the so-called period of Mobilization for the Suppression of the Communist Insurgency. Most favored further changes in government policy toward allowing direct transport links with the Mainland (68 percent), direct investments by Taiwan businessmen in the Mainland (63 percent), and exchanges of official visits at the ministerial level (63 percent). The poll was conducted by the Public Opinion Polling Center of the *United Daily*, the largest newspaper in Taiwan in terms of circulation and influence (*Central Daily News*, 1991b).

7. The news of the possible upgrading of Japan's relations with Taiwan, as first reported by the *Asahi Shimbun*, was personally brought back by Taiwan's Vice Minister of Foreign Affairs John Chang, after an official visit in Tokyo (*Tsu-li Tsao-pao*, 1991).

## References

Alexandroff, A. 1981. *The Logic of Diplomacy.* Beverly Hills, Calif.: Sage.

*Central Daily News.* 1991a. March 7, Overseas ed., p. 1.

*Central Daily News.* 1991b. April 30, Overseas ed., p. 1.

Chen, F. 1990. "An Assessment of Trends in Asian Pacific Regional Security in the 1990s." *Guoji zhanlue yan jiu* [International Strategic Studies]. January.

Dell, E. 1987. *Politics of Economic Interdependence.* New York: St. Martin's.

Deng, X. 1984. "One Country, Two Systems." *Liaowang Weekly* 42.

Eurostat. 1982. *Europe in Figures.* Lanham, Md.: Unipub.

Feng, B. 1989. "The Role of Hongkong in the Course of China's Economic Development." *Jingji yanjiu [Economic Research]* 4: 64–70.

Gaddis, J. L. 1986. "The Long Peace: Elements of Stability in the Postwar International System." *International Security* 10: 99–142.

Gelber, H. 1990. "China's New Economic-Strategic Uncertainties and Security Prospects." *Asian Survey* 30: 646–648.

Gilpin, R. 1987. *The Political Economy of International Relations*. Princeton, N.J.: Princeton University Press.

Howe, C. 1990. "China, Japan, and International Interdependence." *China Quarterly* 124: 662–693.

Hsiung, J. C. 1990. "Mainland China's Paradox of Partial Reform: A Postmortem on Tiananmen." *Issues and Studies* 26: 29–43.

Hsiung, J. C. 1989. "Balance of Power in the Pacific Century." In B. Joei. (ed.), *From Pacific Region Toward Pacific Community*. Taipei: Tamkang University Press.

Hsiung, J. C. 1985a. *Beyond China's Independent Foreign Policy*. New York: Praeger.

Hsiung, J. C. 1985b. "The Hong Kong Settlement: Effects on Taiwan and Prospects for Peking's Unification Bid." *Asian Affairs* 12: 47–58.

Huan, X. 1985. "The New Technological Revolution and China's Response." *Social Science in China*, Spring.

Huntington, S. P. 1991. "America's Changing Strategic Interests." *Survival* 33: 3–17.

IBRD. 1990. *World Development Report*. Washington, D.C.: author.

IISS. 1990. *The Military Balance: 1990–1991*. London: Brassey's.

*Japan Times Weekly*. 1990. "Japan to Mend China Ties While World Eyes the Gulf." Sept. 24–30, p. 1.

Jervis, R., R. N. Lebow, and J. G. Stein. 1985. *Psychology and Deterrence*. Baltimore, Md.: Johns Hopkins University Press.

Jiang, Z. 1991. "China on Its March Towards the 21st Century." *Beijing Review* 34, 21: 11–16.

Jing, J. 1989. "The Economic Relations Between the Mainland and Taiwan, and the Concept of an Economic Bloc." *Chinese People's University Reprint Series* F14: 59–64.

Kennedy, P. 1987. *The Rise and Fall of the Great Powers: Economic Change and Military Conflict from 1500 to 2000*. New York: Random House.

Keohane, R. O., and J. S. Nye. 1977. *Power and Interdependence: World Politics in Transition*. Boston: Little, Brown.

Langer, W. 1950. *Encyclopedia of World History*, 3rd rev. ed. Boston: Houghton Mifflin.

Linder, S. B. 1986. *The Pacific Century: Economic and Political Consequences of Asian Pacific Dynamism*. Stanford, Calif.: Stanford University Press.

Makin, J. H. 1989. "American Economic and Military Leadership in the Postwar World." In J. H. Makin and D. C. Hellmann (eds). *Sharing World Leadership? A New Era for America and Japan*, pp. 3–40. Washington, D.C.: American Enterprise Institute.

Mearsheimer, J. 1990. "Back to the Future." *International Security* 15: 6–56.

*New York Times*. 1984. Sept. 27.

Pollack, J. D. 1990. "The Sino-Japanese Relationship and East Asian Security." *China Quarterly*. 124: 714–729.

*Renmin Ribao*. 1991a. "Proposal of the CCP Central Committee on the Formulation of the Ten-Year Plan for National Economic and Social Development; and the Eighth Five-Year Plan." January 29, Overseas ed.

*Renmin Ribao*. 1991b. "Strive for the Realization of the Strategic Goals of the

Second Step." January 31, Overseas ed.

Sarbrosky, A. N. 1989. "From Bosnia to Sarajevo." In B. Russett, H. Starr, and R. Stoll. (eds.), *Choices in World Politics*. New York: W. H. Freeman.

Shen, C. S. 1991. "The Hatching of the 'National Unification Program': Notes for History on the Making of a Historic Document." *Global Views Monthly* 6: 64–66.

Silk, M. A. 1990. "Silent Partners: Taiwan Businessmen Are Bullish in China." *China Business Review* 17, 5: 32–41.

Tao, B. 1984. "U.S. Fight for Supremacy in the Asian Pacific Region." *Shijie zhishi [World Knowledge]*. 2: 6–18.

*Tsu-li Tsao-pao* [Independent Daily]. 1991. May 6, p. 2.

USCLTIS (U.S. Commission on Long-Term Integrated Strategy). 1988. *Discriminate Deterrence*. Washington, D.C.: Government Printing Office.

U.S. Department of Commerce. 1990. *Statistical Abstract of the United States*, 11th ed. Washington, D.C.: author.

U.S. Department of State. 1988. "The European Community's Program to Complete a Single Market by 1992" (pamphlet). Washington, D.C.: Department of State, Bureau of European and Canadian Affairs.

Wang, N. T. 1991. "Taiwan's Economic Relations with Mainland China." *Asian Affairs* 18: 99–120.

Wang, S. 1986. "The Economic Development of the Asian Pacific Region, and China's Strategy." *Guoji Shangwu Yanjiu [International Commercial Research]* 2:1–6.

Yuan, Y. 1984. "The Fluctuating Stability in Asia Pacific." *Shijie Zhishi [World Knowledge]* 9: 2–5.

## 5

# Thailand's Political Economy: Change and Persistence

## *Gerald Fry*

### *Migrating Images of the Thai Political Economy*

In a book titled *Thailand: The War That Is, The War That Will Be,* Los Angeles journalist Louis Lomax (1967) viewed Thailand as the next Vietnam. He confidently predicted that Thailand would become engulfed in a violent civil war and become the next communist domino in Southeast Asia. Although Lomax's book, based on an "extensive" three weeks in Thailand, was rightly ignored by both the Thais and serious U.S. scholars, it was probably one of the most widely read nonfiction works on Thailand in recent decades. Even in the late 1970s, several serious Western scholars were still predicting a violent civil war in Thailand (Bradley et al., 1978). In the late 1970s it was also common to hear jokes about Vietnamese tanks rumbling into Thailand only to be stopped by Bangkok's infamous traffic jams. The persisting mainland Southeast Asian refugee problems and the media attention to this issue also tend to cause many to associate Thailand with the currently serious economic problems of Vietnam, Cambodia, and Laos. In Steven Schlosstein's (1991: 203–204) recent volume on the new "little" dragons of Indonesia, Thailand, and Malaysia, he also presents an image of Thailand as an extremely violent society, despite the country's legitimate reputation for Buddhist "softball politics," in which coups and irregular political changes are usually nonviolent.

A second image, closely linking Thailand with the political and economic problems of Vietnam, is that of political instability, reinforced by the media impression of the bloody (by Thai standards) October 14, 1973, student "revolution" and the October 6, 1976, rightist military coup. There have been twenty-one coups or attempted coups (ten having been successful) since 1932, roughly one such incident every 2.8 years (*Matichon Sudsabadaa*, 1991a: 5). Ironically, the October 6, 1976, coup occurred exactly on the same day that the Gang of Four was arrested in the People's Republic of China, a remarkable political coincidence given the impact of these dramatic political changes in both countries. Although coups in both 1981 and 1985 against the Prem government were unsuccessful, the "Saturday Surprise" coup of February 23, 1991, reinforced Thailand's image of being coup prone (see Stowe, 1991, for a valuable historical perspective on Thai coups).

A third political image—a legacy of the mythical *The King and I* and media accounts of the extravagant life-style of Field Marshall Sarit, who died shortly after President Kennedy's assassination in the United States—is one of "oriental splendor and despotism." Despite its gross distortions of Thai history and of King Mongkut, the musical drama of *The King and I* and the subsequent Hollywood film have provided false images of Thailand for millions of Westerners.

A final image, related to the economy, is that of the rice bowl of Asia— a predominantly agricultural country with little modern industrial infrastructure. In this image, Thailand's dependent economy is based predominantly on the production of three commodities: rice, tin, and rubber.

As will be seen in this chapter, many of these old images are now false and misleading. Thailand's political economy has changed dramatically during the past fifteen years at a pace far faster than nearly all had envisioned. Who in 1977 would have predicted that a little more than a decade later Thailand would lead the dynamic Pacific Basin in the rate of growth of manufactured exports and lead the world in economic growth (during the four years 1987–1990); that rice would represent only a relatively small share of approximately 6 percent of Thailand's foreign exchange earnings (NSO, 1990: 93; TDRI 1990: 4); that Thailand would not experience a single irregular nonparliamentary political change during a thirteen-year period (1978–1990); or that Thailand's communist insurgency would be virtually eliminated (Murray, 1984)?

## New Images: Is Thailand a Pacific Basin Tiger and NIC?

In 1988 numerous popular Western magazines such as *Fortune* (March 28) and *Newsweek* (July 11) provided glowing accounts of Thailand as the newest tiger in the Pacific Basin and as the newest Asian NIC (newly industrializing country). Thailand was praised for its impressive export performance, attractive foreign investment climate (Nikkei, 1988), and dynamic entrepreneurs. Prominent Thai economists and industrialists such as Phaichitr

Uatrakul and Amnuay Virawan have been much more cautious and humble in their own assessment. Writing in *Leaders*, Amnuay (1988) states that Thailand is still far from being a NIC. In a thoughtful article, Peter Warr (1987: 60–74) of the Australian National University contrasts Western perceptions of the Thai economy with those of Thai economists writing in the vernacular. The Thais are much less optimistic, focusing on important structural, distributional, and bureaucratic issues. Warr (1987: 60) mentions that "at times, it seems doubtful that the Thai and foreign writers are referring to the same economy at all."

Actually, both perspectives are correct. In aggregate terms, the Thai economy has been performing exceptionally well, as is indicated in this chapter in the section on the new economic realities of Thailand. But at the same time major regional disparities and distributional inequalities persist. With respect to Thailand's status as a potential NIC, there is no doubt that the Bangkok metropolitan area is a NIC with a per capita income comparable to that of Taiwan and higher than that of South Korea. Yet remote rural parts of the north and northeast are far from being NICs (Fry, 1990; Sanitsuda, 1991). Thus, Thailand is and is not a NIC. As is so often the case, Thailand does not neatly fit our simplistic Western categories of binary logic.

## Emerging Political Realities

As Thailand approaches a new century, a complex but workable political system of "half-leaf" democracy and grand coalitions has emerged (Neher, 1988; also see Likhit, 1985, on modern Thai political history). Thai democracy is half-leaf because the senate, whose members hold office for four years, is appointed by the king upon recommendation of the government. Although a new constitution was drafted by a committee established by the National Peacekeeping Council (NPC), which carried out the February 23, 1991, coup d'etat that contained numerous changes, Thailand's half-leaf democracy principle persists.

Having the senate appointed is designed to enhance political order and avoid radical change. Also the prime minister, elected by the combined vote of the appointed senate and elected house, does not have to be an elected member of parliament. Prem Tinsulanonda, Thailand's longest serving "civilian" prime minister (1980–1988, eight years and five months), preferred to stay above partisan electoral politics by neither joining a political party nor running for elected office. For three days following the July 24, 1988, national elections, students and other activists staged rallies protesting the renomination of Prem as prime minister by parliament because of his nonelected status. The persisting influential role of the military in Thai politics, as illustrated in the February 1991 coup, is still another important element accounting for the half-leaf nature of Thai democracy. In addition to the military, the other four major influential groups comprising the Thai polity are the monarchy, the civilian bureaucracy, intellectuals, and more recently wealthy business individuals directly involved in elective politics (Sippanondha, 1990).

Several recent policy issues are also reflective of Thailand's current realities of political economy. The first concerns the building of a controversial dam, Nam Choan, in Kanchanaburi Province in western Thailand. EGAT, Thailand's electrical generating authority, argued for the construction of this dam based on the need for agricultural irrigation and the growing need for cheap electricity by Thailand's rapidly growing manufacturing and industrial sector. A combination of forces—including the international environmental community, the local environmental movement, student interest groups, and technical analyses by Thailand's major autonomous think tank, the Thailand Development Research Institute (TDRI)—led to a shelving of the dam project (Schiemer, 1988: 4). The extensive and open policy debate on this issue and the resultant interest aggregation again reflect an important and persisting element of openness in modern Thai politics.

A second issue—one of Thailand's most critical policy issues—concerns relative regional and personal income disparities (Chulaphob et al., 1988; Suganya and Somchai, 1988). The northeast, where one-third of the Thai population lives, is the most arid part of the country with the poorest soil conditions and the most serious deforestation. It continues to lag significantly behind the rest of the country economically. Absolute regional income disparities have grown dramatically during the past two decades (see Table 5.1). Mirroring these economic disparities are similar patterns related to elite mobility and educational opportunity (Amrung et al., 1990). Those from remote northeastern provinces such as Srisaket, Surin, and Buriram have little opportunity to become part of Thailand's business or bureaucratic elites (Fry and Setboonsarng, 1989).

Responsive to the persisting problems of the northeast, His Majesty King Bhumipol launched in March 1987 the *Isaan Khiaw* (The Greening of the Northeast) project. The goal of this five-year project was to reverse the above trends and to ensure adequate water and irrigation services to the northeast. Despite the idealism of this project and His Majesty's support, there were persisting controversies concerning the implementation of the project, particularly the extent of the army's role in the project. General Chavalit personally viewed this as a priority project for himself and the Thai army when he was Thai army commander. Chavalit's involvement in promoting this project has given him considerable political visibility in Thailand's populous northeast. With its vast financial, manpower, and logistic resources, the military had the potential to have a major impact on the project. A number of civilian politicians, deeply concerned about the long-term political implications of this project, lobbied to have the civilian National Economic and Social Development Board (NESDB) assume coordinating responsibility for the project. The NESDB, the army, the universities, the business community, and international development agencies all became involved in the project. A publication titled *The Green Field Newsletter,* published by the Internal Security Operation Command (ISOC), provided periodic updates on the status of this significant project. The project was "completed" in 1991.

Table 5.1    Regional Income Distribution in Thailand, 1960–1987
(per capita in current baht)

| | 1960 | 1970 | 1980 | 1981 | 1982 | 1983 | 1984 | 1985 | 1987 |
|---|---|---|---|---|---|---|---|---|---|
| Thailand | 2,160 | 3,849 | 14,743 | 16,469 | 17,359 | 18,584 | 19,551 | 20,263 | 23,022 |
| Bangkok | 5,630 | 11,234 | 41,300 | 46,891 | 49,539 | 52,150 | 56,092 | 59,003 | 74,418 |
| Central Thailand | 2,564 | 4,662 | 15,646 | 18,508 | 19,448 | 19,554 | 20,861 | 21,133 | 23,638 |
| South Thailand | 2,700 | 3,858 | 13,745 | 13,496 | 13,419 | 15,058 | 15,200 | 15,358 | 17,832 |
| North Thailand | 1,496 | 2,699 | 9,866 | 11,064 | 11,355 | 12,375 | 12,781 | 13,353 | 13,170 |
| Northeast Thailand | 11,082 | 1,822 | 6,012 | 6,581 | 7,185 | 8,107 | 8,009 | 8,124 | 8,383 |
| Ratio of Bangkok to Northeast | 5.2 | 6.2 | 6.9 | 7.1 | 6.9 | 6.4 | 7.0 | 7.3 | 8.9 |
| Ratio of Central to Northeast | 2.4 | 2.6 | 2.6 | 2.8 | 2.7 | 2.4 | 2.6 | 2.6 | 2.8 |
| Absolute disparity between Bangkok and Northeast | 14,548 | 9,412 | 35,288 | 40,310 | 42,354 | 44,043 | 48,083 | 50,879 | 66,065 |

*Sources:* Keyes (1987: 159) and TDRI (1990: 2).

Also noteworthy since the fall from power of the Gang of Five in 1977 is the dominance of softball politics, the essence of which is the gentle treatment of former political enemies or adversaries. Illustrative of softball politics is the current political prominence of both former communist insurgents and former Young Turks involved in the abortive

coup attempts in 1981 and 1985. Softball politics has certainly contributed significantly to Thailand's impressive success in defusing an insurgency that at its peak in 1979 had strength comparable to that of the New
People's Army (NPA) in the Philippines today (Saiyud, 1986: 188). The
political strategies articulated by such military leaders as Prem, Saiyud, and
Chavalit are described in detail in a fascinating volume written by General
Saiyud Kerdphol (1986) titled, *The Struggle for Thailand: Counter-
insurgency 1965–1985.*

Another key feature of contemporary Thai politics is the involvement
of prominent intellectuals and technocrats in governance. Field Marshall
Sarit in the early 1960s began utilizing such technocrats as advisers and
administrators of new technical policy-oriented agencies, and the 1980s and
1990s have seen a special emphasis on the utilization of such talent. The
cabinet appointed after the February 1991 coup is dominated by prominent intellectuals and technocrats and is without question the most brilliant
in Thai history. Its accomplishments, given its limited time in office,
may be unparalleled in modern Thai politics (see Handley, 1991a: 20–21).
Highly respected Thai intellectuals and scientists, such as Sanoh Unakul,
Anat Arbhabhirama, Sanga Sabhasri, Meechai Viravaidya, Phaichitr
Uathavikul, Sippanondha Ketudat, Kaw Sawasdipanich, Kasem Suwannagul,
and Saisuree Jutikul, are members of the new cabinet, and several played
important roles in various Prem governments and policymaking decisions. Phaichitr, for example, was deeply involved in the controversial
"devaluation" of the Thai baht in November 1984. Phaichitr's political
courage in pushing this controversial policy helped facilitate Thailand's
subsequent emergence as one of the Pacific Basin's most dynamic new
exporters. Sippanondha, another of the new cabinet members, was chair
of the Educational Reform Movement and has been a key player in
the development of the Eastern Seaboard Project, designed to divert
development away from the extended Bangkok metropolitan area.
Sippanondha (1990) is the author of a new book providing a critical
assessment of Thailand's alternative political, economic, and sociocultural
futures.

As Thailand moves toward the next century, two important political
events show both the persistence and "impermanence" of Thai politics
(Morell and Morell, 1972; Pridi, 1957; Wijeyewardene, 1991: 9). The
first was the 1988 national election, which brought to power Thailand's
first (since 1976) elected member of parliament (MP), Chatichai, as
prime minister. Second, the "Saturday Surprise" military coup of
February 1991 overthrew the democratically elected Chatichai government and was the first successful coup since 1977, when the repressive
and unpopular Thanin regime was overthrown by a coup group led by
Kriangsak.

## The July 1988 Election: A New Transition

On July 24, 1988, nearly seventeen million Thais went to the polls to select 357 members of a new parliament. The July 24 election was the seventeenth national election since the country abolished its absolute monarchy and became a constitutional monarchy in 1932. As expected, the major political parties supporting then Prime Minister Prem Tinsulanonda won a majority of seats (58 percent) in the new parliament. In Thailand's multiparty system, sixteen parties competed in the election. Gaining the most seats (87) in the election was the Chart Thai (Thai Nation) party. The Chart Thai (sometimes referred to as the "generals' party"), which was established in 1974, is one of Thailand's oldest parties. Its earlier leadership belonged to the Phin-Phao clique of the 1950s. It is considered a rightist, probusiness party.

Chart Thai's leader, Chatichai Choonhaven, chosen as the prime minister, was an experienced politician and former diplomat who had held ministerial portfolios in a number of previous governments. Like his predecessors, Kriangsak and Prem, he was a former Thai military officer, having joined the diplomatic corps in 1958. Chatichai's father was Field Marshall Phin, a leading politician in the late 1940s and 1950s and a former deputy prime minister and army commander. Never having achieved the post of prime minister, one of Phin's last political dreams was for his son, Chatichai, to assume this position of leadership. Several decades later his dream was realized—though soon to be spoiled, ironically, by an unexpected *military* coup.

The major surprise of the 1988 Thai election was Prem's decision not to accept a sixth term as prime minister. Prem, obviously after careful thought, decided to go out as a winner. Reflective of the wisdom of his decision, on the evening of July 28, Thai television Channel 7 featured a documentary titled "Eight Golden Years and a Man Called Prem."

## The "Saturday Surprise" Coup of February 1991

The coup of February 1991 confirmed the view of skeptics who doubted the so-called "maturing" of Thai politics. It reflects the pattern in many dynamic Asian economies for political development (as defined in Western terms) to lag significantly behind the pace of economic change. Although there were a number of interrelated causes for the coup, the fundamental issue was the growing economic power of civilian-business-political elites, relative to the Thai military, which has traditionally dominated politics since the shift to a constitutional monarchy in 1932 (Riggs, 1966; Suchit, 1987).

With the rising financial power associated with Thailand's remarkable economic growth record of the past four years, Chatichai's financial base for competing in the 1992 elections would have been formidable. Also, Chatichai had initiated bold new and potentially highly successful foreign policies to facilitate Thai economic penetration of neighboring countries such as Vietnam, Cambodia, Laos, and Myanmar (Burma). The major rationale for the coup presented to the public was the pervasive and endemic corruption, which was alleged to have reached unprecedented levels during the Chatichai government. Numerous interviews conducted by me in Bangkok following the coup indicated that it was actually popular among many of Bangkok's urban masses. Many middle- and upper-level government bureaucrats had become frustrated as well by their perception of excessive interference with the bureaucracy and related nepotism being allegedly fostered by the Chatichai regime. The level of satisfaction with the coup reflects a rather unique aspect of the Thai political culture, which seems to tolerate such irregular forms of shifts in political power, particularly if the changes bring the system more toward equilibrium. Despite such public attitudes among the urban masses, many students and intellectuals (e.g., Sulak Sivaraksa) were severely upset with the coup and its adverse effects on Thai political development and participation. They strongly disagreed with General Suchinda (a key leader of the coup group, Thai army commander, and a potential future prime minister) when he stated that the coup was one step backward to go ten steps forward (Wijeyewardene, 1991: 13).

In the months following the February coup, the major issue in Thai politics was the nature of the new constitution (Thailand's fifteenth) being drafted by a committee of the National Peace–keeping Council (NPKC). A popular democracy campaign eventually emerged that challenged the attempt of the NPKC to adopt an inadequately democratic constitution. A mass popular rally at Sanam Luang in Bangkok on November 19, 1991, drew more than 70,000 citizens, the largest demonstration since the student "revolution" of 1973 (*The Nation*, 1991: 1). As a result of such a show of "people power," the draft constitution was modified to become more responsive to popular demands. The number of appointed senators, for example, was reduced from 360, equal to the number of elected members of parliament, to a smaller 270. Also, the constitution was changed to prohibit government officials or military officials from serving in the new cabinet. Thus, General Suchinda, Thai supreme commander and army chief and a key member of the February coup group, would be ineligible to be the next prime minister, unless he resigned his army positions.

Despite these modifications, many intellectuals and politicians were still dissatisfied with the constitution approved by the National Legislative Assembly (appointed by the NPKC) on December 7, 1991, and presented to the king on December 9. These critics felt that the new constitution gave too much power to the new senate to be appointed by the NPKC for a four-year term. The senate, for example, can join with the lower house in passing a no-confidence motion against an existing government. General Harn Lernanond of the New Aspiration party called the passing of the new constitution a "quiet coup" because it gave so much power to the NPKC through their control of the new senate (*Bangkok Post Weekly Review*, 1991: 3).

Reflective of the softball nature of Thai politics, the deposed prime minister of Thailand, Chatichai, was able to return to Thailand and has been encouraged by his supporters to compete in the March 1992 elections. Not only did Chatichai return to Thailand, but on October 11, 1991, he was invited to a party at the home of "Big Jord" (General Sunthorn), leader of the coup group that overthrew him seven months earlier (*Lakthaj*, 1991: 1–4).

With a new national election scheduled for March 1992, General Chavalit Yongchaiyudh, formerly head of the Thai military, has clear political ambitions and would certainly be open to a call from the new parliament to become prime minister. General Chavalit, formerly a powerful Thai military leader, has been a leading voice of the Democratic Soldiers' Movement (1981) and helped orchestrate Thailand's highly successful anti-insurgency program, which emphasized political rather than military action. Thailand's Personality Development Centre in conjunction with Chulalongkorn University's Social Research Institute chose Chavalit as Thailand's man of the year for 1987–1988. Chavalit, having formerly resigned from the military during the Chatichai administration, is currently the leader of Thailand's New Aspiration party, which has already attracted to its fold substantial numbers of MPs who earlier were with other parties (*Matichon Sudsabadaa*, 1991b: 10).

Also, Bangkok's dynamic and popularly elected governor, Chamlong Srimuang, leader of the Palang Dharma (Moral Force) party, is offering an alternative to Thailand's traditional parties. His party presents the image of a clean and green Buddhist vision. Chamlong, an advocate of voluntary simplicity, is sometimes referred to as "half-monk, half-man." As his party grows in influence, he too is a likely future candidate for prime minister. Given the newness of Chamlong's party and its lack of a political base outside Bangkok, its winning "only" fourteen seats in the 1988 election was actually quite respectable.

A critically important element in Thailand's unique system of political economy is the monarch, one of the three pillars of the Thai polity along with nation and religion (Buddhism). King Bhumibol Adulyadej has been a key source of stability and commitment. In July of 1988, King Bhumibol became the longest reigning monarch in recorded Thai history, which dates back to the thirteenth century. He may well be the world's most popular political leader. Because he purposefully avoids overt involvement in partisan politics and major policy debates, he remains above conflictual partisan politics and related antagonisms.

## March 22, 1992, National Election

Thirteen months after the "surprise" military coup of 1991, Thailand returned to democracy with its sixteenth national election, held on March 22, 1992. Two thousand seven hundred forty-two individuals competed for seats in the 360-member House of Representatives—with so many parties competing in the election, as expected, no single party emerged with a majority. The largest number of seats, 79 out of 360, was gained by the new Samakkhitham (Justice Unity) Party, backed by the military officers who carried out the 1991 coup. With such a small plurality, a "grand coalition" of parties is needed to govern. Thus, a coalition of five parties was formed, comprising a majority 195 seats; and Mr. Narong Wongwan, leader of the Samakkhitham Party, was nominated to become Thailand's next prime minister. Out of the 2,742 candidates for parliament, Narong, a veteran civilian politician from a northern Thai province, had the third-highest number of popular votes.

Soon after the announcement of the choice of Narong, a serious snag developed: News emerged internationally via a U.S. State Department spokesperson that Narong had been denied a visa for the U.S. in July 1991, because of alleged links to the drug trade. Given this skeleton in Narong's closet, considerable controversy emerged as to the suitability of Narong to be prime minister, despite his impressive popularity among the voters in his constituency and his party's having won a plurality in the election. The coalition parties reconvened and instead nominated General Suchinda Kraprayoon to be prime minister. His nomination was approved by the king on April 7, 1992. General Suchinda, commander of the Thai army, was one of the two key leaders in the February 1991 coup. The Thai constitution does not require that the prime minister be a member of parliament, but does not permit the prime minister to hold concurrently any military or civil service post. Thus, Suchinda had to resign from his military post. Student groups and opposition political parties indicated their strong disapproval because of Suchinda's nonelected status and predicted eventual political unrest because of this undemocratic outcome.

Perhaps the biggest surprise of the election was the showing of the Moral Force Party of Chamlong Srimuang, particularly in the Bangkok area, where his party won a surprising landslide victory, capturing 32 of the 35 seats being contested. Nationwide his party gained 41 seats, dramatically up from their 14 seats of four years ago. Chamlong and his party will be a key opposition group in the new parliament. The dominance of Chamlong's party reflected a strong regional factor in this election. In each of the five major regions of Thailand, a different political party dominated, contributing to the highly dispersed electoral outcomes and potential fragility of the new governing coalition.

## Changing Economic Realities

As a result of an average growth in real GNP of more than 6 percent per year during the past twenty-eight years and the world's most rapid economic growth (36 percent) during the 1987–1990 period, Thailand's income per capita is now approaching $1,500. Between 1982 and 1988, exports of manufactured goods increased a dramatic 318 percent (TDRI, 1990: 4). With such economic growth, Thailand's imports have grown substantially as well, increasing 187 percent during the same time period. The country's economy is becoming increasingly internationalized, with foreign trade now accounting for 60 percent of GDP (TDRI, 1990: 3–4). Thai exports of consumer electronics to the United States went from a minor $7 million in 1988 to $310 million in 1990 (*National Journal,* 1991: 1623).

Thailand has also achieved impressive success in diversifying its international export markets, even more so than other Pacific Basin economies such as that of Taiwan (*Taiwan Statistical Data Book,* 1990: 220, 222). For example, in 1990, 23 percent of Thailand's exports went to the United States, 20 percent to the European Community, 17 percent to Japan, 7 percent to Singapore, 5 percent to Hong Kong, 2 percent to Malaysia, and 26 percent to a wide range of other areas including Canada, Latin America, West Africa, and China (Handley, 1991b: 34). Thus, this nation has achieved a rather remarkable level of export diversity, reflecting its new commitment to broad-based internationalization and avoidance of overdependence on any one nation such as the United States or Japan. Such diversity reduces vulnerability and enhances long-term chances for economic survival and prosperity.

Reflecting such economic conditions, the Thai stock market has been quite robust in the late 1980s. It registered a phenomenal 406 percent percent increase between January 1987 and March 1990, one of the highest in the world (TDRI, 1990: 12). International investors can now easily participate in the Thai stock market through mutual funds available in New York, London, and Tokyo. As part of this economic boom, more than a thousand new factories have been recently built in the extended Bangkok metropolitan area. Six factories are now producing Nike shoes there; and the world's major producer of computer hard disks has a major manufacturing operation in Thailand with approximately 13,000 employees. With so much capital flowing into Thailand from Japan, Hong Kong, Korea, and Taiwan

(Ramstetter, 1988), a number of new projects are being planned, including the current implementation of a major petrochemical complex on the eastern seaboard, a new sixty-three–story World Trade Center, a new athletic stadium seating 100,000, several major skytrain projects, and possibly a new international university. With a minimum wage of $4 a day, many transnational corporations, such as Nike, Seagate Technology, Dole Pineapple, Sharp, Mitsubishi, and Volvo, have moved important production facilities to Thailand.

Thailand's success in diversifying both its industrial and agricultural sectors is remarkable. Although it is still a major world rice exporter, rice, tin, and rubber combined now account for only 13 percent of its foreign exchange earnings (NSO, 1990: 93; TDRI, 1990: 5). In 1988, tourism was more than twice as important as rice as a source of foreign exchange earnings. Textiles and integrated electronic circuits now represent 18 percent of Thailand's foreign exchange earnings. Overall, as table 5.2 indicates, manufactures (26 percent) are almost as important as agricultural products (28 percent) in Thailand's export mix. In terms of the domestic economy, manufacturing's 26.1 percent of GDP is now more than double agriculture's 12.4 percent (Handley, 1991b: 34). By comparison, manufacturing in Taiwan is now 35 percent of GDP (*Chung Yang Jih Pao,* 1990: 1) and in Indonesia it is 18 percent of GDP (*Japan Times,* 1991: 21).

Despite Thailand's steady economic growth, it has largely avoided the inflationary patterns typical of many developing countries. Thailand's success in this regard is largely due to the legacy of "conservative" economists such as Ungtakorn Puey, who prevented Thai politicians from free access to the printing presses of the Bank of Thailand (for the views of Thai economists, see Rangsan and Nipon, 1988; Vichitvong, 1978). Rather conservative fiscal policies in recent years have further contributed to the Thai success in controlling inflation. In recent years the Thai government has also pursued a vigorous policy of privatization. Unprofitable state enterprises are being closed or turned over to the private sector. For example, the famous and historic Erawan Hotel in the center of Bangkok was a victim of this privatization policy in 1988.

## Reasons for Thai Economic Success

There are a multitude of reasons underlying Thailand's remarkable economic success story. First, Thailand is extremely fortunate to have a rich agricultural base. It is one of the few developing countries that is consistently a net exporter of food. In this sense, it differs from the four little tigers (South Korea, Taiwan, Hong Kong, and Singapore), all of which lack natural resources. In fact, Thailand often leads the world as the nation importing the *least* amount of food. In a recent analysis, the Food and Agricultural Organization (FAO) in Rome estimated that Thailand could potentially feed 350,000,000 people with ease (Amnuay, 1988). Thus, wages in Thailand can be low, as individual workers have access to a varied, low-cost, high-quality diet. This condition provides Thailand with a persisting special comparative international advantage because wages are so closely tied to basic food prices.

Table 5.2   The Diversification of Thailand's Exports, January–June 1989

| Export | Percentage of Export Earnings |
| --- | --- |
| Agricultural Products | |
| Rice | 9.8 |
| Rubber | 5.6 |
| Tapioca Products | 5.1 |
| Sugar | 4.5 |
| Frozen Fowl | 1.2 |
| Canned Pineapples | 0.9 |
| Maize | 0.7 |
| Coffee | 0.5 |
| Marine Products | 7.1 |
| Manufactured Products | |
| Textiles and Footwear | 13.7 |
| Precious Stones & Jewelry | 4.5 |
| Integrated Electronic Circuits | 3.4 |
| Furniture | 1.6 |
| Plastic products | 1.5 |
| Wood products | 0.8 |
| Artificial flowers | 0.5 |
| Minerals | |
| Tin | 0.7 |
| Other | 37.9 |

*Source:* TDRI (1990: 5).

Second, Thailand has clearly benefited from the "conservative" economic and monetary policies described above. These have been developed by a cadre of extremely well-trained economists educated at the world's best universities.

With such policies, Thailand has maintained a stable currency, avoided serious inflation, and kept its international debt to a manageable level. Thus, Thailand has an excellent international credit rating and one of the world's most favorable investment climates. In a survey of top executives in Tokyo, Thailand was rated as the second most preferred site for overseas Japanese investment (Nikkei, 1988).

A third most fortunate factor has been Thailand's success in dealing with what was once an explosive population growth in the late 1960s. Fertility rates and population growth rates have declined dramatically during the past fifteen years. The rate of fertility decline in Thailand's northern region is unprecedented in recent demographic history (Cochrane, 1979). One Thai economist and a current cabinet minister, Meechai Viravaidya, has developed a world reputation as a proponent of the condom and has been a key figure in pushing a highly successful community health and family planning program in Thailand. The Thai success contrasts markedly with the serious population problems faced by such developing countries as the Philippines, Mexico, and Kenya.

A fourth key factor has been Thailand's success in integrating its Chinese ethnic minority into its economic and political system (Paisal, 1988: 44–47). This effort has provided Thailand with a pool of dynamic entrepreneurs who have been given full opportunities to pursue their economic interests. Over time, such individuals have also become more prominent in the country's multiple party system. Fortunately, Thailand has avoided the racial problems that exist in other Asia Pacific economies, such as Myanmar, Malaysia, and Fiji.

A fifth key factor underlying Thailand's development success has been its strong commitment to human resource development. As in Taiwan and South Korea, there has been a rapid expansion in educational facilities at all levels during the past several decades. These countries clearly recognize human capital as the wealth of nations. Thailand normally spends 18–20 percent of its national budget on education. It now has more than 300 colleges and universities, including such internationally renowned institutions as the Asian Institute of Technology (the MIT of Asia). Thailand's two open universities, Ramkhamhaeng and Sukhothaithammatirat, each have more than 400,000 students. A major educational reform movement initiated in 1974 after the 1973 student "revolution" has facilitated a steady expansion of both formal and informal education. The nation's literacy rate, as a result, is now estimated to be at 91 percent. Thus, Thailand has a highly trainable and literate labor force.

Another important factor relates to the favorable nature of Thailand's agricultural sector. Never having been a colony, Thailand has no legacy of latifundia or large plantations. Traditionally, Thai farmers have owned their own land. Although land tenancy is now a serious problem in some areas near Bangkok and Chiangmai (Girling, 1981: 69), the common pattern in most parts of Thailand, and particularly in the poorest northeast, is for farmers to have their own land. Even in then-socialist Hungary, there was praise among researchers for Thailand's land tenure system, which contrasts with patterns so common in most of the capitalist less-developed societies (O'Reilly, 1983). As in Japan, South Korea, and Taiwan earlier, this type of land system has facilitated agricultural diversification and economic growth.

A final and critically important factor is Thailand's decision to emulate the outward, export-oriented development strategy pursued earlier by the Asian NICs—namely, South Korea, Taiwan, Hong Kong, and Singapore—rather than follow the internal import-substitution strategies emphasized by a number of Latin American nations. Thailand, along with its ASEAN (Association of Southeast Asian Nations) neighbors, Indonesia and Malaysia, in fact now has certain advantages compared to international competitors such as Taiwan (Bello and Rosenfeld, 1990), which they have emulated. Taiwan's increased cost of labor and an appreciated currency reduced its competitiveness in its traditional export markets, but it is not yet in the science and technology league of Japan. Thus, there are concerns in Taiwan about the threat of deindustrialization (Chen, 1988; *Chung Yang Jih Pao,* 1990: 1). Thailand will eventually face similar issues and dilemmas, but probably not until the beginning of the next century.

## The Thai Model of Political Economy and Its Broader Theoretical Implications

The Thai case provides a rich natural "laboratory" for critically assessing competing theories that seek to explain the complex relations among the goals of growth, equity, and stability (both political and economic) in developing nations. Although there are certainly unique elements of the Thai political economy, this case can help inform such theoretical debates. The Thai case, for example, seems to support strongly those scholars, such as Kuznets (1989) and Coale (1958), who emphasize the potentially positive contributions of reduced fertility for economic growth. Had Thailand persisted with its pronatalist policies of the 1960s, it is doubtful that it could have had near the economic success it has experienced during the last two decades. The Thai case also seems to support clearly Kuznets's well-known inverted-U curve, suggesting increasing income disparities during the middle phases of economic growth (Chulaphob et al., 1988).

With respect to Thailand's noteworthy success in defusing its once serious and threatening communist insurgency, its policies and strategies seem to mirror the policy formulations suggested by James S. Coleman (1990: 502) in his cogent analysis of factors explaining the revoking of authority. Thailand, with its significant investments in education and its underlying wet rice cooperative culture, also confirms the importance of human and social capital stressed by Coleman (1990: 297, 306).

Theoreticians such as Samuel Huntington (1968; Huntington and Nelson, 1976), who emphasize political order and stability rather than inequality and inequity, should be pleased with the empirical evidence from Thailand. Despite the instability suggested by Thailand's coup image, political order and stability along with economic stability have been paramount values in the Thai political economy of development. Since World War II, the Thai currency has perhaps been the most stable of any developing country and Thailand similarly has probably had the least inflation of any developing country over that same period of time. This country has had the same monarch since 1946, and furthermore, a patron–client–oriented and military-dominated bureaucratic polity has been a political constant since the shift from an absolute to a constitutional monarchy in 1932. At times of impending political disorder or chaos, such as October 14, 1973, or October 6, 1976, direct or indirect interventions by either the monarch and/or the military have restored peace, stability, and order.

In a major study of political performance, Gurr and McClelland (1971) offer the criteria of durability, civil order, legitimacy, and decisional efficacy as a means to measure political performance empirically. By their criteria, Thailand's performance has been largely successful, and a popular and responsive monarch has provided impressive and important legitimacy, which has contributed to both the order and durability of the political system. With respect to decisional efficacy, the record is more mixed. Basic decisionmaking related to industrial policy and development strategies has been largely effective, although there has been noticeable weakness in decisionmaking related to environmental degradation, public infrastructure, and the growing hyperurbanization and dominance of Bangkok.

The Thai case, however, directly contradicts other major theories. It fails to provide any support for the deprivation and frustration theories of revolution (Gurr, 1970). Also, it contradicts the liberal model of development (Huntington and Nelson, 1976: 19), which postulates that economic development will lead to greater socioeconomic equality and democratic political participation. Such a theory is highly inconsistent with the recent "unexpected" February 23, 1991, coup, which overthrew an elected government of a country that had just experienced the most successful decade of economic growth in its history—accompanied by growing regional and personal income disparities, not greater equality. The theories of Mancur Olson (1982) appear to provide a more persuasive explanation of the recent coup in Thailand and the country's system of political economy. Prior to the coup, Thailand was moving rather quickly to a much more pluralistic society, with business interests, political parties, and labor groups growing in power and influence. Also, local grassroots environmental and related groups were growing in confidence and influence (*Third World Resurgence,* 1991: 29). The military coup and subsequently introduced policies have clearly weakened such groups relative to the public and military bureaucracies claiming to represent an "all-encompassing national interest." Also since the coup, the military has taken strong action to try to minimize the influence of highly powerful special interest groups at the local level, which have in the past acted freely with few constraints (Brown, 1991: 2). Despite the definitional problems related to the concept of corporatism (Zeigler, 1988), that approach certainly seems to have much more explanatory power in the Thai case than the liberal model articulated by Huntington and Nelson (1976).

In many respects, the Thai model of political economy reflects what Sippanondha (1990) calls the middle path, a key concept in Thai Buddhism. The Thais have tended to avoid extremes in both political and economic worlds and value greatly equilibrium. Swings away from the center toward the left in 1973–1976 (Morell and Samudivanija, 1981) and toward the right in 1976–1977 were unable to sustain themselves. Thailand's radical insurgency eventually collapsed. Its mixed capitalistic economy has strong private and public sectors. Despite increased privatization, it has been politically impossible to dismantle a number of powerful state enterprises. Thailand's rapid economic growth, as discussed earlier, has not solved the problem of serious regional income disparities, which persist and have actually dramatically increased, particularly in absolute terms. Nevertheless, Thailand has developed a substantial middle class; and levels of inequality are substantially lower than in many Latin American and African societies. With respect to the democracy-authoritarianism continuum, Thailand has also been generally toward the center. Its system of half-leaf democracy and soft-ball politics has provided substantial room for political openness and debate and has contributed to limiting sociopolitical conflict. Its system has been free from the extent of authoritarianism experienced by such countries as South Korea, Taiwan, and ASEAN neighbors such as Singapore, Malaysia, and Indonesia. Despite the image of political instability suggested by numerous coups, actually the Thai polity has been highly stable, primarily resulting from the presence of a stabilizing and beloved monarch, a well-trained and competent public bureaucracy, and a relatively powerful and increasingly professional military force.

Thus, Thailand, like its Pacific Basin neighbors, Japan, South Korea, Taiwan, and Singapore, has had the political order essential for economic dynamism. It presents a rather unusual mix of stability/order, growth, inequity, and environmental degradation. In its economic dynamism and political stability it contrasts significantly with the Philippines and numerous Latin American countries such as Peru and Bolivia. Although each country must seek its own model of political economy, the Thai emphasis on a middle path and equilibrium has implications that may well transcend its national boundaries. Chile, for example, after experimenting with the extremes of first the left and then the right, now, following national elections in December 1989, seems on a middle path of political economy with, like Thailand, an emphasis on internationalization and diversification. Other nations such as Peru and Ethiopia, which have experienced intense human suffering as a result of extreme paths, may eventually turn toward more moderate paths of development and political change. Costa Rica in Latin America also represents a middle-path approach to the political economy of development.

## Prospects for the Future

As Thailand's economy has become more international and export-oriented, its interdependence with the global economy and economic policies in the United States, Europe, and Pacific Basin nations has increased significantly. These interdependencies have led to some tensions in Thai-U.S. relations. The Jenkins bill, for example, greatly alarmed the Thai textile industry even though it was eventually vetoed by President Reagan. The U.S. Food Security Act of 1985 (Reynolds, 1986: 13–16) adversely affected Thai rice farmers with its subsidies to U.S. rice farmers. U.S. pressure on the Thai parliament to pass legislation protecting intellectual property rights has further exacerbated tensions and was the ostensible reason for the dissolution of the Thai parliament in April 1988. Recently, Washington has put pressure on Thailand to open its protected cigarette market to U.S. firms, and there have been conflicts over aviation rights. In the Thai vernacular press, there was also disappointment expressed that the United States basically ignored the ninety-day war between Laos and Thailand (January–March 1988) and showed little support for the Thai position, whereas the Soviet Union, Vietnam, and Cuba were allegedly actively supporting Laos during this conflict.

Given the decades of close friendship between the United States and Thailand, however, these snags are unlikely to endanger their relations seriously. Nevertheless, the Thais have legitimate fears regarding potential protectionist pressures from the United States and the possible loss of most-favored-nation status. Thus, Thailand's continued exceptional export performance is contingent upon retaining free access to the markets of the industrialized nations in North America, Europe, and Japan.

Even more than its relationship with the United States, Thailand's future prospects are linked importantly to its key Pacific Basin neighbors such as Japan and other members of ASEAN. Particularly during the past decade,

Japan has become the major external economic player in Thailand in trade, investment, and aid.

Thailand has been an integral member of ASEAN since its inception twenty-four years ago. In the fall of 1991, Prime Minister Anand initiated the idea of an ASEAN Free Trade (AFTA) agreement, even though Thailand's tariffs tend to be higher than its ASEAN neighbors. Both Singapore and Brunei indicated enthusiasm for the idea. Indonesia was more cautious; and Malaysian Prime Minister Mahathir seemed preoccupied with promoting his idea of an East Asian Economic Grouping (EAEG). Both the initiatives of Anand and Mahathir were based on the same fundamental premise—that the Asian countries must respond to the challenge of the new 1992 EC agreement and the North American Free Trade agreement by cooperating more closely among themselves. The Thai initiative called for a gradual movement to AFTA over, for example, a ten-year period. The initial Japanese response to the AFTA idea was positive because the Japanese see a single ASEAN unit of currently 314 million consumers as a massive market for trade and investment.

Thailand is also an active member of the Asia Pacific Economic Cooperation (APEC) group and in that context has argued for greater Thai access to South Korean and Japanese markets. Given the rapid growth in intra-Asian trade, Thailand's excellent relations with its Asian neighbors and its history of brilliant diplomacy augur well for its future economic relations in the dynamic Pacific Basin.

There are, however, possible internal constraints that could affect Thailand's ability to maintain its current economic dynamism. Despite the rapid quantitative expansion of its educational system, Thailand has shown inadequate commitment to the development of highly qualified technical, engineering, and scientific manpower (Yoshihara, 1988: 125). Thus, there is intense competition among firms for such highly trained individuals. For example, its secondary school enrollment ratios are the lowest in ASEAN (Ungphakorn, 1991: 2). The country also faces serious bottlenecks with respect to its physical infrastructure as well, particularly in the areas of urban roads, public transportation, ports, and communications.

If protectionist tides do not emerge against its exports, Thailand's long-term export potential is impressive. Its combination of low wages, low food prices, increasing automation and productivity, a literate and trainable labor force, and a large domestic market augur well for its international competitiveness. Thailand's success in beginning to develop new markets for its products in areas such as Africa and other parts of mainland Southeast Asia are also noteworthy. Thus, there is little doubt that Thailand will indeed become another Pacific Basin tiger.

Regarding Thailand's long-term future, a key policy question relates to the problem of environmental deterioration both in Bangkok and in rural areas (Anat et al., 1987; Phanu et al., 1990; Sippanondha, 1990). Excessive deforestation with related soil deterioration has adversely affected remote rural areas, particularly in the northeast. Traditionally, Thai farmers have expanded production by increased acreage through the cutting of forests. This is no longer feasible environmentally, and forceful policies are essential to preserve Thailand's rich rain forests and fragile ecosystem. Hyperurbanization in Bangkok, with its related traffic congestion and health problems, is also a serious policy issue (Fry, 1983: 14–32; Ginsburg et al., 1991). A mass transit rail system now being planned is imperative to enhance Bangkok's quality of life and to reverse the pattern of environmental decay.

A final and critically important question relates to the future of Thailand's political development. In the years ahead there will certainly be pressures to reform the Thai political system in order to bring it closer to full-leaf democracy and in line with the principle of one-person, one-vote. The power of money and finance in Thai electoral and parliamentary elections persists as a thorny problem and was one ostensible rationale for the February 1991 coup. This situation has resulted in political apathy, particularly among some more educated Bangkok voters, resulting in disappointingly low voter participation (only 37.5 percent voted in the July 24, 1988, national election) in the capital itself (*The Nation,* 1988: 2). In that regard, an intriguing question is whether Maha Chamlong's new Moral Force party can transcend a certain degree of latent political cynicism by inspiring greater political participation and a new type of genuinely Buddhist political economy of development and leadership, which appear essential for confronting the challenges that Thailand faces as it approaches a new century of accelerated technological, economic, environmental, and cultural change.

## Note

I am indebted to several Thais for their valuable help in preparing this chapter. First, I thank Voraporn Bovornsiri of Chulalongkorn University for having provided me with extensive data on the outcomes of the July 24, 1988, national election. Discussions with Thai political scientist Vichai Tunsiri about the meaning of that election were also helpful. Tatsanee Setboonsarng helped in preparing statistics and doing bibliographic work. Hsiu-Hua Lai provided assistance in compiling data on economic conditions in Taiwan.

The "migrating images" metaphor at the beginning of the chapter is borrowed from Johnson (1975).

## References

Amnuay, V. 1988. "Thailand: Tiger, Tiger, Burning Bright." *Leaders* 11: 124–125.

Amrung, C., S. Chantavanich, and G. Fry. 1990. *Evaluating Primary Education: Qualitative and Quantitative Policy Studies in Thailand.* Ottawa: International Development Research Centre.

Anat, A., D. Phantumavanit, J. Elkington, and P. Ingkasuwan (eds.). 1987. *Thailand: Natural Resources Profile.* Bangkok: Thailand Development Research Institute.

*Bangkok Post Weekly Review.* 1991. "Passage of Charter 'a Quiet Coup.'" December 20, p. 3.

Bello, W., and S. Rosenfeld. 1990. *Dragons in Distress: Asia's Miracle Economies in Crisis.* San Francisco: The Institute for Food and Development.

Bradley, W., D. Morell, D. Szanton, and S. Young. 1978. "Thailand, Domino by Default?: The 1976 Coup and Implications for U.S. Policy, with an Epilogue on the October 1977 Coup." Athens, Ohio: Center for International Studies, Southeast Asia Program.

Brown, A. 1991. "The Coup and Thai Democracy." *Thai-Yunnan Project Newsletter* 12: 1–3.

Chen, T. C. 1988. "Tai wan hui fa sheng chan yeh kung tung hua ma?" ["Will Deindustrialization Happen in Taiwan?"] *Chung Kuo Lun Tan* [China Tribune] 26: 78.

Chulaphob, S., D. Putamasiriwat, T. Ashakul, and K. Chimkul. 1988. *The Long-Term View on Growth and Income Distribution.* Bangkok: Thailand Development Research Institute.

*Chung Yang Jih Pao* [Central Daily News]. 1990. April 9, International ed., p. 1.

Coale, A. 1958. *Population Growth and Economic Development in Low-Income Countries.* Princeton, N.J.: Princeton University Press.

Cochrane, S. 1979. *The Population of Thailand: Its Growth and Welfare.* Washington, D.C.: World Bank.

Coleman, J. S. 1990. *Foundations of Social Theory.* Cambridge, Mass.: Belknap.

Democratic Soldiers' Movement. 1981. *Ko Senoo Naew Thang Kae Panhaa khong Chaat khong Tahaan Prachaatipatai [Proposals for Solving National Problems by the Democratic Soldiers].* Bangkok: H.J.K. Chutimakaanphim.

Fry, G. 1990. "The Other Thailand: Prospects and Problems Related to the Development of the Northeast." In L. Chen (ed.), *Proceedings of the Fourth International Conference on Thai Studies.* Kunming, PRC: Institute of Southeast Asian Studies.

Fry, G. 1983. "Bangkok: The Political Economy of a Hyperurbanized Primate City." *The Asian Journal of Public Administration* 5: 14–32.

Fry, G., and T. Setboonsarng. 1989. "An Elite Production Function for Thailand: A Political Geography Perspective." Paper presented at the annual conference of the Northwest Regional Consortium for Southeast Asian Studies, University of British Columbia.

Ginsburg, M., B. Koppel, and T. G. McGee. 1991. *The Extended Metropolis: Settlement Transition in Asia.* Honolulu: University of Hawaii Press.

Girling, J. L. S. 1981. *Thailand: Society and Politics.* Ithaca, N.Y.: Cornell University Press.

Gurr, T. 1970. *Why Men Rebel.* Princeton, N.J.: Princeton University Press.

Gurr, T., and M. McClelland. 1971. *Political Performance: A Twelve Nation Study.* Beverly Hills, Calif.: Sage.

Handley, P. 1991a. "Clearing the Decks." *Far Eastern Economic Review.* December 19, pp. 20–21.

Handley, P. 1991b. "Growth Without Tears." *Far Eastern Economic Review.* July 18, pp. 34–35.

Huntington, S. P. 1968. *Political Order in Changing Societies*. New Haven, Conn.: Yale University Press.

Huntington, S. P., and J. Nelson. 1976. *No Easy Choice: Political Participation in Developing Countries*. Cambridge, Mass.: Harvard University Press.

*Japan Times*. 1991. "Indonesia: The Years of Living Prosperously." August 11, p. 21.

Johnson, S. 1975. *American Attitudes Toward Japan, 1941–1975*. Washington, D.C.: American Enterprise Institute.

Keyes, C. F. 1987. *Thailand: Buddhist Kingdom as Modern Nation-State*. Boulder, Colo.: Westview.

Kuznets, S. 1989. *Economic Development, the Family, and Distribution: Selected Essays*. Cambridge: Cambridge University Press.

*Lakthaj*. 1991. "Chatichai 'Khliarcaj' Big Jord Rab Naathii Samkhan Pya Baanmyuang" ["Chatichai and Big Jord Level with Each Other, Accepting Important Duty to the Country"]. October 14–20, pp. 1–4.

Likhit, D. 1985. *Thai Politics: Selected Aspects of Development and Change*. Bangkok: Tri-Sciences Publishing House.

Lomax, L. 1967. *Thailand: The War That Is, the War That Will Be*. New York: Vintage Books.

*Matichon Sudsabadaa*. 1991a. "Pathiwat 23 Kumphaa '34" ["Revolution of 23 February"]. March 3, pp. 5–18.

*Matichon Sudsabadaa*. 1991b. "Saamakhiithaam-Khwaamwangmaj Poed 'Talaadnad' S. S. Suung Sud Hua La 5 Laan" [Justice Unity Party–New Aspiration Party Open 'Weekend Market' for MPs, Highest Going for 5 Million]. June 30, p. 10.

Morell, D., and S. Morell. 1972. "The Impermanence of Society: Marxism and the Political Philosophy of Thailand's Pridi Banomyong." *Southeast Asia: An International Quarterly* 2: 397–424.

Morell, D., and C. A. Samudivanija. 1981. *Political Conflict in Thailand: Reform, Reaction, Revolution*. Cambridge, Mass.: Oelgeschlager, Gunn & Hain.

Murray, C. 1984. "The Domino That Didn't Fall." *Atlantic* 254: 34–48.

*The Nation*. 1991. "Politicians Reject Concessions." November 20: 1.

*The Nation*. 1988. July 25, p. 2.

*National Journal*. 1991. "Japan Outstrips the U.S. in Southeast Asia." June 29, p. 1620–1625.

NSO (National Statistical Office). 1990. *Statistical Yearbook Thailand 1990*. Bangkok: author.

Neher, C. 1988. "Thailand in 1987: Semi-Successful Semi-Democracy." *Asian Survey* 28: 192–201.

Nikkei Advertising Research Institute. 1988. *Country Image Survey: Present State and Future Prospects of Foreign Direct Investment by Japanese Corporations*. Tokyo: author.

Olson, M. 1982. *The Rise and Decline of Nations: Economic Growth, Stagflation, and Social Rigidities*. New Haven, Conn.: Yale University Press.

O'Reilly, F. D. 1983. *Thailand's Agriculture*. Budapest: Akademiai Kiado.

Paisal, S. 1988. "Happy Together: Chinese in Thailand Gain Affluence and Influence but Avoid Antagonism." *Far Eastern Economic Review*. February 18, pp. 44–47.

Phanu, K., T. Panayotou, and K. Charnprateep. 1990. *The Greening of Thai Industry: Producing More and Polluting Less*. Bangkok: Thailand Development Research Institute.

Pridi, B. 1957. *Khwaampenanpicang khong Sangkhom [The Impermanence of Society].* Bangkok: Kwien Tong Publishing Company.

Ramstetter, E. D. 1988. "Taiwan's Direct Investment in Thailand: The Potential for Technology Transfer." *Development & South-South Cooperation.* December, pp. 113–127.

Rangsan, T., and P. Nipon (eds.). 1988. *Setakit Thai: Bon Seen Taang Haeng Santhiprachayathaam [Thai Economics: On a Path to a Philosophy of Buddhist Peace],* 2 vols. Bangkok: Faculty of Economics, Thammasat University.

Reynolds, S. 1986. "Food Security Act of 1985 Expects to Boost U.S. Rice Exports." *Rice Outlook and Situation Report.* May, pp. 13–16.

Riggs, F. 1966. *Thailand: The Modernization of a Bureaucratic Polity.* Honolulu: East-West Center Press.

Saiyud, K. 1986. *The Struggle for Thailand: Counter-insurgency 1965–1985.* Bangkok: S. Research Center.

Sanitsuda, E. 1991. *Behind the Smile: Voices of Thailand.* Bangkok: Thai Development Support Committee.

Schiemer, F. 1988. "Nam Choan Dam Will Damage Precious Aquatic Resources." *The Nation.* February 4, p. 4.

Schlosstein, S. 1991. *Asia's New Little Dragons: The Dynamic Emergence of Indonesia, Thailand, and Malaysia.* Chicago: Contemporary Books.

Sippanondha, K., with R. Textor. 1990. *The Middle Path for the Future of Thailand: Technology in Harmony with Culture and Environment.* Honolulu: East-West Center Press.

Stowe, J. 1991. *Siam Becomes Thailand: A Story of Intrigue.* Honolulu: University of Hawaii Press.

Suchit, B. 1987. *The Military in Thai Politics.* Singapore: Institute of Southeast Asian Studies.

Suganya, H., and J. Somchai. 1988. *Thailand's Income Distribution Poverty Profile and Their Current Situations.* Bangkok: Thailand Development Research Institute.

*Taiwan Statistical Data Book.* 1990. Taipei: Council for Economic Planning and Development.

TDRI (Thailand Development Research Institute). 1990. *Thailand Economic Information Kit.* Bangkok: author.

*Third World Resurgence.* 1991. "Thai Coup's Effects on Peoples' Movements." June, pp. 29–30.

Ungphakorn, P. M. 1991. "Secondary Enrollment Ratios in Thai Schools Lowest in ASEAN." *Bangkok Post Weekly Review.* December 27, p. 2.

Vichitvong, N. P. (ed.). 1978. *Readings in Thai Political Economy.* Bangkok: Bangkok Printing Enterprise.

Warr, P. 1987. "Thai Economic Performance: Some Thai Perspectives." *Asian-Pacific Economic Literature* 1: 60–74.

Wijeyewardene, G. 1991. "The New World Order in Mainland Southeast Asia." *Thai-Yunnan Project Newsletter* 13: 9–14.

Yoshihara, K. 1988. *The Rise of Ersatz Capitalism in South-East Asia.* Oxford: Oxford University Press.

Zeigler, H. 1988. *Pluralism, Corporatism, and Confucianism: Political Association and Conflict Resolution in the United States, Europe, and Taiwan.* Philadelphia: Temple University Press.

## 6

# Guerrilla Capitalism and the Limits of Statist Theory: Comparing the Chinese NICs

### Danny Kin-Kong Lam & Ian Lee

The extremely rapid industrialization of the East Asian newly industrializing countries (NICs) over the last several decades has created much theoretical interest in the question of whether their success can be attributed to a common set of factors. Statist theory, with its emphasis upon state industrial policies (Johnson, 1982), is now probably the most popular explanation for these East Asian "economic miracles." However, statist theory cannot explain the very diverse economic policies adopted by the East Asian NICs, which range from Hong Kong's official policy of laissez-faire to South Korea's highly statist policies.

One fundamental weakness of statist explanations is that, by their very nature, they ignore factors that are not centered on the role of the state. Moreover, the efficacy of state policies can clearly be brought into question. On the one hand, state policies did create or help facilitate the development of many industries in the Chinese NICs—Hong Kong, Singapore, and Taiwan. On the other hand, the record of these industries has been relatively mixed, ranging from outright failure to moderate success. Thus, one needs to look further to discover the core of the "East Asian development model."

In contrast to differing and not always effective state industrial policies, a common feature of the private sector is easy to discern. All these states possess a large sector of small- to medium-scale businesses, which, by and large, have been left alone or ignored by the state. In spite of this neglect, they have become astonishingly successful. Small- to medium-scale firms account for a disproportionate share of the Chinese NICs' exports and are generally regarded as the most dynamic sector of these economies. Inasmuch as state policies and actions did not play a critical role here, they cannot explain how this pattern of business originated and succeeded. This chapter argues, therefore, that the key to understanding the parallels in development among the Chinese NICs lies not in state policies, but in the common patterns of business practiced by small- to medium-sized firms, which we term "Chinese capitalism." This pattern evolved later into a strategy of business called "guerrilla capitalism." It is a common trait shared by Chinese firms in the NICs, which, we contend, accounts for their success.

## Chinese Capitalism and Guerrilla Capitalism

The rise of the Chinese NICs has been difficult to reconcile with development theory. The problem is that only a handful of states have been exceptionally successful, but many other states have, from the same starting point in the 1950s, been relatively unsuccessful. One reason for this lies in the universal nature of conclusions about economic growth and transformation. Thus, these theories—whether liberal, market-oriented theories or statist theories—are supposed to be applicable to any state under any regime. They do this by relying upon abstract generalizations. A principal abstraction shared by all development theories is the assumption that industrialization and development must follow one model. It is an implied convergence model that presumes firms, industries, and individuals face the same costs, benefits, and returns across all states. Nothing could be further from the truth in the case of Chinese businesses.

Chinese enterprises in the NICs practice a form of business that is distinguished by the following factors:

1. domination of the economy by small- to medium-scale family-owned firms,
2. flexibility and responsiveness of management to customer and market needs,
3. extensive sharing of resources and information among friends and associates,
4. mutually interlocking ownership among small firms, and
5. the tight coupling of businesses to market conditions and a corresponding lack of commitment to any particular product or industry. This is a common pattern, which we term Chinese capitalism.

As the Chinese NICs developed over time, firms evolved into adapting a strategy of guerrilla capitalism. This is a refinement of the above pattern made possible by a large wave of migration from all of the Chinese NICs in the 1950s and 1960s. Overseas Chinese, primarily in North America and Europe, became a conduit to facilitate entrepreneurship by their friends and relatives back home. This created a trade in technology from developed countries to the Chinese NICs, and at the same time provided the Chinese NICs with a sophisticated understanding of the markets in the wealthiest nations in the world. The NICs, therefore, have been enabled to exploit market opportunities in developed countries while still benefiting from their relatively low-cost manufacturing potential in order to develop sophisticated industries. Chinese firms exploited these opportunities using the strategy of a guerrilla force: seek out an opportunity for high profit margins in a particular good, develop a formula, exploit it by rapidly flooding the market before the established firms can respond, make profits over the short term, and then leave the market for another one before competition forces the prices down to the point where NIC firms are no longer profitable without large-scale investments in technology or infrastructure. It is this strategy that explains the success of Chinese firms in exploiting the market opportunities available in the Western world.

## Textile Exports and Their Consequences

All of the Chinese NICs experienced a sustained expansion of their textile industries in the 1950s and 1960s. This was caused by a variety of factors, from the rapid increase of prices for textiles in Japan as the economy recovered after World War II to the rise in textile demand in the United States created by the Korean and Vietnam wars. Thus, all of the Chinese NICs benefited from their strategic location and low cost. Not only were Chinese textile exports inexpensive, but Chinese firms shared the common attribute of willingness to fill small customized orders while offering prompt delivery with high quality. Thus, basic cost advantages were magnified by these qualitative factors (Morawetz, 1981: 107–115).

The reason Chinese firms were willing to "bend over backwards" in meeting customer demands was their relative poverty at that time. It is easy to be flexible when one is desperate for any business. Thus, small- to medium-sized firms who are more concerned with getting an order than wringing the maximum economies of scale from operating their factory at capacity would naturally be more flexible. Moreover, during those years, U.S. military and civilian procurement generated a large demand for quality products built to stringent specifications. The reward for firms able to meet these specifications was large orders for goods that were promptly paid in U.S. dollars. Another factor was that both Taiwan and Hong Kong received many Japanese subcontracts and had the opportunity to learn from dealing with the Japanese during their occupation. The Japanese, even in those days, demanded exacting standards for the goods shipped to them both in terms of promptness of delivery and quality. As the Japanese fine-tuned their production processes in the 1950s and 1960s, a "spillover" effect was created in the NICs. Thus, in the early 1960s, export orders represented the most profitable outlet for the output of textile factories. Consequently, this sector rapidly became "export oriented" in Hong Kong. Taiwan's exports of textiles also improved at about the same time when the negative incentives in the price structure were gradually eased in the 1960s. The government of Taiwan "promoted" exports in the broad sense of the term, but the real work of meeting customer needs and learning how to work to stringent specifications was carried out by the firms themselves.

Many small firms were able to enter the textile industry with relatively little capital because it is not capital-intensive at the assembly stage (however, it is a capital-intensive industry at the synthetic fiber manufacturing stage) and because there were relatively few restrictions on individuals to start small businesses in the Chinese NICs, except for the normally small bribes and favors officials extracted to obtain the requisite business permits and licenses. Initially, these firms might have started out as subcontractors. Then, as they grew larger to become medium-sized firms, they began to be able to compete for business on their own. Due to a variety of factors that led to the persistence of small firms, discussed below, they came to dominate the export sector of the economy.

The dominance of small firms in the export sector enhanced the competitiveness of the entire industry by establishing a high standard of flexibility and customer service. As with any competitive market, it was necessary for all firms to at least match the flexibility of their competitors. When there are so many firms in the market, the unwillingness to customize and meet customer needs can be fatal. On the other hand, in the United States at the same time, firms became more and more bureaucratized and unionized, with strict work rules and regulations governing wages and conditions of work, which made flexibility more difficult to achieve. These forms of institutional barriers to flexibility were unknown in Taiwan's small-scale private business at that time.[1]

From the perspective of liberal economic theory, small size is not necessarily an asset if there are significant economies of scale in production. Although it is true that scale economies are vital if one talks about large production runs, in the real world such large production runs are all too rare. This was especially true of textile exports from the Chinese NICs in the 1960s to 1970s. The fashion industry is inherently engaged in producing a highly diversified, heterogeneous product in which production runs are small. Indeed, few textile items except basic raw materials such as cloth can be produced in continuous processes rather than through batch or piece production. Consequently, small firms in the Chinese NICs were actually not at a large disadvantage because, although the absolute scale economies available to small firms were small, their relative scale economies compared to the size of the average batch order were highly competitive.

The paradox is why small businesses in the Chinese NICs that grew up during this time did not face the constraints on small businesses that exist in the Western world.[2] The classic problems faced by small business include undercapitalization, lack of management skills, lack of technology, and the inability to exploit scale economies. As we have noted above, scale economies may not be relevant to the prevailing pattern of business in the textile trade. However, the issues of undercapitalization and lack of technology remain. These problems are attenuated, however, by the way foreign buyers deal with overseas firms about which they may not know very much. Buyers going to the Chinese NICs wanted, first of all, assurance that the firms with which they were dealing had the capacity to fill their orders. This is normally verified by buyers visiting a potential supplier's factories and making a visual inspection of his facilities. Although this is but a minimum level of assurance that the firm has the competence to fulfill a contract, it is, nevertheless, a typical ritual in dealing with foreign buyers. However, often when a firm succeeds in winning a major bid, that single order is frequently much larger than its capacity. Because the bidding process favors firms that already do a reasonable volume of business, the existing plant would more than likely be occupied by other orders. Because orders in this business are heterogeneous, and volume tends to change quantitatively and qualitatively almost daily, it is impossible to do what would be logical—schedule production into smooth runs that operate concurrently with each other. The solution to this in a Western firm would be to have a large amount of "idle capacity" on hand. However, this requires investment in fixed capital that is not possible because of the undercapitalization of most small firms.

Small Chinese firms did not respond to a lack of capacity in the customary North American fashion. If a U.S. firm had no surplus capacity and the buyer could not wait for a delivery, it would not normally seek business that was beyond its ability to produce in the short term. This contrasted with many Chinese firms, especially the small ones that thrive on bidding on contracts that they knew they could not fill themselves. They were able to do this because they did not allow their own capacity to limit their business. They adopted what can be termed the strategy of a guerrilla. They audaciously bid for many orders without regard to their ability to fill the order. In order to meet contracts they could not fill, they relied on subcontractors. In the odd instance they could not fill an order even with subcontracting, they were content to squander their "reputation" and "goodwill" by not filling the order at all.

An extensive network of subcontracting relationships among firms in an industry is a common pattern in Chinese business. From the point of view of a firm winning a lucrative foreign order that it could not fill, this network effectively engaged the capacity and competence of the industry available to them through subcontracting. This enhanced the efficiency of the industry in two ways. First, it allowed the winning contractor to make trading profits through his knowledge of the local industry and being able to match it up with a customer need. Moreover, the winning contractor would tend to subcontract to firms that had excess capacity, which they would sell at marginal rather than full cost. Second, subcontracting assured the continued existence of other firms even when they failed to spot the same market opportunity. In other words, rather than a zero-sum game typical of the bidding process in Western nations, in Chinese business the loser could also benefit from having less lucrative, but still profitable subcontracting work.

Because foreign buyers were not well connected in the local industry, as long as the prime contractor met quality specifications, there was no way the buyer could actually tell if the goods were in fact produced by the prime contractor. Frequently, they were not. This process explains how a layer of small firms could circumvent the limitations that would normally be placed on them by undercapitalization and the inability to handle large orders. This intricate subcontracting network makes Chinese industry able to respond more as a unified organism rather than as disparate units. By facilitating the growth of small enterprises, this process allowed them a more gradual process of slowly "growing up" to become large businesses. Compared to Western firms, which have to succeed from the beginning, this is a more gradual and realistic way to learn a business.

The system of Chinese industrial organization encourages the formation of small firms. In Hong Kong and Singapore, many of the senior managers of Chinese firms will eventually resign and start their own businesses because of the limited prospects of working for a family-owned firm. On the other hand, in Taiwan, entrepreneurship is enhanced by the Japanese model of fission, which occurs in this manner: As a firm grows larger, often a senior manager is "spun off" to start a new firm on his own. This new firm will represent a subunit of the old firm. The old firm would not only help the new one with loans for equity, but also retain an equity interest in it. The new firm is at once guaranteed orders for its goods through its continuing relations with the old firm. At the same time, the new "boss" is free to look for other business. This pattern both reduces bureaucracy and satisfies the craving in Taiwan that "everyone wants to be boss."

## Capital Ownership Patterns

The consequence of this pattern of intense entrepreneurship is that over time, an extensive, overlapping myriad of friendship, interlinking ownership, and subcontracting relationships is created among firms. The network of subcontracting relationships extends into another pattern of industrial organization unique to Taiwan and Hong Kong. Whereas industries on the Western model typically consist of an integrated factory with a collection of capital equipment collectively owned by one firm, Hong Kong's and Taiwan's industry during the formative years was dominated by a pattern of capital ownership in which each piece of capital equipment was owned by one entrepreneur (Myers, 1984: 515). For example, an assembling factory for electronics circuit boards built on the Western model would own a group of machines that undertook board masking and etching, drilling, perhaps automated component inserters, wave soldering machines, and even possibly a computerized testing machine at the end of the line. Conversely, in the Chinese NICs, each of these pieces of equipment would be owned by a separate entrepreneur.

There are serious disadvantages to this type of piece-oriented capital ownership. For one, extensive quality control of goods that pass through so many independent subcontractors is almost impossible. Second, a manufacturer is always at the mercy of a bottleneck anywhere in the process. Third, the chance of being able to purchase the services of the ideal type of machinery to do the job by an entrepreneur is remote because it is more than likely not available. But looking at it from the Chinese perspective, the system as a whole is inherently flexible. No one is "stuck" with a fixed investment in an integrated and specialized plant that might be idle much of the time during periods of slack demand. Moreover, machinery in a Western plant is idle much of the time because it is not possible to perfectly match scale economies of a collection of discrete capital equipment. In contrast, in the Chinese pattern of capital organization, capital equipment is not "locked into" one industry. Chinese industrial owners tend to see their capital equipment as machines with the capability to produce a wide range of commodities rather than equipment for specific industries. Therefore, there are few institutional barriers to capital mobility (i.e., metal stamping machines that normally stamp buckles can be readily adapted to stamp automobile parts if needed). In other words, no Chinese owner of a stamping plant for automobile parts is going to turn down business stamping computer casings if there is surplus machine capacity and if the price is right.

This pattern of capital ownership enhances the ability of businessmen to respond rapidly to new market demands providing that the industry is relatively concentrated geographically. This is true of all the Chinese NICs. It contrasts with a much more geographically dispersed form of industrial organization on the Western model, in which it is neither practical nor feasible to have as extensive a pattern of subcontracting or discrete capital goods ownership available "for hire."

The implications of this form of capital ownership for industrial flexibility in the Chinese NICs are very important. Following the Western model of capital ownership, specific manufacturing services can be purchased from discrete sources such as custom machine shops, but the prices for custom work is comparatively high. If an entrepreneur in North America wished to manufacture ten units of a prototype, it would be very costly out of pocket unless he had access to corporate resources that can command those services on an in-house basis. On the other hand, a small entrepreneur in Taiwan who wanted to create a new product need only find capital to pay for the cost of using the manufacturing services he needs, which can be purchased from other entrepreneurs, as opposed to investing in specialized equipment and tooling "up front." The costs of this form of custom work are typically much lower than the costs of ordering a small batch of custom-made parts from a manufacturer in the United States. This allows small batch runs of products to be made, tested, marketed, and sold before an entrepreneur has to commit to larger scale tooling and investment. In effect, the start-up cost is lower in the Chinese NICs than comparable costs of entry into an industry where one has to purchase a turnkey facility from scratch. Thus, the pattern of capital ownership contributes greatly to flexibility in manufacturing in the Chinese NICs. The commercial environment in these states makes it easy to start a business and permits an entrepreneur to invest larger sums only after it has "grown up." Once a small firm grows up, it would then gradually take on the more "mature" form of an integrated business over time.

## *Blend of Chinese and Western Management Skills*

The second major problem faced by small firms is a lack of management skills. In a Western enterprise, substantial administrative skills are necessary to plan, organize, and best utilize the limited resources of a small firm. Small firms are most frequently those with the weakest management skills in the West; therefore, they often fail. This makes the success of small Chinese firms more problematic for theories of development—they ought to be the ones most prone to failure, yet they seem to be at the cutting edge of the NICs' success. One of the problems with the Western conception of management skills is that it is very much based on the idea of best utilizing resources in an essentially static framework of analysis. Thus, managers consistently aim to wring the highest output out of a relatively static, unchanging market and production environment. Because of the rapid change in the economy of the Chinese NICs, the pattern of long-term planning and bureaucratization common to Western firms is a handicap for all but the largest firms.

Sophisticated management skills such as organization building, marketing, and planning are less important for small businesses in the NICs because their operations are smaller. Similarly, sophisticated managerial accounting, control, and organization are not needed because the entrepreneur, as the owner, is able to make decisions independently of other managers. Accountability and management systems that simulate the idealized owner-entrepreneur in Western corporate organizations are unnecessary in small owner-operated firms in the NICs. Moreover, there are cultural barriers to the development of a Western-style, functionally divided form of firm organization.

A cultural barrier to adapting a Western form of functionally specialized firm organization divided into branches (such as sales, marketing, production, accounting, and general management) is the Chinese culture and the business environment that it engenders. The Chinese are a group-oriented people who place a premium on trust of insiders and, conversely, distrust of outsiders. Therefore, people who are related are, by definition, more trustworthy than outsiders. In fact, the distrust of outsiders is so intense that frequently outsiders—even those with technical skills that are greatly needed in a firm—are not brought into the firm because they cannot be trusted. This is not simply an unjustified paranoia. In all the Chinese NICs, there are few moral or effective legal barriers to someone in a position of trust embezzling funds and disappearing—to Hong Kong if they are from Taiwan, or vice-versa, or elsewhere beyond the reach of the law. In fact, it happens frequently despite substantial safeguards by firms. Thus, in a typical Chinese firm, the owner-entrepreneur is normally surrounded by his immediate family members as his most trusted assistants. No outsider is trusted. There are, however, exceptions to the rule. Those who are not family relations but occupy positions of trust normally begin in very junior positions; only over a period of many years do they gain the status of being an insider. Finally, as insiders, their status becomes indistinguishable from that of family members.[3]

Chinese firms, therefore, are not just small because of economic constraints, they stay small because there are barriers to the formation of corporate forms of organization, which, although not impossible, are difficult for most to overcome (Pye, 1985: 71). Indeed, many "big businesses" in the NICs are in fact not large-scale firms on the Western model of a corporation. They are, in fact, a collection of small firms in discrete businesses that are often not even remotely related or managed in a coherent fashion (Hamilton and Biggart, 1985: 13–17). The Western hierarchical model of bureaucratic, meritocratic, functionally specialized organization is not the dominant form of firm organization in small- to medium-scale enterprises in locally owned firms in the Chinese NICs. The typical small firms rely on the expertise localized in one man—the owner. This suggests that there are limitations to the size of any one firm that is managed by the owner and his immediate family members. It limits the firm's size to roughly two hundred employees before it encounters major problems with managerial control and coordination.

The inability of Chinese firms to grow large is not entirely a disadvantage. The problems of planning and accounting are less of a burden for them. Moreover, the neglect of formal records, detailed written plans, and accounting also allows a firm to play a "cat and mouse game" with the state's tax collectors more effectively and to circumvent a myriad of regulations that bound business. This is especially a crucial problem for Taiwanese firms as they must all play a game with officials. Few of the smaller firms bother to obtain the numerous permits needed to legally start a business. Thus, they are able to evade most of the more burdensome regulations that saddle large firms. Small firms are better able to evade the tax burden placed on private enterprise in Taiwan.[4] Firms in Hong Kong, on the other hand, have benefited from a relatively low level of taxation. They did, however, have to deal with a degree of official corruption until the late 1970s.

Another factor limiting size is the rapidly changing nature of the business environment in the Chinese NICs. Because of the high degree of uncertainty created by the competitive nature of the marketplace and the need to be flexible, long-term planning is irrelevant to most small- or medium-sized Chinese firms. A very long term plan would be for six months. This lack of foresight is appalling to Western notions of business, but in Chinese firms it is the norm. Given a rapidly changing business environment, it makes sense. It represents an excellent adaptation of local management style and skills to the needs of the local business environment.

As discussed earlier, Chinese firms have historically had a high willingness for accommodating customer demands born of the cut-throat business environment of the 1950s. In its modern form, this was carried over to a general industrial trend of willingness to innovate. By innovation, we mean not necessarily technological innovation, but innovation in spinning off new products or derivatives of products primarily from existing facilities. This contrasts with the North American or European industrial culture in which manufacturers in one industry have a strong inclination to stay within that industry. Manufacturers in the Chinese NICs tend to take a much more relaxed view of these arbitrary psychological boundaries. They are masters of the art of "lateral thinking." As an example, a shirtmaker would think nothing of moving his sewing machines aside and starting to assemble toasters if there were a sudden demand that he could accommodate. Many of the electronics and computer firms today are former textile makers who learned how to assemble computers.

Business in the Chinese sense is not about industrialization or other lofty goals. It is rather about making money. If making money is the objective, then industrialization or enhancement of manufacturing output is neither a necessary nor a sufficient condition toward achieving that goal. In this sense, manufacturing firms in the Chinese NICs are not industrialists in the sense of being specialized in one industry, they are generic manufacturers who possess skills in assembly. Whether they assemble toys, textiles, computers, or vacuum cleaners is irrelevant to them as long as there are good profit margins.

A major hurdle facing small firms is the problem of acquiring and adapting modern technology. For the Chinese NICs that began with a primitive industrial base in the 1950s, this was a serious problem that had to be overcome. However, the colonial legacy for all of them was not entirely negative. For Taiwan, the Japanese occupation resulted in a legacy of infant industries, initiated by the Japanese, and excellent infrastructural facilities. Similarly, Hong Kong and Singapore inherited an excellent infrastructure from Britain. As Japan's economy recovered in the 1950s, its textile industry became increasingly uncompetitive on the world market. It was natural for the obsolescent technology to be sold to entrepreneurs in the Chinese NICs. Thus, all of the latter countries were able to obtain a low-cost, reliable source of technology for their industries. The success of "low technology" industrial activity provided all the Chinese NICs with a foundation on which to build a more sophisticated industrial base through a process that we term "guerrilla capitalism."

## Guerrilla Capitalism

Guerrilla capitalism is an expansion of the pattern of business discussed above. It is a refinement and enhancement of Chinese capitalism based on two new factors. First, the creation of a network of multinational market linkages through the overseas Chinese community caused a flow of technology and market knowledge from the developed world to the Chinese NICs. Second, multinational corporations unintentionally transferred their technology and know-how to local managers. Thus, these parallel processes added to the skills and industrial capabilities available in the Chinese NICs, and at the same time exposed them to market opportunities in the developed markets of the world.

In order to understand these phenomena, one must turn to the impact of outward migration on these economies. However, as the economies of the Chinese NICs improved in the 1970s and 1980s, this outward migration became complemented by an increase in "returnees." Although many of them were fresh graduates with relatively few usable skills, there were among them a large number who possessed both advanced degrees and years of practical experience in Western firms. This group of emigrés provided a direct link with the markets of developed nations, particularly the United States, while bringing to the economy a degree of know-how that was immediately applicable in the less developed economies of the Chinese NICs at that time.

The availability of a network of family and relations with timely, on-the-spot information about market and business trends and needs in the largest market in the world was instrumental in raising the awareness of new outlets for the low-cost goods made in the Chinese NICs.

It became self-evident to many Chinese that importers and distributors earned large profit margins. Thus, it was possible to either purchase or manufacture many goods in Hong Kong or Taiwan and distribute them at lower prices than those prevailing in the United States. Another unintended consequence of this large wave of migrants was that they brought back not only education but also ideas and technology from their extended stay in the United States. Hence, much of the export industrialization benefited from this free flow of technology and know-how from Chinese students returning from the United States. This provided an infusion of technology and modern management skills into the Chinese NICs' economies that largely explains their ability to upgrade to high-tech products from their base in low-tech goods. Whereas the skills of an engineer with ten years' experience may be only average in the United States, these skills could be put to much better use in the Chinese NICs in the 1970s because of the low labor costs and the shortage of skilled engineers. Because starting a small business was relatively easy, many of the emigrés ended up opening their own businesses.

## *Multinational Corporations and Technology*

The impact of multinational corporations (MNCs) opening assembly plants in the electronics industries in the Chinese NICs is critical to understanding how these countries developed a base in electronics manufacturing. MNC investments in the Chinese NICs in the 1960s and 1970s were heavily concentrated in the electronics industry, which moved offshore because of rapidly rising labor costs in the United States. Faced with low-cost competition from Japan, many electronics manufacturers moved their most labor intensive assembly operations into the Chinese NICs—first Hong Kong, then Taiwan, and later Singapore. Manufacturers found that not only were labor costs low compared to other Third World states, but labor was also more productive. As Morawetz (1981: 149) observed, "On average, output per worker in the garment industry appears to be 30 to 50 percent higher in East Asia than in Colombia; as a result, Colombia's labor costs (wages paid per garment produced) are significantly higher than those in Korea and Taiwan and possibly in Hong Kong."

Manufacturers found that Chinese workers possessed a particular skill and deftness in the assembly of textiles, which was in turn transferable to assembling complex electronic components. This facility in assembling textiles, Morawetz (1981: 132) observed, was a function of the generalized societal training in manual dexterity received by the workers as well as their physical characteristics such as the thickness of their fingers and their hand-eye coordination. This skill in assembly work was acquired through learning to write Chinese characters, which trained people to develop a high degree of manual dexterity, self-discipline, and willingness to carry out repetitive tasks precisely. It was the availability of this pool of highly skilled laborers at a reasonable cost that attracted large numbers of electronics assemblers to the Chinese NICs. Eventually, the rather rudimentary assembly work attracted manufacturers of components who wished to take advantage of the same low-cost labor and also to be closer to their customers who had moved to the Chinese NICs earlier.

In many other Third World countries, this offshore manufacturing benefited the host country only to the extent that it employed local labor, whereas for the Chinese NICs it resulted in multiple spinoffs. One of the more interesting characteristics of this phenomenon was the transfer of many skills to the NICs. Because of the prohibitive cost of employing expatriate managers in overseas plants, most MNCs chose to employ lower-cost local managers. However, the local managers turned over very quickly because of competition for their skills from other MNCs opening their own plants. Also, many utilized their tenure at an MNC to acquire skills, knowledge, and contacts in the industry to enable them to start their own businesses. In many cases, after no more than two years of employment with an MNC, a senior local manager would resign, purchase the identical or similar manufacturing equipment from the MNC's suppliers, and open up shop as a direct competitor at an even lower cost. The pattern of piece-oriented capital ownership and other infrastructure supporting entrepreneurship in the Chinese NICs made it possible to lower the cost of entry into any business.

## Guerrilla Industrialism

Many of the small firms opened by former employees of multinational electronics firms later developed into large firms in their own right. Initially, they began as small businesses that supplied the small but growing local market. Because these new Chinese competitors were all undercapitalized, they did not necessarily begin by opening integrated factories on the Western model unless they had backing from local financial sources. They bought the absolute minimum amount of specialized equipment and relied on outside sources for the other services they needed. This gave them tremendous flexibility in what they manufactured. As start-ups, they were inherently less bureaucratic and more anxious to win any business. Consequently, they were willing to tailor products to their customers' specifications and do whatever was required to build up their fledgling businesses. Because the electronics components industry is characterized by a highly heterogeneous product mix and frequent spot shortages of specific components, Chinese entrepreneurs responded to this market environment with an ingenious form of doing business. They took their customary "flexibility" one step further.

Chinese entrepreneurs would constantly search for products with high margins, which not only their own firm but the industry was capable of producing. Thus, if margins were good for one product possibly because of a short-term shortage (e.g., low-power resistors), they would enter that market when the margin was high, knowing that they ultimately would not be the lowest cost suppliers. Once the market reached equilibrium, they were no longer competitive against the major suppliers who had specialized, automated equipment. But by that time they had already made their profits and moved on to other products. Through repeated processes of this type of "raiding" markets, fortunes were made and many of the small businesses prospered. Before long they began to move beyond the local markets. In time, these small local firms acquired the contacts to exploit the trading margins MNCs were enjoying in distributing components made in the Far East. This process of the "trickle down" of knowledge from MNCs allied with the network of kinship relations abroad enabled them to exploit the high prices for electronics components and other manufactured goods in the U.S. market. Thus, a strategy of being a guerrilla was established: Look for a product that a firm thought it could manufacture in the NICs, make it quickly and flood the market with the product, and move on as the price of the product declined in the overseas market in response to competition.

One manufacturer interviewed said he would go to visit a buyer at a major U.S. department store, and just prior to the meeting he would go through the store's catalog and then offer to make certain catalog items. He would then solicit an order by offering to price his products 20 percent below whatever the buyer was paying. In many cases, he would leave the buyer's office with an order. It was only after he won the order that he would purchase a sample of the item from the store to take back to Taiwan to figure out how to manufacture it. This form of guerrilla capitalism had the benefit that it did not require the Chinese NICs to possess large amounts of capital nor to break down large barriers to entry for products in the established markets. One additional benefit of this pattern of guerrilla capitalism in manufacturing was that Chinese manufacturers were able to stay one step ahead of protectionist measures. It was neither practical nor feasible for the Chinese NICs' largest trading partners to stem the flood of imports effectively through regulation, given the length of time it takes for regulations to be changed. Indeed, Chinese firms that made large capital investments that were not redeployable into other products would invite protectionist measures.[5] Even when such protectionist measures were taken, Chinese firms found it natural and easy to move on to producing something else because of the lack of investment in a specialized capital plant.

This pattern of industrialism in the Chinese NICs ultimately created two major groupings of firms. Large foreign multinationals were in the NICs to manufacture a specific product or range of products because of their attractive manufacturing environment for electronics. They were surrounded by a large number of small, locally owned manufacturers of components and supplies and a locally owned electronics industry that manufactured consumer electronics goods primarily for the local market. This is the pattern of industry that existed in Taiwan's electronics industry in the early 1970s. At that time, many industry observers thought that the local industries that assembled low-tech items such as televisions were in decline. However, the market changed in the 1970s. When the computer revolution generated a demand for computer monitors, those lines that assembled low-margin, low-tech televisions became the basis for producing high-tech, high-margin components like computer monitors. Likewise, labor-intensive assembly work for telephones and video games in Hong Kong and Taiwan created a market for the integrated circuit (IC) chips being produced by the Taiwan government's IC manufacturing venture. This pattern of low-technology goods providing a basis for which high tech became possible was repeated in the personal computer (PC) revolution, which so energized the local industry in the late 1970s.

## The Impact of the PC Revolution

In the 1980s, assemblers of video games and telephones in Hong Kong and Taiwan turned to assembling personal computers when they could no longer compete in the telephone market in the late 1970s and 1980s. Singapore, on the other hand, capitalized on the PC revolution by making itself the most attractive site for offshore manufacturing in the Far East. Thus, we see a bifurcation into two strategies in dealing with a similar opportunity. Singapore became a branch plant economy, whereas Hong Kong's and Taiwan's local manufacturers went into manufacturing computer products. Initially, their computer products were by all accounts inferior to the goods produced by the major firms in the United States. In many instances, their computer products were outright illegal copies of major brand-name computers. Indeed, compared to the most efficient U.S.-based manufacturers, the cost of manufacturing for personal computers was higher. Despite this, the oligopolistic nature of computers in the United States allowed Hong Kong and Taiwan manufacturers to make handsome profits for a time because customers in the United States were willing to accept lower quality in exchange for prices less than one-half the going rate for brand-name computers. By 1988, a few years after the first Hong Kong and Taiwan clone computers were made and became very successful as an export product, the margins had diminished sufficiently to reduce the number of manufacturers to only a handful compared to those in 1984.

Many manufacturers went into other businesses. However, the opportunity to learn to manufacture computers from assembling low-technology PCs gave firms in the Chinese NICs the opportunity to improve their skills to become more competitive in the tougher environment, as well as providing a large internal market for computer components, which were to become the basis of the successful high-tech industry in Taiwan and Hong Kong today. As we observed about other commodities, firms in the Chinese NICs were adept at moving from product to product, industry to industry to find profitable opportunities in a guerrilla fashion. The firms that ultimately survive each of the "shake-outs" as markets become flooded are, by necessity, internationally competitive. However, without the "pilot" function performed by the large number of entrepreneurs seeking opportunities in all industries in search of a successful formula, it is unlikely that so many successful formulas would have been found to perpetuate business in the Chinese NICs.

The strategies by Chinese small- to medium-scale firms, however, have been affected by many unique factors in each of the countries. Singapore's industrial policy of promoting offshore manufacturing by MNCs and its high wage policy in the early 1980s suppressed the inherent dynamism of locally owned Chinese businesses. Hong Kong, however, has seen its labor-intensive assembly industries, particularly textiles, electronics, and toys, gradually move to other lower-cost competitors, such as the People's Republic of China. At the same time, the "opening" of the PRC has created a vast market for services to support Chinese businesses, which became the dominant economic activity in Hong Kong by the late 1980s (Lam, 1990: 131–142). In that case, the Chinese guerrilla capitalist moved on to Mainland ventures as opposed to simply producing manufactured goods for export. Taiwan, on the other hand, went through a period of sustained cost increases and currency appreciation in the 1980s that forced most of the labor-intensive industries to move to the PRC or other Asian sites. At the same time, the computer industry became very successful and is now a major component of Taiwan's exports. The Taiwanese low-tech guerrillas have, in many cases, graduated to become high-tech guerrillas who manufacture industrial and commercial equipment that has higher profit margins than consumer goods. This diversity in firm level responses is evidence of the dynamism of the basic industrial and social infrastructure that underpins the Chinese NIC's strong growth over the past three decades.

# Conclusions

We began with the idea that there is a common rationale that can explain the success of the Chinese NICs. The common factors emphasized here are found despite a diverse set of state economic and industrial policies, not because of the consistency in state intervention but because all these countries shared a common culture and background that influenced market behavior. These common attributes, ranging from culture to business practices, were affected similarly by extraneous events such as the demand for low-cost sources of textiles in the Western world in the postwar era, military procurement from the NICs as a result of the Korean and Vietnam wars, and finally, the mass migration of the U.S. electronics industry to the Chinese NICs. None of these events was fundamentally the result of the NIC's industrial policies, although state actions did in many cases contribute to permitting and often facilitating the exploitation of these opportunities by local entrepreneurs. Similarly, the consequences of the mass migration of people from the Chinese NICs to the Western world, so important for providing skills and technology for their later development, were neither anticipated nor facilitated by deliberate policy moves by the NICs. State centric explanations for the success of the Chinese NICs, therefore, are clearly limited. In fact, what happened in the NICs at the firm level is a pattern of adaptability to market opportunities by local entrepreneurs, together with fortuitous events that made possible many opportunities, which were then exploited to the fullest. Although the state did play a critical role in some ways, to attribute the development of the Chinese NICs entirely to state policy and action would be akin to considering *Hamlet* without the ghost.

# Notes

1. Note that this form of flexibility is very different from the idea of capital-intensive "flexible manufacturing" advocated as the solution to industrial decline in the United States. For example, Piore and Sabel's (1986) flexible manufacturing involves the adaptation of capital-intensive high technology CAD/CAM/CAE to allow manufacturers to adapt to changing market demands. The Chinese flexibility is clearly not necessarily a capital- or technology-intensive form of flexible manufacturing.

2. See Chandler (1977) for a summary of the arguments concerning the separation of ownership and control in Western capitalism and also a discussion about the cause of large businesses. He contends that large businesses exist because of the large-scale economies that they are able to exploit more efficiently than smaller firms. However, what the theory does not discuss is what happens over time. Suppose a large firm became dominant in an industry. By effectively monopolizing the industry, it will tend to stifle the dynamics of competition with deleterious effects for the industry over time.

3. There has always been a historical tension in Chinese society between ties of tribal loyalty and the need to recruit talent. In the traditional imperial Chinese system of government, talented but not trusted officials would be checked by a trusted official. See Pye (1985: 70) for a discussion of the distinct insider/outsider feelings in Chinese culture. Also see Chan (1982: 218–235) for his discussion of how a traditional and "modern reform" Chinese firm managed the problem of trust in business relationships.

4. There is no question that tax evasion by businesses in Taiwan is widespread. Another indication of large-scale tax evasion is the proportional share of revenues derived from easy-to-obtain sources, such as customs duties and monopolies, as compared to the harder-to-collect sources, such as income and business taxes. Note that in Western developed countries, the percentage of revenue from the more difficult-to-tax activities is much higher. Because of the low taxes in Hong Kong, tax evasion has not been as severe a problem.

5. The example of the Chinese NICs' success in textile imports and their consequent regulation under the General Agreement on Tariffs and Trade (GATT) is indicative of what actions the NICs' trading partners would take, should any of their industries become consistently too successful.

## *References*

Chan, W. K. K. 1982. "The Organizational Structure of the Traditional Chinese Firm and Its Modern Reform." *Business History Review* 56: 218–235.

Chandler, A. D. 1977. *The Visible Hand: The Managerial Revolution in American Business.* Cambridge, Mass.: Belknap Press.

Hamilton, G., and N. W. Biggart. 1985. "Market, Culture, and Authority: A Comparative Analysis of Management and Organization in the Pacific Basin." Paper presented at the Regional Seminar on Chinese Studies, University of California, Berkeley.

Johnson, C. 1982. *MITI and the Japanese Miracle: The Growth of Industrial Policy, 1925–1975.* Stanford, Calif.: Stanford University Press.

Lam, D. K. K. 1990. "The Economic Dimensions of 1997." *Asian Affairs* 17: 131–142.

Morawetz, D. 1981. *Why the Emperor's New Clothes are Not Made in Colombia: A Case Study in Latin American and East Asian Manufactured Exports.* New York: Oxford University Press.

Myers, R. H. 1984. "The Economic Transformation of the Republic of China on Taiwan." *China Quarterly* 99: 500–528.

Piore, M. J., and C. F. Sabel. 1984. *The Second Industrial Divide: Possibilities for Prosperity.* New York: Basic Books.

Pye, L. W., with M. W. Pye. 1985. *Asian Power and Politics: The Cultural Dimensions of Authority.* Cambridge, Mass.: Harvard University Press.

# 7

# Leadership Change
# and Government Size in
# East Asian Authoritarian Regimes

## Chi Huang

The ancient Chinese scholar Mencius once said, "State policies always shift with the change of the top leader in charge." This line of thinking is obviously not unique to the Chinese. If Plato's idea of "philosopher king" means anything, it must mean that the top state leader matters. And indeed whenever and wherever political leadership turnover occurs, it almost always draws people's attention not just because of the process of change itself but because of its possible impact. New leaders may mean new policies or a change in government performance.

But do new leaders really make a difference—even in authoritarian regimes? The purpose of this chapter is to study the impact of the changes of top-level state leaders on government size in bureaucratic-technocratic authoritarian regimes. Following the logic of the "most similar systems" design, the Republic of China (ROC) on Taiwan and the Republic of Korea (ROK, or South Korea) are included in a multiple interrupted time series design to test if different types of leadership transition have any effect on government size, and if they do, in what ways.

## A Hypothesis About Leadership Turnover and Government Size in Authoritarian Regimes

There is an enormous and still growing literature concerning the size of government. The most often cited and debated theories, such as political party control theory, median voter theory, and political business cycle theory, are obviously developed in the context of Western democracies. These theories generally agree that who takes the top position matters because in democracies these top state leaders presumably reflect party ideology or

125

majority voters' opinions and needs. Yet very little theory in this area can be readily applied to authoritarian regimes. The nature of limited political pluralism in authoritarian regimes (Linz, 1975: 264) severely limits the influence of party competition, elections, and voters on decisions made by state leaders. Given the fact that a majority of countries in the world have an authoritarian form of government despite the recent trend of democratization, theories intended to explain government size should also take into account the characteristics of this regime type.

The shift of political power in authoritarian regimes, although not through competition between or among parties in elections as in liberal democracies, can also imply a change of ideology (or, using Linz's terminology, "mentality") of leaders and a change in the policies of the government and the way it allocates public resources. In other words, leadership change may very well be one of the major sources of longitudinal variation in government size and policy priority in a given authoritarian regime. Unfortunately, there is only limited research on authoritarian regimes that can give us a guide to the impact of state leadership change on government size and policy priority. O'Donnell's (1978) bureaucratic-authoritarian model, for example, discusses the relationship between regime and policy, but says little about the dynamics of changes in the same type of regime. The following discussion, therefore, attempts to shed some light on this topic by putting together two groups of seemingly remotely related literatures: studies about the effects of political succession in totalitarian communist regimes, on the one hand; and studies about the politics of public spending in developing nations, particularly in Latin American countries, on the other hand.

There is some literature concerning the linkage between the "succession connection" and policy output in the Soviet Union. For example, Bunce (1986, 1981, 1980) argues that the concerns of the public always receive special attention during succession periods in both socialist and capitalist systems. During the "honeymoon" period, she shows, leaders have both the incentive and the capacity to bring about policy innovations. Later, policymaking becomes routinized, and the leaders' desire and ability to innovate are diminished considerably. Roeder (1986, 1985) contends that it is intraleadership competition during successions, not the general secretary's incentive alone, that accounts for the alternation of elite-oriented policies and mass-oriented policies. The greater the competition among elites, the higher the general secretary's incentive to satisfy elite demands. Therefore, mass-oriented policies obtain higher priority only after the succession is resolved and the newly ascendant leader consolidates his position—"consolidation connections."

Some careful thinking is necessary before applying either Bunce's or Roeder's arguments to this study. In nonsocialist authoritarian regimes, power shifts usually are even less institutionalized than is the case in the Soviet Union. Thus, there is a much wider range of ways of succeeding to power, from peaceful transition to bloody coup d'etat, even with the type of regime remaining unchanged. If leaders indeed use the public budget as the "currency" to construct coalitions insuring their political survival, as Ames's (1987, 1977) theory of survival coalition explains the politics of public spending in Latin America, then a different form of political succession, peaceful or violent, may open different options for and impose different constraints on building such coalitions. Thus, variation in the form of leadership change may account for, at least in part, the variation of government sizes across authoritarian regimes over time.

Peaceful transition, such as one resulting from the serious illness or death of an existing leader, usually implies less elite competition. By its peaceful nature, the successor is more clearly identified and at least acquiescently accepted by the previous leader's coalition. But this also means that the new leader inherits greater institutional inertia from his predecessor. Lacking the incentive and the capability to break sharply from the previous leader and his legacy, the rational successors would create their own coalitions by "adding their supporters to the existing coalitions while retaining, at least in the short run, most of those in the previous leader's coalition" (Kimenyi and Shugart, 1989: 173). This process of coalition formation—that is, diluting the power of an older coalition by adding new supporters—implies an increase in the size of the government because old members and public programs endorsed by them cannot be eliminated immediately. This also implies that policy changes envisaged by the new leader can be introduced and implemented only gradually.

On the other hand, an abrupt and violent power shift, such as one resulting from the assassination of an existing leader, a military coup, or even a civil war, usually implies severe conflict within the elite group. Due to the irregular nature of this type of political succession, the successor is usually not readily identifiable, and, even if identified, is not likely to receive immediate acceptance from the old coalition of the previous leader. The emerging successor, after building his own winning coalition during the process of power struggle, may thus have a stronger incentive to break away from, if not condemn, the predecessor and demonstrate his own characteristics. The violent nature of such power transition may also give the new leader greater capacity (and more excuses) to purge members of the old coalition in the name of cleaning up corruption. By twisting the political structure to his own favor and bringing in sweeping changes of faces in powerful positions during and after political succession, the new leader has not only a stronger incentive but a better opportunity to introduce and implement brand new policies of his own.

Based on these arguments, the following hypothesis is developed:

So long as a regime remains authoritarian, a peaceful change of the top state leader is more likely to lead to a gradual growth of government size, whereas an abrupt and violent leader change is more likely to lead to an abrupt and sudden change of government size. It should be noted that this hypothesis specifies only the speed, but not the direction, of change in government size after violent leadership turnover. It is the author's belief that this direction is, to a large extent, determined by the most urgent issues the nation faces when the political succession occurs and immediately afterward.

## Research Design

The preceding hypothesis concerns the causal linkage between leadership change and government expenditures. As some critics of Bunce point out, analysis of such a causal relationship, just like any other causal analysis, requires that one control for extraneous factors that may yield spurious results (Bunk and Minehart, 1984: 561; Roeder, 1986: 220). Despite the recognition of the need for control in studying this topic, few serious attempts have been made to carry it out through careful research designs.

This study applies the logic of "most similar systems" design in the comparative politics tradition (Frendreis, 1983; Meckstroth, 1975; Przeworski and Teune, 1970) to the "interrupted time series" quasi-experiment frequently used in the fields of experimental psychology and policy evaluation (see, for example, Campbell and Ross, 1968; Campbell and Stanley, 1963; Cook and Campbell, 1979). The former involves matching two cases that appear to be very similar in as many respects as possible and yet experience different outcomes. The goal of this design is to identify the difference that is responsible for contradictory outcomes. Those similarities between two cases can be considered relatively "controlled for" and thus ruled out as plausible causes of the different outcomes under study. The interrupted time series design, on the other hand, involves one experimental group (or unit) and multiple observations before and after an intervention (or the occurrence of the studied event). As Achen (1986: 149) points out, the great advantage of such a design is that "past behavior of the subjects usually serves as a good control for their current activities" and thus makes it easier to detect and isolate the effect of the event of interest. The weakness of this kind of single time series design is the threat of history to the internal validity of causality. That is, there is always the possibility that factors other than the event under investigation come to influence the dependent variable at about the same time the intervention occurs. One solution to this problem is to "seek out a similar institution not undergoing the [event], from which to collect a similar 'control' time series" (Campbell and Stanley, 1963: 55). For our case, however, it is difficult to find a nation without leadership turnover for more than two decades during the same period under study.

If we can find two relatively similar countries, each of which has leadership change at different times, then cross-sectional control can still be achieved. That is, when one country experiences intervention the other serves as a control, and when the control nation later experiences the event the original experimental case serves as the control. This design, using the conventional Campbell-Stanley notation, can be diagramed as:

Taiwan       O O OXO O O O O O O O O

South Korea  O O O O O O O OXO O O O

where each O represents an observation of the dependent variable (i.e., government expenditures), and X stands for the occurrence of the independent variable (i.e., top leadership change).

The two countries, Taiwan and South Korea, are selected following the logic of the most similar systems design. In other words, they are chosen for this study because they are relatively similar in terms of their small open economies, lack of natural resources, middle level of economic development, Confucian cultures, and so on (see Chan, 1990; Clark, 1989). Politically, both countries were right-wing authoritarian regimes with disciplined bureaucrats and technocrats until at least the end of the 1980s. Both regimes also face security threats from their communist counterparts, the People's Republic of China and the Democratic People's Republic of Korea, respectively. However, they are different in terms of the foci of this study: the form of leadership turnover and the amount of government spending after the leadership change. Taiwan experienced a peaceful power shift in May 1972 (Jacobs, 1974, 1973; Winckler, 1988), which was followed by an expansionist policy except for fiscal year 1974 (Kuo, 1983), whereas South Korea had an abrupt and violent leadership change during the tumultuous period from October 1979 through August 1980 (Lee, 1981, 1980) and then the new government imposed fiscal restraint as part of its stabilization policy (Bahl et al., 1986; Haggard and Moon, 1990; Kim and Yun, 1988). Time series data of annual government expenditures for both countries from the 1960s to the end of the tenure of the last top state leader (fiscal year 1988 for Taiwan and 1987 for South Korea) have been gathered. By comparing these two time series to infer the effect of leadership change, we have a comparative interrupted time series design.

## *Leadership Change in Taiwan and South Korea*

As stated above, the events of leadership change on which this study focuses are the peaceful transition that occurred in Taiwan in 1972 and the abrupt and violent transition that occurred in South Korea in late 1979 and the first half of 1980. Both are "discrete interventions" in the sense that they constitute some qualitative change in the state of affairs at specific points in time. They are also suitable for our research design because, first, in both cases the power shift did not change the characteristics of their authoritarian regimes, and second, there are enough observations available before and after the events. More recent leadership changes that occurred in 1988 in both countries are also interesting events for investigation. These recent changes may be more appropriately studied under the topic of democratization, but their recentness also means that it is too early to evaluate their effects on government size quantitatively.

The Nationalist government of the Republic of China at Nanking, led by Chiang Kai-shek, moved to the island of Taiwan in 1949 after it was defeated by the Chinese communists on the Mainland. Thus, the island came under the tight control of Chiang Kai-shek, with the security forces, the military, the party (Kuomintang, or KMT), and the Mainlander-dominated bureaucracy, through both coercion and cooptation. During the 1950s, it seemed that Chiang intended to make General Chen Cheng, the chief figure who implemented the successful land reform program on the island, his successor. But Chen Cheng died in the mid-1960s. It soon became obvious that the generalissimo's eldest son, Chiang Ching-kuo, was the heir apparent. Even before Chen died of cancer, Chiang Ching-kuo became vice-minister of defense (1964–1965), and then minister (1966–1969), a position that allowed him to have full control of the military. In 1969, he became deputy premier, with the politically compliant economic technocrat Yen Chia-kan as premier. When Chiang Kai-shek's fifth term as president began on May 21, 1972, he made Yen vice-president and immediately named Chiang Ching-kuo as premier. The appointment was confirmed by the rubber stamp Legislative Yuan on May 26 by a majority of 93.38 percent. Given the fact that Chiang Kai-shek's health was deteriorating and he rarely appeared in public, Chiang Ching-kuo had the smoothest de facto political succession any authoritarian ruler could dream of. He continued to run the country from the premiership even after 1975 when his father died and Yen assumed the presidency. He finally became president in 1978 when Yen's formal term of office expired. This formal change of position had little effect, though, because Chiang Ching-kuo simply named a compliant technocrat, Sun Yun-suan, as premier and took the main policymaking power with him to the presidential office.

In comparison, Park Chung Hee came to power in South Korea in a military coup that toppled the short-lived Chang Myon government. He won the presidential elections in 1963 and 1967, and—after changing the two-term limitation of the Constitution of the Third Republic in order to allow himself candidacy for a third term—he ran and won again in 1971. But his determination to stay in power dictated a fundamental change of the political structure. In October 1972, Park suddenly clamped down martial law throughout the country and handed down a new constitution, which allowed him to be reelected to an unlimited number of six-year terms by an electoral body. By November 1972, this so-called Yushin (Revitalizing Reform) Constitution was approved in a national referendum, and in December Park was elected as the eighth president of South Korea, inaugurating the Fourth Republic. He continued to rule until October 26, 1979, when he was assassinated by his director of the Korean Central Intelligence Agency (KCIA) due to discord within the inner ruling circle.

Ostensibly, the electoral body selected Park's prime minister, Ch'oe Kyu Ha, as president. But the power struggle inside the highly politicized military during Park's rule had just begun. First, Major General Chun Doo Hwan, then head of the powerful Defense Security Command, together with a group of younger officers, launched the "first coup" on December 12, 1979, to arrest his superior Chong Sung Hwa. Then Chun moved further to control the coercive instruments by assuming the directorship of the KCIA in April 1980. Having thoroughly consolidated his position in the military and security forces, Chun launched the "second coup" to arrest student leaders and "corrupted" politicians in May, and used military force to crack down the Kwangju uprising later in the same month. Finally, Ch'oe resigned and Chun forced his own election in August 1980 as president under the Yushin Constitution. In October 1980, a new constitution was approved in a national referendum. Chun was then elected as president again by the new electoral college in February 1981. On March 3, 1981, Chun, for the second time in six months, was sworn in as president and inaugurated the Fifth Republic.

## Operationalization and Data Collection

As Edinger (1975) points out, leadership can be either positionally or behaviorally defined. For this study, it is defined as the top position in a hierarchical power structure. Leadership change refers to either the exit of the incumbent in that position and the entry of a new figure, or the taking over of the actual power of that top position. Peaceful leadership change is a regular transition process without resorting to coercion. Violent leadership change, on the other hand, is a more or less irregular power transition process with observable and massive use of coercive forces.

The dependent variable, government size, refers to the scope of public sector activity. It is sometimes measured in terms of total real government expenditures (G) in the literature of government growth/shrinkage. This is certainly not a perfect measure (see Higgs, 1987: 27–30), but it may be used as a good approximation of overall public sector activity because most government policies involve outlays. As Wildavsky (1988: 2) says, "A budget . . . may be characterized as a series of [policy] goals with price tags attached."

However, government size is a relative rather than an absolute concept. An absolute dollar amount, even in its real values, does not reflect this relative nature. One reasonable adjustment is to measure the size of government relative to the entire economy (i.e., gross domestic product [GDP]). This measurement, G/GDP, focuses on the proportion of available resources allocated by the government. The obtained percentages also provide a common basis of comparison across nations. However, as Alt and Chrystal (1983: 222–223) point out, this measure has the potential danger of confounding the trends of GDP with the trends of government spending. That is, the accelerations of expenditures as a percentage of GDP may be due to rising spending or declining GDP or both.

The size of a government is also relative to the size of the population it serves. As Roeder (1985) points out, an expanding population also increases the demand for government services such as public utilities, education, and health, which means a higher aggregate amount of government expenditures in both nominal and real values. To take this into account, a natural adjustment is to use per capita real government expenditures as a measure of government size. One disadvantage of this per capita measurement is that some components of government spending, such as national defense, may not be directly related to population size.

Because each measure has its advantages and disadvantages and because there is no agreement upon the superiority of one over the other, this study uses both of them. If they show similar results in our analysis, then we have greater confidence in our conclusions.

Gathering reliable time series data for developing countries is always challenging. During the process of data collection, efforts are made to meet three criteria: measurement validity, accounting consistency, and a sufficient number of observations. Measurement validity is intended to ensure that the data reflect what we purport to measure. For example, total government expenditures should include both current and capital spending of all levels of government, not just the central government. Consistency is examined to avoid the confounding effect of changing accounting practices, which constitute the threat of instrumentation to the internal validity of causality. Once these two criteria are met, the data sources that provide the longest time series are chosen. For South Korea, I chose those data published by the Economic Planning Board (various years, 1990) that contain consistent data from 1968 to 1987. For Taiwan, government expenditures are taken from the Ministry of Finance (various years), figures of GDP in fiscal years are taken from the Directorate-General of Budget, Accounting and Statistics (DGBAS, 1989), and population size is from the Council for Economic Planning and Development (1990). All the data on Taiwan are given for fiscal years, which begin from July 1 of the preceding year and end on June 30 of the designated year. Such consistent data are available from fiscal year 1962 to 1988.

Figures 7.1 to 7.4 show the trends of the two measurements of government size for Taiwan and South Korea. In general, per capita government expenditures in both countries have a consistent rising trend. Government spending as percent of GDP, on the other hand, shows much greater fluctuation. Both countries experienced a rising trend during the 1970s—except in 1973, when the first oil crisis occurred—and then a downward trend after the early 1980s.

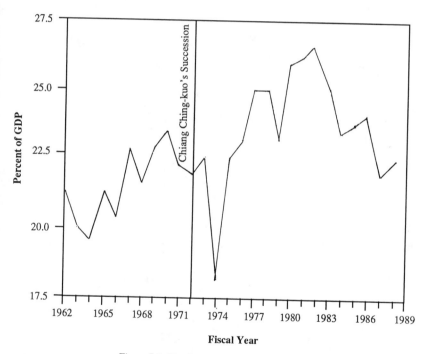

Figure 7.1  Total government expenditures as percent of
GDP in Taiwan (FY 1962–1988).

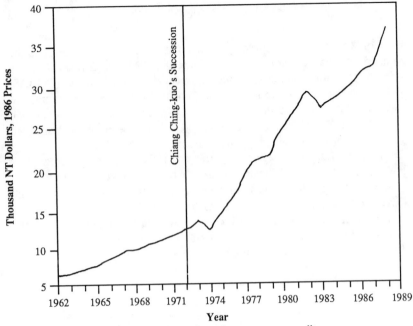

Figure 7.2  Per capita real government expenditures
in Taiwan (FY 1962–1988).

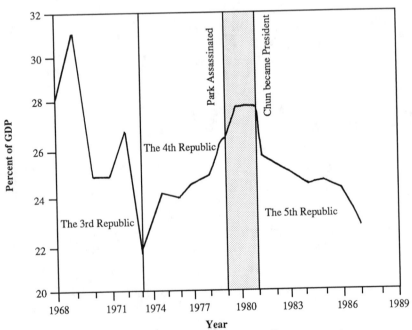

Figure 7.3  Total government expenditures as percent
of GDP in Korea (1968–1987).

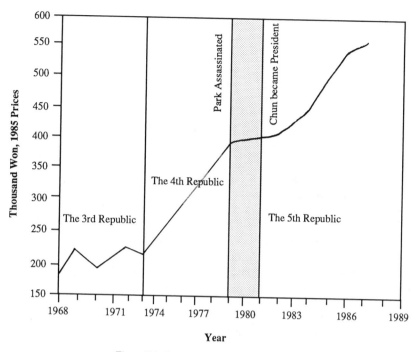

Figure 7.4 Per capita real government expenditures
in Korea (1968–1987).

## *Empirical Analysis*

In the literature, Box and Tiao's (1975) interrupted time series analysis is often used to assess the impact of a discrete intervention on a social process (see, for example, Hibbs, 1977; McCleary and Hay, 1980). However, this method usually requires one to identify and estimate a noise model based on the preintervention series as a benchmark for comparison with the entire series. Given the limitation of annual data available for this study, ten (for the case of Taiwan) to twelve (for the case of South Korea) time points before leadership change occurs are obviously too few to apply Box and Tiao's technique. What we need here is a method that takes advantage of the entire series and is still able to assess the impact of events on the dependent variable.

The method suggested and used by Lewis-Beck (1986, 1980, 1979) meets such needs. Essentially, Lewis-Beck views interrupted time series models as a variation on the classic multiple regression model. Therefore, the method is to regress the dependent variable upon independent variables representing a trend, events, and/or other relevant "third variables." Each event, in turn, is represented by a dichotomous dummy variable (which captures the intercept change) and a postintervention time counter (which captures the slope change).

Based on this approach, the equation I use to assess the impact of Chiang Ching-kuo's peaceful succession in 1972 on government size in Taiwan is specified as follows:

$$Y_t = b_0 + b_1 T_t + b_2 D_{1,t} + b_3 C_{1,t} + b_4 \text{Growth}_t + b_5 \text{Inflation}_t + b_6 D_{2,t} + b_7 C_{2,t} + e_t$$

where

$Y_t$ = dependent variables, either G/GDP or per capita G

$b_0$ = estimated intercept

$T_t$ = a counter for time from 1 to the last observation N

$D_{1,t}$ = a dichotomous dummy variable indicating the "Chiang Ching–kuo era," scored 0 for observations before fiscal year 1973 and 1 for observations on and after fiscal year 1973

$C_{1,t}$ = a postintervention time counter scored 0 for observations before fiscal year 1973 and 1, 2, 3 . . . for observations on and after fiscal year 1973

$\text{Growth}_t$ = economic growth rate

$\text{Inflation}_t$ = inflation rate

$D_{2,t}$ = a dichotomous dummy variable scored 0 for observations before fiscal year 1981 and 1 for observations on and after fiscal year 1981

$C_{2,t}$ = a time counter scored 0 for observations before fiscal year 1981 and 1, 2, 3 . . . for observations on and after fiscal year 1981

$e_t$ = error function

The two economic variables, growth rate and inflation rate, are included in the equation as control variables. They are considered relevant "third variables" because fiscal allocation, besides being treated as the "currency" of building survival coalitions, may also be used by decisionmakers in these two "developmental states" as a macroeconomic policy instrument. The last two variables, on the other hand, are included as if there were a leadership change in Taiwan in 1980. This "intervention" is included to measure the trend of government size in Taiwan after 1981 in order to compare it with the intervention in South Korea, where a leadership change actually occurred in 1980.

Equation (7.2) for South Korea is identical to equation (7.1) except that the two dummy variables and time counters now represent the Yushin Constitution period and the event of Chun Doo Hwan's violent political succession, respectively:

$$Y_t = b_0 + b_1 T_t + b_2 D_{1,t} + b_3 C_{1,t} + b_4 \text{Growth}_t + b_5 \text{Inflation}_t + b_6 D_{2,t} + b_7 C_{2,t} + e_t$$

where

$D_{1,t}$ = a dichotomous dummy variable indicating the Yushin Constitution period, scored 0 for observations before 1973 and 1 for observations on and after 1973

$C_{1,t}$ = a time counter scored 0 for observations before 1973 and 1, 2, 3 . . . for observations on and after 1973

$D_{2,t}$ = a dichotomous dummy variable indicating the Chun Doo Hwan era, scored 0 for observations before 1981 and 1 for observations on and after 1981

$C_{2,t}$ = a postintervention time counter scored 0 for observations before 1981 and 1, 2, 3 . . . for observations on and after 1981

Other variables are the same as defined in equation (7.1).

## Leadership Change and Government Size in Taiwan

Statistical results for the case of Taiwan are presented in Table 7.1. For both measurements of government size—total government expenditures as a percentage of GDP (G/GDP) as well as per capita real government expenditures—there is a statistically significant rising trend before fiscal year 1973. For the period after the peaceful leadership change that occurred at the end of fiscal year 1972, both measurements indicate a negative sign in intercept change and a positive sign in slope change. But for the ratio of government outlays to GDP, neither estimate is statistically significant. For per capita government expenditures, on the other hand, there is no significant change in intercept but there is a significant increase in slope. This indicates that the per capita government spending in Taiwan grew faster after Chiang Ching-kuo's succession than during the Chiang Kai-shek era. These results show that for the period from fiscal year 1963 to 1972, each year saw an average growth of NT$0.78 thousand (about US$22.3 in 1986 prices). During the next nine years, however, per capita government spending increased by an average NT$1.84 thousand ($b_1 + b_3$ = NT$0.78 thousand + NT$1.06 thousand, or about US$52.6) annually. This was more than two times the rate of growth during the 1960s and early 1970s. But this rising trend leveled off after fiscal year 1981. On average, per capita government outlays increased by only NT$1.19 thousand (about US$34.02) every year during the fiscal years 1982 to 1988.

Table 7.1    Leadership Change and Government Expenditures in Taiwan

|                        | G/GDP              | Per Capita G       |
|------------------------|--------------------|--------------------|
| Constant               | 21.97[a]           | 5.03[a]            |
|                        | (1.21)             | (1.36)             |
| Trend                  | 0.47[a]            | 0.78[a]            |
|                        | (0.13)             | (0.14)             |
| Dummy 1                | -1.53              | -1.87              |
|                        | (1.20)             | (1.35)             |
| Counter 1              | 0.07               | 1.06[a]            |
|                        | (0.23)             | (0.25)             |
| Growth                 | -0.24[b]           | -0.004             |
|                        | (0.10)             | (0.11)             |
| Inflation              | -0.16[b]           | -0.03              |
|                        | (0.05)             | (0.06)             |
| Dummy 2                | 0.93               | 0.37               |
|                        | (1.20)             | (1.35)             |
| Counter 2              | -1.34[b]           | -0.65[b]           |
|                        | (0.25)             | (0.28)             |
| N                      | 26                 | 26                 |
| Adjusted $R_2$         | 0.73               | 0.98               |
| Durbin-Watson          | 2.28               | 1.73               |

*Notes:* Figures in parentheses are estimated standard errors.
a. Statistically significant at .01 level, two-tail test.
b. Statistically significant at .05 level, two-tail test.
G/GDP = total government expenditures as percent of GDP
Per Capita G = per capita real government expenditures
Trend = counter for time from 1 to N
Dummy 1 = dichotomous dummy variable scored 0 before 1973 and 1 on and
          after 1973
Counter 1 = counter of time scored 0 before 1973 and 1, 2, 3 . . . after 1973
Growth = economic growth rate
Inflation = inflation rate
Dummy 2 = dichotomous dummy variable scored 0 before 1981 and scored 1 on
          and after 1981
Counter 2 = counter of time scored 0 before 1981 and 1, 2, 3 . . . after 1981

The results for government expenditures as a percentage of GDP show a slightly different trend. Before fiscal year 1973, each year saw an average growth of 0.47 percent of GDP absorbed and allocated by the government. From 1973, when Chiang Ching-kuo assumed leadership, until 1981, the percentages on average grew at about the same rate as in the 1960s (neither intercept nor slope effect is significant during this period). With the exception of fiscal year 1974, when the country was hard hit by the first oil crisis and thus fiscal restraint was imposed, this steadily rising trend continued for the next eight years of President Chiang's tenure, reached its peak (26.8 percent) in fiscal year 1982 and then began to decline afterwards. By fiscal year 1988, when President Chiang died, the percentage dropped to 22.5. This measurement of government size, G/GDP, also indicates that the ROC government was sensitive to the economic growth and inflation rates. The negative and statistically significant coefficients attached to these two economic variables seem to imply that decisionmakers in Taiwan had tended to use government outlays as a fiscal instrument to stabilize economy (also see Huang, 1989; Huang and Tang, 1988).

## Leadership Change and Government Size in South Korea

Table 7.2 contains the statistical evidence about the effect of violent leadership change on government size in South Korea. In general, both measures of government size indicate a fast rising trend during the Fourth Republic when Park Chung Hee was in control (1973–1979) and then a dramatic decline during the Fifth Republic when Chun Doo Hwan was the president (1981–1987). In terms of per capita real government expenditures, there was a rising trend even before Park Chung Hee further tightened his control with the Yushin Constitution at the end of 1972. Starting from 1973 to Park's assassination in late 1979, per capita real government expenditures on average climbed by 30.69 thousand won (about US$35.25 in 1985 prices) every year. After Chun Doo Hwan consolidated his power and started the Fifth Republic in early 1981, there was a sharp and significant drop in the intercept by 33.16 thousand won (about US$38.1 in 1985 prices), although the slope remained at about the same magnitude (i.e., the negative slope coefficient of the second counter is statistically insignificant).

The measure of government expenditures as a percentage of GDP indicates distinct trends in three different periods: an average 1.02 percent declining rate from 1968 to 1972, a significant 4.31 percent drop in intercept accompanied by a subsequent 0.72 percent average increase rate from 1973 to 1979, and then an immediate and sharp reversal of this trend by an annual average drop of 0.62 percent since Chun took power in 1980. By 1987, when

Chun ended his seven-year term as president, he had almost reversed the ratio
of government expenditures to GDP back to the level of 1974.

Table 7.2    Leadership Change and Government Expenditures in South Korea

|  | G/GDP | Per Capita G |
|---|---|---|
| Constant | 30.43[a] | 142.43[a] |
|  | (2.70) | (25.11) |
| Trend | -1.02[b] | 10.75[b] |
|  | (0.43) | (4.03) |
| Dummy 1 | -4.31[b] | -65.51[a] |
|  | (1.61) | (14.97) |
| Counter 1 | 1.74[a] | 19.94[a] |
|  | (0.43) | (4.04) |
| Growth | -0.05 | 2.14 |
|  | (0.13) | (1.17) |
| Inflation | 2.71 | 80.85 |
|  | (6.05) | (56.31) |
| Dummy 2 | 1.02 | -33.16[b] |
|  | (1.33) | (12.34) |
| Counter 2 | -1.34[a] | -4.94 |
|  | (0.37) | (3.46) |
| N | 20 | 20 |
| Adjusted $R_2$ | 0.72 | 0.99 |
| Durbin-Watson | 2.88 | 2.41 |

*Notes:* Figures in parentheses are estimated standard errors.

a. Satistically significant at .01 level, two-tail test.

b. Satistically significant at .05 level, two-tail test.

G/GDP = total government expenditures as percent of GDP

Per Capita G = per capita real government expenditures

Trend = counter for time from 1 to N

Dummy1 = dichotomous dummy variable scored 0 before 1973 and 1 on and
         after 1973

Counter1 = counter of time scored 0 before 1973 and 1, 2, 3 . . . after 1973

Growth = economic growth rate

Inflation = inflation rate

Dummy2 = dichotomous dummy variable scored 0 before 1981 and scored 1 on
         and after 1981

Counter2 = counter of time scored 0 before 1981 and 1, 2, 3 . . . after 1981

## Does Leadership Change Make a Difference?

If we examine the analysis results for each individual time series, it seems that the pattern fits our hypotheses quite closely. Following Lewis-Beck's (1986: 217) interpretation of significant intercept change as the short-term effect and slope change as the long-term effect of intervention, we find that the peaceful leadership change that occurred in Taiwan in 1972 led to either no change in government outlays as a percentage of GDP or to a more gradual and longer-term increase in per capita government spending. But the violent leadership change that occurred in South Korea in 1979–1980 led to an abrupt and sudden drop in the level of per capita government spending and a longer-term decrease in the ratio of government outlays to GDP.

However, by comparing the time series and statistical results in Tables 7.1 and 7.2, and linking them to the research design discussed above, the picture looks somewhat different. The major advantage of a comparative time series design is to allow us to rule out many plausible alternative explanations of causality. Given the fact that the two selected units are relatively similar, if the experimental unit has the expected responses after the intervention whereas the control unit does not, then we have stronger confidence in attributing the effect to the intervention. If we examine the peaceful leadership turnover that occurred in Taiwan in 1972 and treat South Korea during the same period as a control group, we find that from 1973 to 1980 both countries experienced rapidly expanding government size in per capita measurement. In terms of government expenditures as a percentage of GDP, Taiwan showed no significant change in growth rate whereas South Korea had significant short-term and long-term changes during this period. Both results are contrary to our expectations. That is, South Korea (the control case) had an even more dramatic increase in both measurements of government size than did Taiwan.

Because we cannot argue that the experimental case experiences expected change whereas the control case did not, the causal linkage between peaceful leadership change and gradual growth in government size in Taiwan becomes tenuous at best. There are too many possible explanations for the common trends in these two countries during this eight-year period. An obvious one is that both countries were responding to a common shock from the external environment—the first oil crisis, which occurred in late 1973. After a very short period of fiscal restraint, decisionmakers in both countries attempted to use expansionist policy to restructure their economies. It may not be a pure coincidence that both governments invested aggressively in building heavy and chemical industries during the mid-1970s in order to reduce their reliance on imported industrial raw materials.

After the violent leadership turnover in 1979–1980, South Korea experienced an immediate, sharp, and persistent decline in the level of per capita government expenditures as well as in the slope of government expenditures as a percentage of GDP. If we treat Taiwan during this time period as a control case, we find that Taiwan did not experience any significant intercept change in per capita government spending (but its slope did level off slightly) and had a more fluctuating decline in the ratio of government outlays to GDP only after fiscal year 1983 (see Figure 7.1). Although the per capita measurement of government size lends some support to our hypothesis about the abrupt and sudden impact of violent leadership turnover, the contrast between the government outlays to GDP ratios of the two cases is not obvious enough to allow us to attribute the more dramatic and persistent decrease in government size in South Korea after 1981 to its violent leadership change alone. It is possible that leadership turnover provided the new leader with both the incentive and the capacity to purge his opponents from important positions under the name of "purification," thus allowing him to implement his own idea of "right" policies. But it is also possible that the post-1981 trend in both Taiwan and South Korea simply reflected their common reaction to the second oil crisis by trimming—although in different degrees and at different speeds—the size of government. Besides, Park Chung Hee's administration had already announced an economic stabilization plan in April 1979—about six months before his assassination—to deal with the acceleration of inflation (Haggard and Moon, 1990: 219). It is likely that a decrease in the South Korean government's expenditures still would have occurred, but probably less dramatically, if Park Chung Hee had not been assassinated and had remained in power after 1979.

## Conclusions

By adapting the literature concerning the effect of leadership change in totalitarian regimes on policy priorities to authoritarian regimes, I have hypothesized that peaceful leadership change leads to gradual growth in government size whereas violent leadership change leads to abrupt and sudden change in government size. Following the logic of most similar systems design, time series data on Taiwan and South Korea were collected to form a comparative interrupted time series quasi-experiment. The results of this analysis and comparison, however, indicate that the relationship between peaceful leadership turnover and gradual increase in aggregate government size is inconclusive at best. The empirical analysis does lend some support to the linkage between violent leadership turnover and immediate and sudden change in government size, but only in the per capita measurement of government spending. Therefore, we cannot say that our hypothesis about leadership turnover and government size is fully substantiated by the empirical data. This conclusion reminds us that some findings supporting the impact of peaceful leadership change on government size (e.g., Kimenyi and Shugart, 1989) should be reexamined in a more rigorous research design.

However, this study does indicate some important factors that can and should be taken into account in future research. First, the sharp difference in the trend of government size in South Korea between the Third Republic and the Fourth Republic implies that regime change, even with the same top state leader in charge, may also affect fiscal policies. To some extent, regime change also gives leaders both the incentive to break from the past in the name of various "reforms" and the capability to impose new rules to implement the "right" development policy to manage the most urgent issues the nation is facing (see Cheng, 1990). In this sense, the sharper and more persistent decline in government size during Chun's rule (the Fifth Republic) in South Korea may reflect the cumulative effects of both regime change and leadership change. Second, neither Bunce (1986, 1981, 1980) nor Roeder (1986, 1985) emphasizes the constraints that the international environment may impose on new leaders. However, the cases of Taiwan and South Korea illustrate how vulnerable these small open economies have been to fluctuations in the world market. External factors may affect the policy agenda of new leaders in authoritarian developing nations. Third, the impact of leadership turnover should be evaluated in different policy areas, such as elite-oriented policies (including military and administrative spending) and mass-oriented policies (such as health, education, housing, and welfare spending). It is likely that the general trend of aggregate government size might remain similar between the two cases but that policy priorities would shift due to leadership turnover. Therefore, we need to identify the key elements in a winning coalition and link them with priorities in fiscal allocation. The coalition members who are most crucial to a top state leader's political survival should obtain a larger share of public spending as rewards than do less vital allies.

If the last point is correct, then the recent trend of democratization in both Taiwan and South Korea may lead to substantial increases in government spending in the mass-oriented policy areas because voters and election results now play crucial roles in distributing political power. Median voter theory and political business cycle theory may become relevant in explaining the impact of leadership change in these fledgling democracies after the late 1980s.

## Note

Researching and writing this chapter was supported by a Leadership Research Grant from the Department of Political Science at Texas A&M University.

## References

Achen, C. H. 1986. *The Statistical Analysis of Quasi-Experiments*. Berkeley, Calif.: University of California Press.

Alt, J. E., and K. A. Chrystal. 1983. *Political Economics*. Berkeley, Calif.: University of California Press.

Ames, B. 1987. *Political Survival: Politicians and Public Policy in Latin America*. Berkeley, Calif: University of California Press.

Ames, B. 1977. "The Politics of Public Spending in Latin America." *American Journal of Political Science* 21: 149–176.

Bahl, R., C. K. Kim, and C. K. Park. 1986. *Public Finances During the Korean Modernization Process*. Cambridge, Mass.: Harvard University Press.

Box, G. E. P., and G. C. Tiao. 1975. "Intervention Analysis with Applications to Economic and Environmental Problems." *Journal of the American Statistical Association* 70: 70–79.

Bunce, V. 1986. "The Effects of Leadership Succession in the Soviet Union." *American Political Science Review* 80: 215–219.

Bunce, V. 1981. *Do New Leaders Make a Difference? Executive Succession and Public Policy Under Capitalism and Socialism*. Princeton, N.J.: Princeton University Press.

Bunce, V. 1980. "Changing Leaders and Changing Policies: The Impact of Elite Succession on Budgetary Priorities in Democratic Countries." *American Journal of Political Science* 24: 373–395.

Bunk, G. G., and T. G. Minehart. 1984. "How Important Is Elite Turnover to Policy Change?" *American Journal of Political Science* 28: 559–569.

Campbell, D. T., and H. L. Ross. 1968. "The Connecticut Crackdown on Speeding: Time Series Data in Quasi-Experimental Analysis." *Law & Society Review* 3: 33–53.

Campbell, D. T., and J. C. Stanley. 1963. *Experimental and Quasi-Experimental Designs for Research*. Chicago: Rand McNally.

Chan, S. 1990. *East Asian Dynamism: Growth, Order, and Security in the Pacific Region*. Boulder, Colo: Westview.

Cheng, T. J. 1990. "Political Regimes and Development Strategies: South Korea and Taiwan." In G. Gereffi and D. Wyman (eds.), *Manufacturing Miracles: Paths of Industrialization in Latin America and East Asia*, pp. 139–178. Princeton, N.J.: Princeton University Press.

Clark, C. 1989. *Taiwan's Development: Implications for Contending Political Economy Paradigms*. New York: Greenwood.

Cook, T. D., and D. T. Campbell. 1979. *Quasi-Experimentation: Design and Analysis Issues for Field Settings*. Chicago: Rand McNally.

Council for Economic Planning and Development. 1990. *Taiwan Statistical Data Book, 1990*. Taipei: author.

DGBAS (Directorate-General of Budget, Accounting and Statistics). 1989.

*National Income Statistics in Taiwan Area, The Republic of China, 1989.* Taipei: author.

Economic Planning Board. 1990. *Korean Economic Indicators.* Seoul: author.

Economic Planning Board. Various years. *Major Statistics of Korean Economy.* Seoul: author.

Edinger, L. J. 1975. "The Comparative Analysis of Political Leadership." *Comparative Politics* 7: 253–269.

Frendreis, J. P. 1983. "Explanation of Variation and Detection of Covariation: The Purpose and Logic of Comparative Analysis." *Comparative Political Studies* 16: 255–272.

Haggard, S., and C. I. Moon. 1990. "Institutions and Economic Policy: Theory and a Korean Case Study." *World Politics* 42: 210–237.

Hibbs, D. A., Jr. 1977. "Political Parties and Macroeconomic Policy." *American Political Science Review* 71: 1467–1487.

Higgs, R. 1987. *Crisis and Leviathan: Critical Episodes in the Growth of American Government.* New York: Oxford University Press.

Huang, C. 1989. "The State and Foreign Investment: The Cases of Taiwan and Singapore." *Comparative Political Studies* 22: 93–121.

Huang, C., and D. P. Tang. 1988. "Causality Among National Income, Government Expenditure, and Government Revenue in Taiwan." Paper presented at the Annual Meeting of the American Association for Chinese Studies, Hoover Institution, Palo Alto, Calif.

Jacobs, J. B. 1974. "Taiwan 1973: Consolidation of the Succession." *Asian Survey* 14: 22–29.

Jacobs, J. B. 1973. "Taiwan 1972: Political Season." *Asian Survey* 13: 102–112.

Kim, W. S., and K. Y. Yun. 1988. "Fiscal Policy and Development in Korea." *World Development* 16: 65–83.

Kimenyi, M. S., and W. F. Shugart, II. 1989. "Political Succession and the Growth of Government." *Public Choice* 62: 173–179.

Kuo, S. W. Y. 1983. *The Taiwan Economy in Transition.* Boulder, Colo.: Westview.

Lee, C. S. 1981. "South Korea in 1980: The Emergence of a New Authoritarian Order." *Asian Survey* 21: 125–143.

Lee, C. S. 1980. "South Korea 1979: Confrontation, Assassination, and Transition." *Asian Survey* 20: 63–76.

Lewis-Beck, M. S. 1986. "Interrupted Time Series." In W. Berry and M.S. Lewis-Beck (eds.), *New Tools for Social Scientists: Advances and Applications in Research Methods,* pp. 209–240. Beverly Hills, Calif.: Sage.

Lewis-Beck, M. S. 1980. "Can Government Regulate Safety? The Coal Mine Example." *American Political Science Review* 74: 745–756.

Lewis-Beck, M. S. 1979. "Some Economic Effects of Revolution: Models, Measurement, and the Cuban Evidence." *American Journal of Sociology* 84: 1127–1149.

Linz, J. J. 1975. "Totalitarian and Authoritarian Regimes,." In F. I. Greenstein and N. W. Polsby (eds.), *Handbook of Political Science,* vol. 3, pp. 175–411. Reading, Mass.: Addison–Wesley.

McCleary, R., and R. A. Hay, Jr. 1980. *Applied Time Series Analysis for the Social Sciences.* Beverly Hills, Calif.: Sage.

Meckstroth, T. W. 1975. "'Most Different Systems' and 'Most Similar Systems': A Study of the Logic of Comparative Inquiry." *Comparative Political Studies* 8: 132–157.

Ministry of Finance. Various years. *Yearbook of Financial Statistics of the*

*Republic of China.* Taipei: author.

O'Donnell, G. 1978. "Reflections on the Patterns of Change in the Bureaucratic-Authoritarian State." *Latin American Research Review* 13: 3–38.

Przeworski, A., and H. Teune. 1970. *The Logic of Comparative Social Inquiry.* New York: Wiley.

Roeder, P. 1986. "The Effects of Leadership Succession in the Soviet Union." *American Political Science Review* 80: 219–224.

Roeder, P. 1985. "Do New Soviet Leaders Really Make a Difference? Rethinking the 'Succession Connection.'" *American Political Science Review* 79: 958–976.

Wildavsky, A. 1988. *The New Politics of the Budgetary Process.* Glenview, Ill.: Scott, Foresman.

Winckler, E. A. 1988. "Elite Political Struggle, 1945–1985." In E. A. Winckler and S. Greenhalgh (eds.), *Contending Approaches to the Political Economy of Taiwan,* pp. 151–171. Armonk, N.Y.: M. E. Sharpe.

## 8

# The State, Foreign Investment, and Sustaining Industrial Growth in South Korea and Thailand

*Russell Mardon & Won K. Paik*

Initiating and, more importantly, sustaining industrial transformation in late developing nations has proven to be a very difficult and complex task. During the latter half of this century nearly every developing country has officially enacted and pursued policy intended to transform its agriculture-based economy to one based upon industrial production. A multitude of approaches and strategies has been tried, but most have failed.

The East Asian capitalist nations have been the principal success stories for the past few decades. First, Japanese industrialization, initiated early in this century, reemerged in the 1950s and moved through the production cycle successfully to become a dominant force in the world economy. In the 1960s and 1970s, South Korea and Taiwan successfully initiated industrialization programs. They are presently attempting to move through higher levels of the production cycle by integrating higher technological processes into their industrial production. In the 1980s, the Southeast Asian nations of Indonesia, Thailand, and Malaysia became the leading edge of the third wave of Asian nations experiencing rapid industrial growth (Chan, 1990).

These three groups of nations are clearly at different phases of industrialization. However, they all appear to be following a similar trajectory of climbing upward along what has been called the "international product cycle" (Harris, 1986; Thorelli and Sentell, 1982; Vernon, 1966). In the initial stage of industrial development, the economy is driven by the production of labor-intensive goods (e.g., textiles, processed food, consumer electronics, toys, hand tools, and so on) combined with the initiation of heavy industrial production (e.g., steel, oil refining, and chemicals) through import substitution programs. During this phase of the production cycle, comparative advantage in labor cost is an essential factor of economic growth. This is the current phase for the Southeast Asian nations (Moon, 1989).

As an economy moves through the initial stage of industrial development, the supply of labor becomes less plentiful and labor costs rise. This process begins to erode a comparative advantage based primarily upon low labor costs. If industrial development is to be sustained, the economy must undergo a restructuring process. Economic restructuring, in essence, is a nation's reaction to changes in the comparative costs of production and the demands and conditions of the world market. It adapts a nation's production, finance, and trade systems to the prevailing market and resource constraints, so that a new equilibrium between the national economy and the international market can be achieved (Chu, 1989: 649). At this phase of the production cycle, labor-intensive sectors must utilize more technology to move upscale to higher quality items and higher value-added market niches in order to facilitate industrial adjustment. For example, textile production must move upscale in its quality of materials and workmanship in order to gain market share in the higher cost and more profitable clothing markets. At the same time, heavy industries developed through import substitution during the early stages of industrial development must become competitive on international markets and begin to earn foreign exchange. This is the location on the production cycle to which South Korea and Taiwan graduated relatively successfully in the 1980s.

During this phase, relatively low labor costs compared to more industrialized economies are important, but it is the combination of relatively low labor costs with increasing levels of productivity—due to the integration of more technologically intensive production processes—that allow for economic growth to continue.

As the industrialization process progresses further, labor costs continue to rise, and eventually the entire labor-intensive sector of the economy is no longer competitive in international markets. Other countries entering the early phases of the production cycle with low labor costs begin to gain market share in these sectors (e.g., China, the Southeast Asian nations, and India). Labor-intensive sectors then must be phased out or, preferably, relocated in other countries where labor costs remain low. Japan moved through this phase in the 1960s when it relocated much of its labor-intensive production to other Asian nations. Presently, South Korea and Taiwan are moving through this phase. Again, a restructuring of the production base of the economy is necessary in order to sustain economic growth.

At this level of economic development high-tech production processes must be integrated into the economic structure. In order to sustain economic growth, the cost of labor is relatively insignificant. Rather, it is the development of technology-intensive sectors and processes with high levels of productivity that becomes the most significant factor for sustaining growth.

It is this movement to technology-intensive production that is the most difficult phase to transcend in the production cycle. Somehow, the developing economy must formulate relatively high levels of capital to conduct research and development into new technologies, to train highly technical personnel, and to invest into very capital-intensive production processes. It is also at this phase that the developing economy finds itself competing directly with producers from the advanced industrial countries who already control global market share in these sectors. Certainly, Japan has passed through this phase and has become a world leader in technology-intensive sectors (i.e., electronic machine tools, computers, and office machines). South Korea and Taiwan now find themselves attempting to ascend to this higher level of the production cycle. If they are successful in gaining market share in these sectors, their economic growth can be sustained. If they cannot successfully develop these capital- and technology-intensive sectors, their economies will stagnate.

The fact that the East and Southeast Asian capitalist economies have experienced rapid industrial growth is clear. However, the explanation and analysis of the underlying cause of this growth, and the potential to sustain this growth through the many phases of the production cycle, constitute a controversial issue in international political economy debate.

## Theoretical Discussion

The dominant explanation of the causes of Asian economic development emerging from the liberal school of economics is that their success is largely due to these nations having adopted rational market-oriented policies. This, in turn, has allowed these economies to expand in line with their comparative advantage. The major emphasis of this line of argument is on the significance of export-oriented regimes that have created and sustained an economic environment in which industrial development is driven by international market prices (Balassa, 1982, 1981; Bhagwati, 1982; Chen, 1979; Krueger, 1979; Westphal, 1978; World Bank, 1983). In this view, the role of the government in economic affairs is seen as being limited to making correct policy choices that effectively oriented the domestic economy to international market forces.

Liberal analysis views foreign direct investment (FDI) as a precondition to the initiation and maintenance of industrial development. Its proponents argue that developing economies that are open to foreign investment will receive the benefits of foreign capital, technology, and marketing expertise that are absent from domestic sources. Although foreign ownership and control of the means of production may be the end result, FDI is viewed as a positive force in that it will lead to industrial growth and to the integration of the developing economy into the world market. From this perspective, the successful performance of the East Asian economies is primarily the result of the market discipline that an export-oriented strategy imposes on government policy, combined with the efficient integration of foreign capital into the domestic economy. It is assumed that the continuation of these market rational policies will allow the developing economy to industrialize further and move up in the production cycle.

An alternative explanation for the successful economic performance in East Asia is the developmental state perspective. Proponents of this view argue that the industrialization process has been systematically led by a highly centralized and resourceful state apparatus. The argument centers upon state intervention in domestic economic affairs to plan sectoral development, to mobilize and distribute resources, to grant financial and other privileges to industrial firms, and to control labor forces. These actions are taken in order to create production that is competitive in international markets (Amsden, 1991, 1989; James et al., 1989; Johnson, 1987, 1981; Jones and Sakong, 1980; Mardon, 1990a, 1990b; Paik and Mardon, 1991). This perspective argues that late industrializing nations are inherently at a competitive disadvantage in relation to advanced industrialized economies, thereby making industrialization dependent upon state intervention in order to mobilize resources and to provide other necessary inputs. The state must provide infrastructure, technological leadership, marketing assistance, special tax and production privileges, and other missing factors of production that will permit the economy to grow rapidly by reducing private sector costs below their market levels and by facilitating economies of scale in production. Under this process, it is argued, returns are significantly increased as the rate of economic growth accelerates (Alam, 1989; Dietz, 1991).

From the developmental state perspective, as from the liberal perspective, foreign capital and technological integration into the development process are seen as essential to rapid industrial expansion. However, the question of domestic versus foreign ownership of the means of production is a critical issue in relation to how the rewards of economic growth will be divided. Foreign capital inputs, according to the developmental state perspective, will best serve national development objectives if state policy breaks down the various components of the "production bundle" (see Chan, 1991: 80), and merges them individually into the domestic economy in a pattern that fits the needs of domestic entrepreneurial expansion. That is, rather than permitting foreign investment to provide and control capital, technology, managerial operations, labor, and marketing, these components should be "decoupled" from the foreign direct investment bundle and selectively integrated to fit the growth needs of the domestic producers. For example, if the need of a particular domestic firm's expansion is primarily capital, the state's function is to assist that firm to raise capital on international markets and to restrict foreign direct investment to that sector only. This will protect the market share enjoyed by the domestic firm and, theoretically, allow profits generated in this sector to be reinvested into the developing economy rather than to be repatriated by foreign investors. If the need for a domestic firm's expansion is advanced technological processes, the role of the state is to assist in arranging a technology transfer through license or through a joint venture with a foreign firm.

In this manner, the domestic market is largely reserved for domestic producers, and capital accumulation is channeled back to domestically controlled investment. As domestic firms increase capital accumulation and production, they should become more competitive on international markets and begin to move up the production cycle. According to the developmental state perspective, it is the state's control over its territory and market that allows it to implement a policy that effectively decouples the foreign investment production bundle and facilitates the growth of domestic firms. The growth of domestic firms leads to the maximization of domestic capital accumulation. This, in turn, facilitates sustained economic growth. Thus, in direct contrast to laissez-faire economics, coping with a dependency upon foreign capital is seen as a potential problem—one that different developing nations have met with varying success (Crone, 1983; Evans, 1987).

This chapter will proceed with an examination of the industrialization processes in South Korea and Thailand. Both of these nations have experienced rapid economic growth in the recent past. However, the role of the state and the manner in which foreign capital has been integrated into the domestic economies of these two nations vary greatly. South Korea's model of development is more representative of a developmental state. Thailand, although certainly not a laissez-faire economy, is more representative of a liberal model of development. These different paths to development have resulted in vastly different patterns of domestic and foreign ownership and control over the means of production. In the final section of this chapter, we will explore how these different ownership patterns may significantly affect the capacity of each of these economies as they attempt to move through the production cycle.

## South Korea: A Case of Economic Nationalism

During a three-decade period (1961–1990), South Korea experienced a significant economic transformation from a poor, agriculture-based society to a diversified industrial economy. In 1961, Korea's GNP per capita was below $100 (United Nations, 1966: 730–733), manufacturing accounted for less than 15 percent of GNP, and the value of exports and domestic savings each equaled less than one percent (Bank of Korea, 1973). By 1990, Korea's GNP per capita exceeded $5,000, manufacturing accounted for 32 percent and financial and other services 55 percent of GNP, and exports exceeded $62 billion (Korean Economic Planning Board, 1991). As shown in Table 8.1, South Korea's GNP grew at an annual rate of about 9 percent during the period between 1967 and 1987. During the same time period, exports increased at about 30 percent annually, whereas FDI concentration remained very low (increasing only 1.75 percent annually).

Table 8.1 Major Economic Indicators, South Korea, 1967–1987

| Year | GNP Growth (percentage change) | Export Growth (percentage change) | Productivity Index (1980=100) | Foreign Direct Investment Concentration (percentage of total investment) |
|---|---|---|---|---|
| 1967 | 6.6 | 28.0 | 10.1 | 1.64 |
| 1968 | 11.3 | 42.2 | 13.4 | 0.88 |
| 1969 | 13.8 | 6.7 | 16.3 | 1.05 |
| 1970 | 7.4 | 34.2 | 17.8 | 0.87 |
| 1971 | 9.1 | 27.8 | 20.5 | 1.59 |
| 1972 | 5.3 | 52.1 | 23.5 | 5.00 |
| 1973 | 14.0 | 98.6 | 31.4 | 5.16 |
| 1974 | 8.5 | 38.3 | 40.0 | 1.86 |
| 1975 | 6.8 | 13.9 | 47.6 | 4.39 |
| 1976 | 13.4 | 51.8 | 60.9 | 1.02 |
| 1977 | 10.7 | 30.2 | 74.1 | 0.64 |
| 1978 | 11.0 | 26.5 | 91.1 | 0.87 |
| 1979 | 7.0 | 18.4 | 101.8 | 0.57 |
| 1980 | -4.8 | 16.3 | 100.0 | 1.00 |
| 1981 | 6.6 | 21.4 | 112.7 | 0.93 |
| 1982 | 5.4 | 2.8 | 118.3 | 1.09 |
| 1983 | 11.9 | 11.9 | 137.0 | 1.27 |
| 1984 | 8.4 | 19.6 | 157.5 | 1.68 |
| 1985 | 5.4 | 3.6 | 164.4 | 1.98 |
| 1986 | 12.3 | 14.6 | 195.0 | 1.04 |
| 1987 | 12.0 | 36.2 | — | 2.26 |
| Average | 8.7 | 29.8 | 76.7 | 1.75 |

*Sources:* Bank of Korea, various years; Korea Economic Planning Board, various years; World Bank, various years

Liberal explanations of the Korean economic development process argue that rational policy adjustments and the continued liberalization of trade policy resulted in a balance in incentives for the production of import-competing and exportable goods. The decreasing interference of the state in the operation of the market, combined with the export orientation of production, led to the sustained success of the Korean economy (Krueger, 1979; Westphal, 1978). It is true that the South Korean government has increasingly liberalized its economic policies, especially during the past decade, and that the outward orientation of production has allowed South Korean producers to exploit changing market conditions. However, to attribute South Korea's economic success to market forces and liberal adjustments is to ignore the highly active role of the government in leading the economy through the production cycle.

In South Korea, comprehensive sectoral planning has been carried out by the government through the Economic Planning Board. Sectoral planning is not unusual in developing countries, but in Korea it has had special significance because of the government's almost total control over finance capital and the manner in which its allocation has been coordinated with development plans (Kim, 1970; Mardon, 1990b; Mason, 1980). From 1961 to 1982, all commercial banks in South Korea were owned and controlled by the government. Still today, all high-ranking bank officials must be approved by the minister of finance. This gives the government control over the principal decisions related to, and the basic flow of, investment. Through this control, investment patterns have been oriented toward the planned sectors and projects. The government, especially during the earlier stages of industrial development, literally selected the firms that would be responsible for developing a particular project or sector. It would then direct subsidized finance to that firm, place production and export quotas on that firm, and assist it in obtaining the necessary technology and markets (Chu, 1989; Mardon, 1990b). Monopoly rights and tariff protection would be provided to producer firms in the domestic market, and export financing would be provided when needed. Producer firms that were successful received preference in being selected in future government-planned and government-financed projects. Those that were not successful were liquidated by government directives to state-controlled banks.

South Korean government planning between 1962 and 1982 was extremely comprehensive and effectively implemented. To examine the pattern of these plans is to travel through the production cycle. In the early period (1962–1971), the primary targets were industrial infrastructure development, labor-intensive export production, and import substitution of basic chemical, petroleum, and steel processes. The government channeled finance to these sectors and strictly limited investment into nongovernment planned projects (Mardon, 1990b). During this period, the South Korean textile, footwear, and electronic assembly sectors were targeted as export industries and were built up rapidly, taking advantage of low labor costs.

During the 1972–1982 period, South Korean development plans placed emphasis on the further expansion of labor-intensive exports and called for high levels of investment to improve the technological base and output of the heavy industry and chemical sectors. Iron and steel, advanced consumer electronics, automobiles, shipbuilding, petrochemicals, and machine tools were initiated and nurtured through government subsidized finance, tax privileges, market protection, and other assistance.

By the 1980s, the South Korean economy had expanded significantly. Labor costs had risen to a level that caused South Korea to begin losing its comparative advantage in labor-intensive export production. However, technological development within South Korean firms had allowed consumer-oriented exports to become increasingly based upon more sophisticated processes. This development increased productivity levels, and allowed South Korean consumer-oriented exports to move upscale to more value-added market niches. In addition, South Korea's heavy and chemical industries had become more competitive in international markets. Its steel, automobiles, ships, machine tools, and fertilizers began to be exported in increasing quantities.

During the 1962–1982 period, the investment criteria utilized by the Korean Economic Planning Board were not strictly based upon market mechanisms or cost benefit analysis. Rather, investment allocation was principally influenced by government decisions at the planning level. Allocations flowed to those domestic industries viewed by government planners as the ones most likely to earn foreign exchange, to reduce the level of required imports, or to create forward or backward linkages with other targeted industries. However, as the economy grew and became more complex, central economic decisionmaking became increasingly less efficient. Miscalculations by the government in the late 1970s created significant imbalances in the structure of heavy industrial production. After 1982, once industrial infrastructure and basic industries were in place and operational, the government found it to be more efficient to let the market play an increasing role in determining investment decisions. Government planning began to rely less on numerical targets and began to allow a higher level of private sector involvement in determining the flow of financial resources. However, the government continues to assist domestic firms through plans that emphasize research in and the development of more technology-intensive production. Domestic firms continue to receive subsidized finance, monopoly rights, protection, tax holidays, and other incentives for developing industries such as computer electronics, fiber optics, telecommunications, digital machinery, and other high-tech undertakings.

Through sectional planning, control of credit allocations, and other financial and political mechanisms, the state shaped the basic pattern of industrial development. Under this system the inflow of foreign capital was strictly controlled. A major concern of the government was to assure that production and markets in South Korea would be controlled to the largest extent possible by domestic producers. Its development planning was highly detailed in identifying specific sectors, projects, and technologies in which foreign inputs would be necessary to meet production targets as well as those in which they were not needed. The Economic Planning Board and the Foreign Capital Deliberation Committee screened all incoming foreign capital and technology, and only those inflows perceived to be complementary to the state's industrial development strategy were allowed to enter the South Korean economy (Koo, 1984: 7). The empirical pattern of foreign investment and technology closely matched the government's development plans (Mardon, 1990a). Those sectors and projects in which domestic technological knowledge was sufficient for production needs were closed to foreign penetration. Those sectors and projects in which foreign technological assistance was necessary were designated as "open" to foreign penetration.

In its attempt to channel foreign inflows into a pattern that would facilitate the growth of domestic enterprises, the South Korean government has followed a policy intended to decouple foreign capital and technology from foreign direct investment. Whenever possible, it has actively utilized foreign capital for infrastructure development and for private domestic firms investing in government-targeted projects. In planned projects in which domestic producers lacked the necessary technical knowledge, government agencies actively searched global markets and attempted to arrange licensing agreements. With the proper combination of loans and technology, rapid industrial expansion would be accompanied by maximum levels of domestic ownership and control over the production apparatus. Foreign direct investment was preferred and allowed by the government only for those projects in which it would provide a technology that was necessary to develop a planned sector and that technology was not available domestically or through a licensing agreement (Haggard and Cheng, 1987: 113; Mardon, 1990a).

In addition to decoupling the principal components of foreign direct investment and controlling its sectoral flow, the South Korean government has actively pursued policies designed to shape the activities of foreign capital once in the domestic economy in order to maximize technology transfer to domestic firms and to protect the domestic firms' market share. Under the Foreign Capital Inducement Act (a law that regulates all incoming foreign investment), foreign investors entering South Korea must negotiate elaborate investment agreements with the government. These agreements specify the conditions under which the foreign firm may operate in South Korea. In general, the government imposes upon a foreign investor the following conditions: (1) a joint venture formed with a South Korean partner whereby the latter will have or will obtain, in a specific period of time, financial and operational control over the enterprise; (2) an agreement as to the levels of capital invested, output and export levels, level and rate of technology transfer, and access to foreign markets that the investor will provide; and (3) an agreement on the divestiture of foreign-held equity to the domestic partner at a specified future date (Mardon, 1990a). In addition, foreign investors cannot raise capital in the domestic market, purchase a domestic enterprise, or increase their market share in a particular sector at the expense of a South Korean producer.

These governmental policies are strictly enforced and have directly facilitated the development of domestic entrepreneurial firms. Between 1966 and 1988, less than two percent of total investment in South Korea was foreign direct investment (International Monetary Fund, various years). Foreign direct investment has been excluded from most sectors that produce consumer goods and from the primary product sectors as well. In contrast, such investment has largely been concentrated in the development of chemicals, electronics, and tourism; in most cases these investments are joint ventures with Korean partners and require significant technology transfer and personnel training (Mardon, 1990a).

As a result, South Korea's consumer markets and export trade have become dominated by the large corporations, or *chaebols,* such as Hyundai, Samsung, Gold Star, and Dae Woo. These corporations today are multinational, with effective global marketing of their goods and production sites located in several countries (even though in 1962 they were small service-oriented firms or did not even exist). These, and a handful of other South Korean corporations, were the primary benefactors of the government's development policy. The four major *chaebols* alone account for approximately one-third of all South Korea's exports and have received more than 10 percent of all commercial loans since 1965 (*Business Korea,* 1984: 51). In total, only 15 percent of South Korea's $62 billion in exports in 1990 were produced by foreign-invested firms (Korean Economic Planning Board, 1991). South Korean producers control approximately 90 percent of the domestic market share in most consumer goods sectors, as well as in steel, automobiles, construction, petroleum, food processing, and consumer electronics. The larger South Korean corporations are presently involved in research and development and are attempting to lead a drive that will make their country competitive in semiconductors, telecommunications, biotechnology, and other high-tech industries. These firms initiated production and later acquired international competitiveness in these diverse sectors after receiving substantial government financial and political assistance. If the South Korean economy continues to move successfully through the production cycle, it will be these domestic corporations that lead the process.

A good example of government policy toward foreign capital in labor-intensive export sectors can be seen in the production of textiies and consumer electronics. In the 1960s, Japanese corporations in these sectors were searching for offshore production sites. South Korea could offer a well-disciplined labor force at relatively low costs. It presented tax and other financial incentives to the Japanese firms, although joint ventures with a local partner and divestiture agreements were required. These foreign investments immediately produced exports and employment, but, more importantly for sustaining economic growth, they began a process in which domestic firms gradually entered the manufacturing and export production sectors. These firms received substantial financial and political assistance from the government, and technological and managerial knowledge from their foreign partners.

In the latter 1970s, many of the triggering mechanisms of the divestiture agreements were reached. The government supported the South Korean corporations in exercising the equity purchase options by providing low-cost finance. In many cases, the foreign companies were opposed to giving up their majority position and control of the enterprises. However, the South Korean government pressured them to abide by the original agreement. Several foreign companies disposed of all of their equity rather than becoming minority partners. Mashushita, Toshiba, Sony, and others sold off their ventures in South Korea and moved elsewhere. The Japanese textile giants—Teijin and Toray—were forced to reduce their share of large local operations and to relinquish financial and operational control. A Korean-owned and Korean-controlled industry for producing consumer goods was thus established.

The South Korean government's foreign investment policy and action were also significant in establishing domestic production in the heavy and chemical industry sectors (Mardon, 1990a). The petroleum-refining industry serves as an excellent illustration. In 1962, South Korea designated oil refining as one of the first major import-substitution projects. However, no native firm possessed the necessary technology. The Gulf Oil Corporation was approached to develop a refining operation in South Korea, but it was reluctant because of the government's insistence on a joint-venture relationship. In order to persuade Gulf Oil to enter into a joint venture with the Korean Oil Company, the government offered Gulf highly favorable terms, including monopoly rights on providing crude for the operation, tax concessions, and a guaranteed minimum profit level of 15 percent. By 1973, Gulf had remitted more than $10 million in profits (Chang, 1985: 137). The partnership served as an import-substitution project, but, more importantly, it also offered the opportunity for South Korean engineers, technicians, and managers to learn the oil-refining process.

As the South Korean economy grew, the need for refined petroleum increased, and Gulf Oil offered to expand its capacity. However, the government wanted to diversify ownership over refining operations. By that time, economic growth had made South Korea more attractive to foreign investors and allowed the government to open bidding for a second refinery. In 1965, a joint venture was formed with Caltex, and the government selected Gold Star Corporation to establish South Korea's second refinery.

The demand for refined petroleum grew along with the economy. In 1968, Union Oil Corporation entered into a joint venture with Korean Explosive Corporation. In 1976—after the first oil shock—in an attempt to expand its supplies to Middle East oil sources, the South Korean government persuaded the National Iran Oil Corporation to form a fourth joint refining venture with Ssangyong Corporation. In the first two ventures, Gulf and Caltex had been granted financial and operational control under the terms of the investment agreement, and they supplied all the technological know-how. The South Korean state granted operational control to Union, but only 50 percent of the decisionmaking power in financial matters. Under the terms of the National Iran Oil Corporation–Ssangyong venture, the local partner held total operational control and 50 percent of financial control.

In the late 1970s, Seoul began a program to gain national control over petroleum-refining joint ventures. By this time, South Korea had gained the necessary technical expertise to operate a refining operation. When, after the fall of the shah, the new Iranian government agreed to sell its equity, the South Korean government provided financing to Ssangyong to purchase the Iranian share. After the second oil shock, in 1979, several oil corporations found themselves in short supply of crude and in need of restructuring their worldwide portfolio. Gulf and Union were willing to sell their equity shares at relatively low prices. Because the South Korean partners now possessed the necessary technical knowledge, foreign participation was no longer needed in refining operations. The government encouraged the domestic partners to purchase the foreign interest by extending subsidized financing. By 1983, the only foreign-invested firm in South Korea's oil-refining sector was Caltex, and it was required to renegotiate its original investment agreement so as to grant operational and financial control to Gold Star. A fifth oil refining operation was established in 1986 as a joint venture between British Petroleum (BP) and the Kukdong Corporation. BP holds 40 percent of equity and supplies the raw materials for the venture; Kukdong holds financial and operational control of the venture.

Today, South Korea refines 100 percent of its domestic oil requirements, purchases most of its crude on a contractual basis or on the international spot market, hauls the bulk of it in its own ships, and holds total financial and operational control over its petroleum-refining sector. All of these refining operations are owned by large diversified domestic corporations. The capital earned and technological knowledge gained from these operations are applied to the expansion of these firms in other sectors. Such policies and actions led to the establishment of Korean-owned and Korean-controlled production in a wide range of heavy and chemical industry sectors.

## Thailand: An Open Policy Toward Economic Development

Thailand has also experienced substantial economic growth over the past three decades (Panayoton, 1986). From the mid-1960s until the late-1980s, as shown in Table 8.2, Thailand's economy grew at an average annual rate of approximately 6 percent. During the same time period, its exports have grown at about 19 percent annually. Moreover, during the past five years, Thailand has been among the fastest growing economies in the world. Between 1985 and 1990, its GNP grew at an annual rate exceeding 9 percent, with growth rates greater than 10 percent during the past three years (World Bank, 1990). Over the last decade, exports and foreign investments have led an economic expansion that has transformed Thailand's largely agricultural economy into a semi-industrial economy.

During the 1960s and 1970s, Thailand's economic growth was primarily fueled by primary products and import substitution. Its exports were centered around agriculture and minerals. During this period manufacturing grew at a relatively modest 10 percent per year. As is common in many developing countries, manufacturing was largely limited to food processing and the production of low-technology consumer goods. By 1980, however, manufacturing made up less than 22 percent of GNP (Bank of Thailand, 1989).

Thailand's rapid growth rates of the past decade are principally the result of a rapid industrial development based upon export production. By 1990, manufacturing accounted for 27 percent of GNP. During the 1985–1990 period, the value of exports increased from $7 billion to $25 billion (Bank of Thailand, various years). At the same time, the share of manufactured goods to total exports increased from 44 percent to more than 68 percent. Prior to 1980, manufactured goods accounted for less than 20 percent of export earnings.

The role of the Thai government in economic affairs has been limited (Institute of Southeast Asian Affairs, 1990; Keyes, 1987; Lepour, 1989;

Wawn, 1982). Trade policy is relatively liberal, and most commodities are imported freely. There has also been little government support for the promotion of particular production sectors or for domestic producers. The government's stated policy and practice has been to give the private sector the primary role in developing the economy. However, there have been certain exceptions to this policy.

Table 8.2 Major Economic Indicators, Thailand, 1967–1988

| Year | GNP Growth (percentage change) | Export Growth (percentage change) | Productivity Index (1980=100) | Foreign Direct Investment Concentration (percentage of total investment) |
|------|------|------|------|------|
| 1967 | 5.1 | 0.48 | 21.2 | — |
| 1968 | 8.3 | -3.44 | 20.5 | — |
| 1969 | 4.8 | 7.53 | 21.3 | — |
| 1970 | 4.9 | 0.43 | 22.6 | — |
| 1971 | 0.2 | 16.94 | 29.4 | 6.87 |
| 1972 | 3.2 | 30.19 | 34.8 | 12.54 |
| 1973 | 3.7 | 43.28 | 32.6 | 10.46 |
| 1974 | 3.2 | 54.53 | 36.5 | 11.69 |
| 1975 | 4.8 | -9.62 | 34.9 | 9.57 |
| 1976 | 9.4 | 35.08 | 48.7 | 5.03 |
| 1977 | 9.9 | 17.11 | 55.6 | 8.70 |
| 1978 | 10.4 | 20.88 | 60.0 | 6.04 |
| 1979 | 5.3 | 30.23 | 65.4 | 5.51 |
| 1980 | 4.8 | 23.13 | 68.1 | 7.01 |
| 1981 | 6.3 | 14.87 | 75.9 | 10.19 |
| 1982 | 4.1 | 4.40 | 85.3 | 4.43 |
| 1983 | 7.3 | -8.30 | 77.1 | 5.30 |
| 1984 | 7.1 | 19.64 | 93.1 | 4.61 |
| 1985 | 3.5 | 10.35 | 100.0 | — |
| 1986 | 4.5 | 20.69 | 116.1 | 22.30 |
| 1987 | 8.4 | 29.17 | 136.7 | 35.20 |
| 1988 | 11.0 | 33.87 | — | 61.10 |
| Average | 5.9 | 18.23 | 58.8 | 13.33 |

*Sources:* Bank of Thailand, various years; International Monetary Fund, various years; World Bank, various years

The Thai government controls rice prices, offers limited protection for import-substitution producers, and, through the Petroleum Authority of Thailand, assumes responsiblity for overseeing the development of natural gas and the growing petrochemical industry. Also, the Crown Property Bureau (which manages the assets of the royal family) and the military have widespread business interests designed to generate funds for these institutions (Wawn, 1982: 139).

The government has also been active in economic planning under the National Economic and Social Development Board (NESDB). The various five-year development plans articulate the government's economic policy objectives. However, they have not had a major impact on economic activity (Wawn, 1982: 140). This is due to several reasons. Politically, the Thai government has been relatively unstable. Several coups d'etat and changes of administration within the last three decades have made decisionmaking inconsistent. The Thai bureaucracy is also structurally uncoordinated. The NESDB is responsible for planning, but it does not control the budget. Unstable government administrations, combined with an ineffective bureaucracy, make the government incapable of establishing decisive economic policy (Janssen, 1988: 75). In addition, private financial institutions are largely independent of government control. Investment patterns follow market-determined patterns, and thereby do not necessarily flow in a pattern that matches government planning. Under this structural relationship, the Thai government neither controls nor leads the direction of its economy (Girling, 1981; Hewison, 1985; Wawn, 1982).

As a result of the Thai government's limited intervention into economic affairs, there have been few attempts to control the pattern of foreign investment or to promote domestic ownership and control of production processes. Capital inflows into Thailand have never been restricted in any systematic manner (Handley, 1990). No Thai law specifically governs the entry of foreign direct investment into Thailand. In general, foreign direct investment enjoys the same rights as a Thai company unless specific legislation provides otherwise. For example, under the Land Code, foreign companies cannot own land in Thailand without the Board of Investment's approval, although long-term leases are available. The Alien Business Law prohibits foreign investment in some sectors (usually those under the control of the Petroleum Authority of Thailand, the Crown Property Bureau, and the military), and requires joint ventures in others (usually in labor-intensive export sectors). However, this law does not apply to most industries, and, with the permission of the government, individual foreign investors can receive exemption from the law. Also, Thai law does not restrict increases in investment by foreign enterprises once established, does not limit the foreign purchase of Thai firms, does not restrict a foreign investor's share of the domestic market, nor does it restrict foreign investors from obtaining investment capital on domestic capital markets. Thai law also does not generally require foreign direct investment to transfer technology or train and promote local managers and technicians (Board of Investment, 1990). Foreign managers are common even in low-technology sectors after ten years of production (Janssen, 1988: 75).

The Thai Board of Investment does review new foreign direct investment coming into Thailand, but its authority is limited to granting or denying tax and other privileges and does not include the authority to deny the entry of foreign investment (Wawn, 1982: 149). In general, the Board of Investment acts merely to facilitate the entry of certain foreign investments with economic incentives. It is staffed by government officials who often have private interests directly related to the foreign-invested firms that they are regulating (Akrasanee and Wattananukit, 1990).

Prior to 1970, political instability in the region and the low level of industrial development limited the level of foreign investment into Thailand. Until 1970, less than 5 percent of total private investment was foreign, and this was primarily in the primary sectors. During the early 1970s, foreign investment began to flow into import-substitution–producing industries. During the latter 1970s, after the discovery of natural gas reserves in the Gulf of Thailand, foreign direct investment went heavily to this and the related petrochemical field (Hewison, 1985: 149). However, by 1980, total foreign direct investment in Thailand equaled less than $150 million. In the early 1980s, foreign investment in labor-intensive export production began to flow into Thailand.

Since 1985, foreign direct investment has flooded into Thailand. In 1986, more than $119 million was invested; in 1987; $323 million; in 1988, $945 million; in 1989, $1.6 billion; and in 1990, $1.8 billion (Bank of Thailand, 1990; Yu, 1991: 8). The majority of this foreign direct investment has gone into labor-intensive export sectors such as textiles, shoemaking, and consumer electronics. Textile exports from Thailand were less than $83 million in 1977 but grew to $800 million in 1985. By 1990, textile exports exceeded $2.5 billion (Bank of Thailand, 1990; Suphachalasai, 1990: 51). Textiles now constitute the largest single export in foreign exchange earnings, making up 26 percent of the manufacturing output and employing more than 500,000 workers.

The rapid increase in foreign direct investment into labor-intensive production has been led by Japanese and Taiwanese companies, and, to a lesser extent, by South Korean and Hong Kong firms. Among the several reasons firms from these nations are relocating in Thailand, the primary one is that changes in their structural relationship with global markets are "pushing" their labor-intensive goods to offshore sites. In the 1970s, Japan's labor costs had risen to a level at which it was no longer competitive in these sectors. At that time, Japanese textile firms such as Toray, Teijin, and Tokai were moving their production to offshore sites. Many of these sites were first located in South Korea, Taiwan, and Hong Kong. Since the early 1980s, however, labor costs have also become uncompetitive in these newly industrializing economies. Particularly since the democratization movements began in the mid-1980s in South Korea and Taiwan, new labor freedoms have sent production costs soaring. At the same time, the currencies of these nations have appreciated considerably against the U.S. dollar, the currency of their primary market, thus further decreasing their international competitiveness (Muscat, 1990; Shale, 1989). In addition, with the voluntary export restraints (VERs) and quotas imposed by the United States on Japanese goods, as well as the ending of the U.S. Generalized System of Preference privileges to Taiwan, South Korea, and Hong Kong, producers in these nations must move to other offshore sites in order to maintain their share of the U.S. market.

Thailand has pulled this investment to its shores largely due to its low labor costs and its government's open approach to foreign investment (Tasker, 1990: 49–51). According to Hisahiko Okazaki, the Japanese ambassador to Thailand, "Japanese need offshore bases for export industries to escape high labor costs, quotas, and the uncompetitive yen. Thailand's wonderful *laissez-faire* policy provides the perfect offshore base" (Tasker, 1990: 49). The basic wage in Thailand is between $90 and $120 per month (Kraar, 1989; Sasada, 1990), approximately one-quarter the cost of labor in South Korea and Taiwan.

In addition to low labor costs and an open market, Thailand, with a population of more than 55 million and a GNP per capita of $1,500 (more than $3,000 in the Bangkok area) offers a relatively large domestic market. The Samsung corporation of South Korea has recently opened an electronics assembly plant in Thailand. It expects to sell 500,000 color televisions, 400,000 refrigerators, and 200,000 video cassette recorders every year, even though Japanese producers already control 70 percent of the Thai market in each of these areas (Rainat, 1988b: 45).

At the macro level, foreign direct investment and open policies have contributed greatly to economic growth in Thailand. The structure of the economy has been transformed, and Thailand is now well advanced into the early phase of the production cycle. However, the Thai industrialization process is largely under foreign ownership and control. The textile sector is primarily owned and operated by foreigners; there are no large-scale Thai corporations in the textile industry (Suphachalasai, 1990: 64). Foreign producers control the consumer electronics sector (Rainat, 1988a: 45). Almost all raw and intermediate materials and machinery are imported, giving little value-added to Thailand except for labor. There is also very little technology transfer or managerial training under this system. The Thai integrated circuit industry is virtually 100 percent foreign owned (*East Asian*

*Executive Reports,* 1988: 21). For example, Japanese trading companies control well over 50 percent of Thai exports and 65 percent of imports (Girling, 1981: 98).

Foreign direct investment also controls more than 50 percent of almost all manufactured goods sectors in the Thai domestic market (Handley, 1990). More than 95 percent of the petroleum industry is foreign owned (Hewison, 1985: 274), and the chemical sector is controlled by Dow (U.S.), ICI (U.K.), and Solvay (Belgium). In addition, five of the ten largest industrial firms in Thailand are 100 percent Japanese owned (Girling, 1981: 100). The remaining five are largely controlled by foreign capital. This large concentration of foreign investment in the domestic market has led to the crowding out of Thai producers. As a consequence of economic growth, increases in land prices, the cost of engineers and skilled technicians, and the overall cost of inputs have driven many Thai producers out of several market sectors. Many local firms have been purchased by foreign investors. Construction and transportation firms have been particularly hard hit. Although economic growth has led to a construction and transportation boom, most contracts have been awarded to firms from the home country of the foreign investor funding the project. Under an open foreign investment system, without systematic protection and financial assistance from the government, capital-short and technologically underdeveloped Thai firms have not been able to compete with foreign multinational corporations (Akrasanee and Wattananukit, 1990: 378). Thailand may be experiencing rapid industrial growth at present, but there are *no* large diversified industrial corporations emerging that are Thai-owned and Thai-operated.

## Conclusion: Sustaining
## Growth Through the Production Cycle

Can economic growth be sustained in South Korea and Thailand? More specifically, will the production structures being established in these economies allow them to effectively pass through the many phases of the production cycle to a point roughly equivalent to the advanced industrial economies? The answer to this question may be determined mainly by the patterns of ownership that have been and are being established.

In the case of South Korea, a developmental state apparatus has sought industrial growth, but a major emphasis was placed upon the development of domestically owned and controlled production. A very active government promoted the growth of domestic firms through financial assistance, protection, tax structures, and foreign investment regulation. In both labor-intensive export and capital-intensive heavy and chemical manufacturing import-substitution sectors, the South Korean government has required joint ventures with indigenous firms as the basic term of entry for foreign investors. These joint ventures have mandatory requirements for technology transfer and usually require the foreign partner to divest equity at a specific time, when the local partner would presumably gain financial and operational control. Many foreign firms refused to accept these terms and located elsewhere. Thus, government policy certainly slowed South Korea's rate of growth in the short term. Those foreign firms that agreed to the Korean terms received economic incentives such as guaranteed domestic market share for a specific period of time and tax holidays (Mardon, 1990a). This approach offered foreign investors benefits that would allow them to recoup their capital investment and return a profit in a short period of time. However, through the joint-venture arrangements and the divestiture policy enforced by the state, South Korean enterprises were pushed and nurtured into becoming large globally competitive corporations.

In order to sustain economic growth through the 1990s and beyond, the South Korean economy must move into more technologically advanced sectors. There is certainly no guarantee that the South Korean economy will be capable of making the complex structural adjustments necessary to become competitive in these industries. However, in South Korea's economy today there are several domestically based large diversified corporate producers. Simply put, their survival is tied to the success of the South Korean economy. These corporations, with substantial government assistance, are now mobilizing for and investing in high-tech research and development and personnel training. If they are successful in developing competitive production in the high-tech areas, much of the future production and profit earned will be based indigenously. This will then allow South Korea to sustain its economic development.

The prospect for Thailand to sustain economic growth over the long run seems far less bright than for South Korea. Due to Thailand's open approach to foreign capital, foreign investors own and control both the export production and domestic consumer goods sectors. There are no large diversified industrial producers emerging in Thailand. Where joint ventures do exist, the foreign partner maintains financial and operational control. There is little transfer of production technology to Thai firms. There are no mechanisms in place to lead to foreign divestiture of equity or financial support for domestic firms to expand.

As long as labor costs remain low, Thailand will remain an attractive offshore production site for foreign investment, and the economy will continue to grow. However, as the capacity of the labor force is exhausted, wages will increase, and when Thai wages become less competitive by world market standards, labor-intensive foreign investment in Thailand will inevitably slow down considerably. At this phase of Thai development, the economy will require adjustment to increase the level of industrial technology. However, there will be few domestic corporations capable of leading this adjustment. Will foreign corporations increase their investment in research and development and personnel training in Thailand? Will foreign corporations bring in technology-intensive production processes? Or, will the foreign firms merely leave Thailand and relocate their labor-intensive operations? Certainly it is too early to answer these questions. However, if past experience is at all indicative, it is highly likely that the foreign firms will choose to relocate. With no large-scale domestic firms to lead the economy to more capital- and technology-intensive production, Thailand's industrial growth will probably not be sustained beyond the labor-intensive stage.

## References

Akrasanee, N., and A. Wattananukit. 1990. "Changing Structure and Rising Dynamism in the Thai Economy." In Institute of Southeast Asian Affairs (ed.), *Southeast Asian Affairs, 1990,* pp. 360–380. Boulder, Colo.: Westview.

Alam, S. M. 1989. *Government and Markets in Economic Development Strategies: Lessons from Korea, Taiwan and Japan.* New York: Praeger.

Amsden, A. H. 1991. "The Diffusion of Development: The Late Industrializing Model and Greater East Asia." *The American Economic Review* 81: 282–287.

Amsden, A. H. 1989. *Asia's Next Giant: South Korea and Late Industrialization.* New York: Oxford University Press.

Balassa, B. (ed.). 1982. *Development Strategies in Semi-Industrial Economies.* Baltimore, Md.: Johns Hopkins University Press.

Balassa, B. 1981. *The Newly Industrializing Countries in the World Economy.* New York: Pergamon.

Bank of Korea. Various Years. *Economic Statistics Yearbook.* Seoul: author.

Bank of Thailand. Various Years. *Monthly Bulletins.* Bangkok: author.

Bhagwati, J. N. (ed.). 1982. *Import Competition and Response.* Chicago: University of Chicago Press.

Board of Investment, Thailand. 1990. *A Guide to Investing in Thailand.* Bangkok: author.

*Business Korea.* 1984. July.

Chan, S. 1991. "Catching Up and Keeping Up: Explaining Capitalist East Asia's Industrial Competitiveness." *The Journal of East Asian Affairs* 5: 79–103.

Chan, S. 1990. *East Asian Dynamism.* Boulder, Colo.: Westview.

Chang, D. J. 1985. *Economic Control and Political Authoritarianism: The Role of Japanese Corporations in Korea, 1965–1979.* Seoul: Sogang University Press.

Chen, E. K. T. 1979. *Hypergrowth in Asian Economies.* London: Macmillan.

Chu, Y. H. 1989. "State Structure and Economic Adjustment of the East Asian Newly Industrializing Countries." *International Organization* 43: 647–672.

Crone, D. 1983. *The Asian States: Coping with Dependence.* New York: Praeger.

Dietz, J. L. 1991. *Latin American Lessons from the Far East: Substance and Illusion.* Fullerton, Calif.: Department of Economics Working Paper No. 9–91, California State University.

*East Asian Executive Reports.* 1988. "Investment Incentives: Can Thailand Now Afford to Be Less Generous?" 10: 8–20.

Evans, P. 1987. "Class, State and Dependence in East Asia: Lessons for Latin Americanists." In F. C. Deyo (ed.), *The Political Economy of the New Asian Industrialism,* pp. 203–226. Ithaca, N.Y.: Cornell University Press.

Girling, J. L. S. 1981. *Thailand: Society and Politics.* Ithaca, N.Y.: Cornell University Press.

Haggard, S., and T. J. Cheng. 1987. "State and Foreign Capital in the East Asian NICs." In F. C. Deyo (ed.), *The Political Economy of the New Asian Industrialism,* pp. 84–135. Ithaca, N.Y.: Cornell University Press.

Handley, P. 1990. "Moneybags Move In." *Far Eastern Economic Review.* April 19, pp. 87–89.

Harris, N. 1986. *The End of the Third World: Newly Industrializing Countries and the End of an Ideology.* New York: Penguin.

Hewison, K. J. 1985. "The State and Capitalist Development in Thailand." In R. Higgot and R. Robison (eds.), *Southeast Asia: Essays in the Political Economy of Structural Change,* pp. 267–294. Boston: Routledge and Kegan Paul.

Institute of Southeast Asian Studies. 1990. *Southeast Asian Affairs.* Boulder, Colo.: Westview.

International Monetary Fund. Various Years. *International Financial Statistics.* Washington, D.C.: author.

James, W. E., S. Naya, and G. M. Meier (eds.). 1989. *Asian Development Economic Successes and Policy Lessons.* Madison, Wisc.: University of Wisconsin Press.

Janssen, P. 1988. "Economic Report: Thailand." *Asian Business* 24: 71–80.

Johnson, C. 1987. "Political Institutions and Economic Performance: The Government-Business Relationship in Japan, South Korea and Taiwan." In F. C. Deyo (ed.), *The Political Economy of the New Asian Industrialism,* pp. 137–164. Ithaca, N.Y.: Cornell University Press.

Johnson, C. 1981. *MITI and the Japanese Miracle: The Growth of Industrial Policy, 1925–1975.* Stanford, Calif.: Stanford University Press.

Jones, L., and I. Sakong. 1980. *Government, Business, and Entrepreneurship in Economic Development: The Korean Case.* Cambridge, Mass.: Harvard University Press.

Keyes, C. F. 1987. *Thailand: Buddhist Kingdom as Modern Nation State.* Boulder, Colo.: Westview.

Kim, S. H. 1970. *Foreign Capital for Economic Development.* New York: Praeger.

Koo, B. Y. 1984. *Industrial Structure and Foreign Investment: A Case Study of Their Interrelationship in Korea.* Seoul: Korea Development Institute.

Korean Economic Planning Board. Various years. *Major Statistics of Korean Economy.* Seoul: author.

Kraar, L. 1989. "Asian Rising Export Powers." *Fortune* 120, 13: 43–50.

Krueger, A. O. 1979. *The Developmental Role of the Foreign Sector and Aid.* Cambridge, Mass.: Harvard University Press.

Lepour, B. (ed.). 1989. *Thailand: A Country Study.* Washington, D.C.: Federal Research Division, Library of Congress.

Mardon, R. 1990a. "The State and the Effective Control of Foreign Capital: The Case of South Korea." *World Politics* 43: 111–137.

Mardon, R. 1990b. "The State and Industrial Transformation in the Republic of Korea." *Journal of Social, Political and Economic Studies* 15: 457–482.

Mason, E. 1980. *The Economic and Social Modernization of Korea.* Cambridge, Mass.: Harvard University Press.

Moon, C. I. 1989. "Trade Friction and Industrial Adjustment: The Textiles and Apparels in the Pacific Basin." In S. Haggard and C. I. Moon (eds.), *Pacific Dynamics: The International Politics of International Change*, pp. 185–208. Boulder, Colo.: Westview.

Muscat, R. J. 1990. *Thailand and the United States: Development, Security and Foreign Aid.* New York: Columbia University Press.

Paik, W. K. and R. Mardon. 1991. "Industrial Policies and Economic Performances of South Korea." *Pacific Focus* 6: 59–76.

Panayoton, T. 1986. "Investment, Growth and Employment in Thailand." *Journal of Business Administration* 16: 117–157.

Rainat, J. 1988a. "Korean Electronic Giants Find a Base in Thailand." *Asian Finance* 14, 7: 44–47.

Rainat, J. 1988b. "Thailand: Asian New Land of Opportunity." *Asian Finance* 14, 10: 32–69.

Sasada, S. 1990. "Japanese Companies Struggle with Labor Problems in Thailand." *Tokyo Business Today* 58, 7: 56–57.

Shale, T. 1989. "Southeast Asia: A New Crop of Tigers." *Euromoney.* September, pp. 91–92.

Suphachalasai, S. 1990. "Export Growth of Thai Clothing and Textiles." *World Economy* 13: 51–73.

Tasker, R. 1990. "Wedded to Success: Thais and Japanese Reap the Rewards from Partnership." *Far Eastern Economic Review* 148, 18: 49–51.

Thorelli, H. B., and G. D. Sentell. 1982. *Consumer Emancipation and Economic Development.* Greenwich, Conn.: JAI Press.

United Nations. Various years. *Yearbook of National Account Statistics.* New York: author.

Vernon, R. 1966. "International Investment and International Trade in the Product Cycle." *Quarterly Journal of Economics* 80: 190–207.

Wawn, B. 1982. *The Economies of the ASEAN Countries.* New York: St. Martin's.

Westphal, L. 1978. "The Republic of Korea's Experience with Export-Led Industrial Development." *World Development* 6: 347–382.

World Bank. Various years. *World Development Report.* New York: Oxford University Press.

Yu, F. 1991. *World Market Report: Thailand.* New York: McGraw-Hill.

# 9

# ASEAN State Industrial Policies and Japanese Regional Production Strategies: The Case of Malaysia's Motor Vehicle Industry

*Kit G. Machado*

Structural changes under way in the world political economy have affected and promise further to affect the power and wealth of states, corporations, financial institutions, classes, groups, and individuals. Which states, organizations, and people move ahead or fall behind in these terms depends largely on the extent to which they are able to advance or maintain their relative position in a fast-changing international division of labor. Worldwide relocation of whole or partial manufacturing processes proceeds apace in many industries. The new international division of labor must be understood as "an on-going process . . . not . . . a final result" (Frobel et al., 1980: 45; see also Caporaso, 1987). No states have been more involved in this process than those of the Pacific Basin. Firms from the world's advanced capitalist states have made substantial new investment in, and relocated numerous manufacturing plants to, most of the less developed states of the region. This process has altered the latters' role in the world economy, and it has contributed to the economic advance made by some of them. Wide dispersal of production sites does not, however, assure commensurately wide dispersal of the economic benefits of production. These are determined primarily by where value is added and how it is shared. These questions are continuously at issue among those at different levels in the global division of labor, as those below the top seek to move up and those on top seek to stay there.

Today, ASEAN (Association of Southeast Asian Nations) states seek to accelerate and deepen industrial development. At the same time, Japanese firms expand and, in some sectors, seek to organize and integrate industrial production throughout the Pacific Basin as part of larger strategies for maintaining or enhancing their position in the international division of labor. The ASEAN states' industrial policies derive from various combinations of international and domestic considerations. Japanese strategies along with other international factors form an important matrix of opportunities and constraints that shapes the outcomes of these policies. This can be seen in various sectors (e.g., electronics and machinery), but it is particularly notable in the motor vehicle industry. The recent development of that industry in Malaysia provides a good example of the intersection between the ASEAN states' industrial policies and Japanese industrial strategies. As part of a larger heavy industrialization drive, the Malaysian government in 1983 formed a national auto firm in joint venture with Mitsubishi. This was, among other things, intended to promote rationalization (i.e., concentration into fewer but larger companies) and localization (i.e., increased use of locally produced parts) in a sector where most other participants were also associated with Japanese auto firms. At the same time, Japanese firms have for both strategic and narrower economic reasons sought to promote regional production of motor vehicles and to control the character and pace of localization. The primary purpose of this chapter is to describe and explain the outcomes of such Malaysian and Japanese efforts to date.

What follows is informed by debates in political economy concerning the prospects for Third World industrialization. Dependency theorists posit a capitalist world system that imposes severe constraints on states seeking to improve their position in the international division of labor and argue that for this reason they may at best achieve dependent and distorted industrial development (see Cardoso and Faletto, 1979; Evans, 1979). Statist and growth coalition theorists, on the other hand, give primacy to domestic factors in determining such states' prospects for industrialization. Both assert that Third World countries can effectively exploit opportunities in the world system to build a solid industrial base. Statists argue that such development requires the efforts of "hard," purposeful, high-capacity states that enjoy substantial autonomy from society (see Deyo, 1987; Haggard, 1990), whereas growth coalitionists assert that it may be furthered by effective public-private sector coalitions even in the absence of a hard state (Doner, 1991). Others, encouraging synthesis, stress that national political economic developments are shaped by both global and domestic factors and that the important matter is to assess their relative weight in particular cases (Ellison and Gereffi, 1990; Frieden and Lake, 1991). This chapter analyzes the effects of global and domestic political economic trends on the development of the Malaysian motor vehicle industry and finds both to have been important.

Malaysia is a particularly suitable subject for this analysis. The country has long exhibited the classic characteristics of economic dependence (Khor, 1983), but it has been systematically attempting to alter this circumstance. It more closely matches the model of the hard, autonomous state than most Third World countries. Malaysia's national leaders and private businessmen have sometimes worked in concert to advance national goals. At the same time, Malaysia's highly complex ethnic situation has an impact on most state undertakings (Milne and Mauzy, 1986). The 1971–1990 New Economic Policy (NEP) called for advancing the economic position of the *Bumiputera* (indigenous Malays) in relation to the large Chinese and Indian communities. This goal has been considered at every turn in pursuing other policy objectives, including industrialization and managing relations with transnational capital (Bowie, 1991; Jesudason, 1989). Examination of the Malaysian case should thus bring the importance of external constraints and opportunities and of domestic characteristics and initiatives into sharp relief.

The balance between global and domestic factors in shaping Third World industrialization efforts is struck most directly in interactions between transnational corporations, on the one hand, and host country states and local partners and suppliers, on the other; but it is also much affected by world and national political economic trends. The focus of this chapter is on the interaction and bargaining between the national and transnational participants in the Malaysian motor vehicle industry as they pursued their respective strategies within the context formed by these trends (for excellent studies of bargaining in the automobile industry, see Bennett and Sharpe, 1985; Doner, 1991). It first briefly analyzes Malaysia's heavy industrial and motor vehicle policies. It next assesses Japan's regional and global economic strategies and its motor vehicle firms' specific strategies. It then examines the intersection of Malaysian policy and Japanese strategies in the transformation of the Malaysian motor vehicle industry through 1990, considering (1) the formation and early development of the Malaysian auto project, (2) the transfer of management control of that project from Malaysian to Japanese hands, and (3) the localization process. Finally, this chapter looks at the intersection of Japanese strategies and both Malaysian and ASEAN policies in the early stages of regional auto production schemes advanced by Mitsubishi, Toyota, and Nissan. I conclude that although Malaysia has effectively exerted influence on Japanese transnational auto firms and thereby derived some real economic benefits and advanced some of its national industrial goals, these gains have been realized at the cost of accepting new forms of dependence for the foreseeable future.

## Malaysian Heavy Industrial and Motor Vehicle Policies

*Policy development and management.* A large-scale, state-sponsored heavy industrialization drive, centered initially on motor vehicle and steel manufacture, was launched in Malaysia in 1981 (Bowie, 1991: ch. 5; Machado,1989–1990, 1987). This was largely the work of Datuk Seri Mahathir bin Mohamad, who became the prime minister that year. He simultaneously defined "learning from Japan" as crucial to national development and vigorously promoted this orientation under his Look East Policy. Heavy industrialization would rely extensively on Japanese capital, technology, and finance, but the priorities would be set by Mahathir. Joint ventures would be established between Japanese corporations and the Heavy Industries Corporation of Malaysia (HICOM). Mahathir had created the latter as a former trade and industry minister and had recruited its top managers mainly from the public sector. In 1981, he took jurisdiction over HICOM with him to the prime minister's department, where it has effectively answered to him. It is not a government agency but a 100 percent government-owned holding company established, like a private firm, under the Companies Act. This fact reduces the governmental control and scrutiny normally exercised over public undertakings (Puthucheary, 1984). The role of HICOM is exemplary of a long-term shift in policymaking power in Malaysia from career bureaucrats to the top political leaders—a shift that was accelerated greatly by Mahathir. Interagency bodies work out the details of narrow industrial policy issues, but the coordinating body for general industrial policymaking is the cabinet. HICOM projects are closely identified with the prime minister, and he has made many key decisions in their development. Political insiders say that dealing with Japanese participants in these projects is the exclusive domain of the prime minister.

*External and domestic factors in heavy industrial policy.* Malaysia's leaders had long attempted to promote manufacturing, but Mahathir's strategy was a new departure in industrial policy. He aimed to push Malaysia into the ranks of the newly industrializing countries (NICs) by the end of this century. His goals were, in part, to reduce Malaysia's economic dependence on world commodity markets and on advanced capitalist states and to increase the benefits to the country of relations with transnational corporations. Malaysia has long been highly vulnerable to fluctuations in primary commodity prices. Long-term trends in the prices of its exports and imports have resulted in a substantial decline in its terms of trade over the past thirty years (Khor, 1987: 76–80). During the first postindependence (1957) decade, industrial development was based on import substitution. In the late 1960s, the promotion of export-oriented manufacturing began. This was based mainly on primary product processing and labor-intensive assembly, packaging, and final processing operations. Many of these industries were foreign owned and operating in Free Trade Zones (FTZs) where they had few links to the rest of the economy. An Industrial Master Plan (IMP) prepared under the auspices of the UN Industrial Development Organization (UNIDO) in the early 1980s was intended to form a coherent framework for further industrial development (MIDA/UNIDO, 1985). Its main goals were rationalization of protected import-substituting industries as well as diversification and deepening of export-oriented industries. The IMP aimed to push modern manufacturing activity beyond FTZ enclaves and to stimulate spin-offs. The intention was to reduce the dependence of Malaysian industries on imported raw materials and intermediate inputs and to foster an expanding network of linkages between these industries. Although the decision to promote heavy industries was made before the IMP was formulated, it was meant to be consistent with IMP goals.

Statists argue that although Third World development strategies may be responses to such external "constraints associated with economic interdependence," their substance is best explained by reference to "domestic politics and policy making" (Haggard, 1986: 346). This clearly applies to the Malaysian case. Mahathir's economic policies were partly responses to external constraints, but his critiques of these problems and his responses to them followed from more than his reading of the economic situation. These derived from his sense of nationalism, from his efforts to mobilize nationalist sentiment to bolster his administration, and, most importantly, from his ideas concerning national development and its requisites and his long-standing concern with what he regarded as serious defects in Malay values and behavior. His views on these matters were originally set forth in his controversial book, *The Malay Dilemma* (Mahathir, 1970). He asserted that rural Malays lacked sufficient individual enterprise, independence, initiative, pride in work, or competitive ability, and he stressed that effecting changes in *Bumiputera* values and behavior was essential to national development. These assumptions also underlay his 1980s Look East Policy, which emphasized the need for Malays to learn from Japanese work ethics and attitudes. Mahathir stressed the rural roots of alleged Malay deficiencies. He argued that the solution was "to urbanize the Malays," and he emphasized that they "must acquire skills through working . . . not be subjected to theoretical lessons" (1970: 105–106). For Mahathir, promoting industrialization to stimulate changes among *Bumiputera* was as important as promoting it to hasten economic development.

Heavy industrialization was also part of Mahathir's effort to further structural change in Malaysia's political economy (Milne, 1986). He was disappointed by the slow progress made in meeting New Economic Policy goals. The NEP required restructuring "society to eliminate the identification of race with economic functions" (Government of Malaysia, 1981: 1), meaning primarily increasing *Bumiputera* participation in the modern sector of the economy. A 1990 target of 30 percent *Bumiputera* ownership and control in the corporate sector was clearly not going to be met. Creation of state industries went well beyond an Industrial Coordination Act–mandated equity restructuring exercise that had given state trust agencies a stake in many private companies after the mid-1970s. Establishing state firms in sectors that had been wholly or partly dominated by the Chinese, often in combination with foreign capital, represented an advance in economic restructuring and in efforts to expand the *Bumiputera* managerial and entrepreneurial classes. Reliance on state firms also followed from the factors that deter private investment in such projects—large initial investments, big risks, long gestation periods before profits can be expected, and low rates of return (HICOM, 1984: 14–15). Moreover, such initiatives created new opportunities for dispensing patronage, which was of growing importance to top leaders of the United Malays National Organization (UMNO), who were seeking to expand further and to cement their political dominance (Gomez, 1990). Mahathir, however, stressed that *Bumiputera* economic problems could not be solved politically without supporting changes in their values and behavior (1970: 31), which must ultimately come through their own efforts (1981: 33). It is these views that are most important to understanding his industrial policies.

*Objectives of the national auto project.* It was Mahathir's decision to promote the manufacture of a national car. He saw this as a central pillar of industrialization and defined it as a key to national "coming of age." He described it as "another step toward enhancing the nation in the eyes of the world [and] a symbol of Malaysians as a dignified people" (*New Straits Times*, 1985). Auto manufacture promised technological advance, the development of engineering skills, and the generation of supply industries with export potential. The auto project was partly an effort to reduce import dependence by forcing rationalization of the industry. After more than a decade of local assembly of imported completely knocked down (CKD) automobile kits, finished vehicles still contained no more than 18 percent local content by value. Automobile assemblers and their primarily Japanese partners had not only consistently resisted government localization policies, but, with government forbearance and protection, they had created an industrial structure that was itself an obstacle to localization. The large number of makes and models of cars being assembled for a very small market made it difficult economically to produce component parts locally (Ariff, 1982; Lim, 1984). Moreover, as local Chinese entrepreneurs dominated auto assembly, it was an obvious target for restructuring.

## Japanese Regional and Global Strategies

*National and corporate strategies.* Forced from Southeast Asia in defeat in 1945, the Greater East Asia Co-prosperity Sphere apparently in ruins, the Japanese soon returned and rapidly became the predominant economic force in the region. During the 1970s, Japan became the largest or the next to largest trading partner of and investor in all of the ASEAN states

(Akrasanee, 1983; Sekiguchi, 1983). As Table 9.1 shows, Japanese firms substantially accelerated investment in the region in the 1980s (JETRO, 1991; Kitazawa, 1987; Saravanamuttu, 1988: Shiode, 1989; Steven, 1990). Today, the Japanese seek to maintain and extend their predominant economic position in Southeast Asia under the best possible terms. They aim to reduce the economic uncertainties inherent in the current period and to maximize their global competitiveness. In pursuit of these goals, they seek to promote greater regional economic integration under their leadership. Top Japanese political leaders made proposals to these ends in the 1960s and 1970s. These proposals were met with little enthusiasm by their neighbors, who perceived them as promising advantages mainly to the Japanese. Tokyo's top leaders have consistently denied that they seek regional economic domination, and have for some time concentrated on supporting ASEAN as well as broader regional arrangements proposed by others (Sudo, 1988a, 1988b). Japanese academics and technocrats simultaneously project colorful images of Asia developing under Japanese leadership. Japan has been variously portrayed as the leader of geese flying in "V" formation and as the "Asian brain."

Table 9.1    Cumulative Japanese Investment in ASEAN and All East Asia (US$ billion)

|  | 1975 | 1980 | 1985 | 1990 |
|---|---|---|---|---|
| Indonesia | 1.19 | 3.90 | 8.02 | 10.40 |
| Singapore | 0.22 | 0.80 | 1.93 | 5.70 |
| Thailand | 0.19 | 0.36 | 0.71 | 3.00 |
| Malaysia | 0.25 | 0.50 | 1.05 | 2.50 |
| Philippines | 0.19 | 0.54 | 0.83 | 1.30 |
| ASEAN | 2.05 | 6.10 | 12.54 | 22.90 |
| Other East Asia[a] | 0.94 | 2.36 | 5.49 | 17.57 |
| Total | 2.99 | 8.46 | 18.03 | 40.47 |

*Note:* Cumulative investment from 1951 to March 31 of the indicated years.

a. China, South Korea, Taiwan, Hong Kong, Brunei

*Sources:* Dobashi (1988: 13); JETRO (1991: 76); *Far Eastern Economic Review* (1991a: 44); and Sekiguchi (1983: 233).

More practically, the Japanese work to build the structural underpinnings for the position they seek in the region one piece at a time. Both government and private sector interests favor and attempt to promote complementation or "agreed specialization" between Japan and its economic partners to optimize complementarity in the division of labor between countries and within specific transnational industries (Aoki, 1986; Dobashi, 1988; *Kikai Shinko Kyokai Keizai Kenkyujo*, 1988; Kojima, 1970; Ohata, 1989; Ozawa, 1979; RIM Studies Group, 1988). The 1987 Japanese Ministry of International Trade and Industry (MITI) New Asian Industries Development Plan sets a framework for investment in and the relocation of export-oriented industries to the region (Unger, 1990). Follow-up Japanese studies done with specific ASEAN governments recommend individual products in which their countries should specialize (*Far Eastern Economic Review*, 1991a: 54; *Wall Street Journal*, 1990). Japanese transnationals design and promote integrated regional production schemes based on an intraindustry international division of labor. Institutions set up to recycle some of Japan's trade surplus in Southeast Asia, such as the Japan-ASEAN Investment Corporation and the ASEAN-Japan Development Fund, finance projects that conform to such goals. Japanese banks are acquiring stakes in local banks in the region to provide better for the needs of Japanese investors there. Many investment, financing, and aid decisions are thus made within the framework of the broader Japanese strategy.

The recent wave of Japanese direct foreign investment, much of it in export industries, is supported by Japanese government agencies, private financial institutions, and trading companies; and it is driving increased integration of the Asia Pacific region. New investments by Japanese transnationals as well as recent relocations of small and medium Japanese firms in other regional states follow from both domestic problems and global strategies. The impact of a severe labor shortage on wages, inflated land prices, and yen appreciation since 1985 have all contributed to increasing production costs in Japan. These mounting costs have had an adverse impact on the price competitiveness of some Japanese manufactured exports in world markets. This has been a particularly important consideration in the decisions of many small and medium Japanese industries to locate elsewhere in Asia where labor is cheaper (Phongpaichit, 1988). It has even been argued that Japan "agreed to yen revaluation in accordance with its own industrial policy for phasing out sunset industries at home and for the purpose of accelerating its direct foreign investment" (Hollerman, 1988: 17). In any case, Japan's wish to hold down its trade surplus with, and to circumvent quotas in, the United States and the European Community (EC) is a further spur to regional investment by its transnationals, as it means that products made by companies under Japanese control can enter these markets from other Asian countries. This consideration has become particularly important as Japanese global strategies have led to the increasing presence of their manufacturing plants in other advanced capitalist states. To enhance price competitiveness in these markets, these plants will be supplied in part by Japanese-controlled companies elsewhere in Asia (Dobashi, 1988).

Hollerman (1988: 8–11) offers a convincing explanation of such trends, arguing that Japan's "domestic industrial policy . . . has evolved into geopolitical strategy [which] coordinate[s] Japan's external relations with the transformation of its indigenous industrial structure, . . . [including] calculated disaggregation . . . of the production process, with some stages being assigned abroad and some retained at home." In this process, "Japan retains for itself the higher value-added operations that yield the best rates of return." At the same time, "export of plants and equipment [establishes a] dependency relationship (in terms of financing, maintenance, management, and distribution of output) . . . between Japan and its clients."

Hollerman (1988: xi) thus contends that Japan aims to become a "headquarters country" able to "impose central management on a world network of joint ventures, subsidiaries, and affiliates" and to "coordinate the relations of its foreign clients with each other as well as . . . with itself." This project is far from realization. The total portion of Japanese industrial production by value located offshore is still only about 5 percent. It is expected to reach the current U.S. figure of around 20 percent by the turn of the century, and in some industries, it is expected to grow much more rapidly. Internationalization of some Japanese industries proceeds apace, and Japanese strategies form an important matrix within which both governments and businesspeople throughout Asia must operate.

*Auto industry strategies.*    Japan's automakers, like its other manu-facturers, have been reluctant transnationals, historically preferring to produce at home and export. Current and feared import restrictions in North American and EC markets have been the primary spur to change. The major Japanese auto firms now have global strategies, looking mainly to replace some exports with cars produced on both continents, where they have invested US$10.5 billion since the mid-1980s (*Far Eastern Economic Review*, 1991c: 59). Nissan, having started the earliest, has gone the furthest with this process. In 1989, it announced that it planned during the next decade to reverse its domestic to overseas production ratio from what it was then (2:1), to make it 1:2 by the turn of the century. About the same time, the firm was reorganized to create what its president called a "tripolar corporate management structure, with integrated opera-tions headquarters in Japan, North America, and Europe, . . . [making] it easier to coordinate our overall activities from a global perspective" (*Asian Wall Street Journal*, 1989). Nissan set out to strengthen the global planning capacity of each of its departments as a step toward establishing its corporate functions on a worldwide basis in order "to reinforce Nissan's ability to coordinate business plans for its overseas operations in harmony with domestic operations" (*Japan Times,* 1990). It also began building a global research and development (R&D) network. Mitsubishi, Honda, and Toyota have, to varying degrees, been moving in the same direction. They are now conducting R&D and producing vehicles alone and/or in linkups with local manufacturers in North America and/or Europe. Mitsubishi, for example, has been partly (now 12 percent) owned by Chrysler since 1971 and is now jointly producing cars with Chrysler in the United States. It has also since 1987 been involved in a cooperative arrangement with Germany's Daimler-Benz and is planning to produce cars in Europe.

Japanese auto firms' Asian regional strategies are similarly inspired, as they also face import restrictions in what they regard as an increasingly promising market. At the same time, however, production of both cars and parts in lower labor-cost states of the region are ultimately intended for export to North America and the EC countries. Parts are also intended for import and use in Japan. In 1988–1989, for example, Nissan was instructing about a hundred of its affiliated parts makers to locate in ASEAN and China to set up a "global buying network" (Steven, 1990: 102). Japanese motor vehicle firms are apparently attempting to reproduce their subcontracting-based domestic industrial structure on a regional basis. Some industry analysts believe, though, that Japanese automobile manufacturing methods (e.g., reliance on "just-in-time" supplies, flexible production, and increasing automation) militate against this in the long run (Hoffman and Kaplinsky, 1988).

This does not necessarily augur well for the ASEAN companies that join with Japanese parts firms to supply Japanese automakers. The latter are basically assemblers and rely heavily on networks of 200 to 300 external suppliers to provide them with components and subassemblies that make up about 70 percent of their total manufacturing costs. Many subcontractors do exceedingly well, but their employees are often among the first to feel economic downturns. Moreover, successful principal-subcontractor relationships center on large measures of trust (Smitka, 1991). It is difficult at this point to imagine Japanese companies entering easily into such relationships with non-Japanese suppliers. Japanese organizations appear to offer two classes of citizenship, one for Japanese and one for foreigners; and it has been argued that the auto firms make this distinction with respect to their offshore suppliers (Womack et al., 1990). In any case, the extent to which the Japanese auto firms' global strategies shape their Asian regional strategies should be borne in mind as we turn to a more detailed consideration of their intersection with Malaysian policies.

# Malaysian Policies and Japanese Strategies in the Transformation of Malaysia's Motor Vehicle Industry

*Formation and early development of PROTON.* Having opted to promote auto manufacture, Mahathir instigated efforts to find a Japanese transnational corporate partner (Doner, 1991: ch. 5; Machado, 1989–1990). HICOM ultimately formed a joint auto venture, *Perusahaan Otomobil Nasional* (PROTON), with Mitsubishi Motor Corporation (MMC) and Mitsubishi Corporation (MC). The establishment and development of PROTON has involved ongoing bargaining between the Malaysian and Japanese partners. At the outset there appeared to be substantial convergence between MMC/MC's corporate interests and Mahathir's definition of Malaysian interests. The terms of the final joint venture agreement favored the Japanese side, but Malaysia got more or less what it initially wanted. PROTON was set up as a HICOM subsidiary under the Companies Act. HICOM required foreign partners to take minority shares in its projects on the assumption that this would commit them to their success. MMC/MC put up 30 percent and HICOM 70 percent of the M$150 million equity in this M$490 million project. MMC was to design and build a plant with an annual capacity of 80,000 (expandable to 120,000) units to manufacture Malaysia's national car, the Saga, a slightly modified Mitsubishi Lancer. The Saga was initially to be built exclusively for the local market. The PROTON plant was to do body stamping, assembly, painting and trim, and final assembly of the car. Bodies were to be added to imported, locally assembled CKD kits. MMC reluctantly agreed under heavy pressure to use in the Saga most locally produced parts used in other makes under the existing local content program. Local production of bodies assured that the Saga would have higher local content than other cars, but they required imported steel, which was to come primarily through MC from Japan. Managerial, technical, clerical, and production jobs would be created, primarily for Malays, and many PROTON managers and workers would be trained by Japanese counterparts in Malaysia or by MMC in Japan.

Production and marketing of the Saga were to be carried out by separate companies, but—in an arrangement unusual in both the Japanese and Malaysian auto industry—they were not under common control. HICOM entered a partnership with a private firm, UMW Holdings, in the Saga marketing company, *Edaran Otomobil Nasional* (EON). HICOM had only a minority share, whereas UMW had effective control of EON. The head of UMW was a successful Chinese entrepreneur who was on the boards of HICOM and some other state-controlled concerns and was considered to be very close to Mahathir. He had acquired the Toyota franchise in 1982 with the intention of taking the dominant place in the local auto market, and PROTON was a major blow to these plans. Some auto industry insiders believe that Mahathir permitted him to take the lead in EON partly to remedy the damage done to his interests. Others believe that Mahathir, and possibly MMC/MC as well, recognizing the lack of marketing experience among PROTON's management, simply wanted to bring in an experienced party to assure the effective sale of the Saga. MMC/MC was not keen on the structure of this arrangement, but accepted it as a local matter. In any case, it was to become the source of a costly schism in the car project.

MMC/MC derived much leverage in negotiating the PROTON agreement from their control of capital and technology. Bennett and Sharpe (1985: 88) argue that these resources are particularly potent for transnationals when Third World states lack alternative sources for them and when they assign particularly high priority to the sectors in which they are to be deployed. Such was clearly the case in Malaysia. Finance and construction arrangements were particularly advantageous to the Japanese partners. As all of the M$340 million in finance for this highly leveraged venture came from associates of the Mitsubishi group, MMC/MC enjoyed greater influence in the project than their minority equity position would suggest. This influence was acquired at very low risk, for all loans were guaranteed by the Malaysian Treasury, as required by the Japanese lenders. The Japanese partners were in charge of contracting for the turn-key plant construction project. The majority of contract payments went to Japanese firms, particularly MMC and MC, who were key suppliers of equipment and machinery. Their equity share in PROTON was equal to about 13 percent of the M$354 million turn-key project. It is likely that their profits were about the same as their equity shares, meaning that the Malaysian side, in effect, paid most of the costs of the project. MMC and MC could also look forward to continuing profits as suppliers of CKD kits and steel for car bodies, even if not as minority shareholders in PROTON.

Bennett and Sharpe (1985: 88–89) argue that Third World states' bargaining power grows with the importance of an investment to potential transnational partners and the extent of competition the latter face in trying to become participants. Malaysia did not enjoy such a position in negotiating the auto agreement. MMC was the only Japanese auto firm willing to meet Malaysia's desire to develop a manufacturing facility. Even then, divisions emerged between a hesitant production side and a more interested commercial side of Mitsubishi concerning the advisability of the project. Hence, there was no competitive selection process. HICOM negotiated the final agreement with MMC after the latter's selection was, in effect, certain. The weakness of HICOM's position was reflected most notably in provisions on key issues such as local content, pricing, and technology, which were all left very vague in accordance with Japanese preferences. The question of export was left as a subject for possible future discussion. The details of such matters have from the outset been the subject of continuous differences between HICOM and

MMC and have had to be negotiated on a case-by-case basis—a circumstance that is seen as disadvantageous by the Malaysian side.

Doner (1991: 109–110) stresses that Third World state bargaining leverage with transnational firms is increased by private sector–state cooperation in areas subject to negotiation. He attributes the weak contract terms received by PROTON primarily to Mahathir's autonomous action in pushing for a quick and secret agreement with MMC/MC. Doner recognizes that given the fierce opposition the project would have encountered from existing auto interests, the prime minister's approach was probably necessary to getting it under way at all. Doner (1991: 110) also believes that had HICOM negotiators tapped expertise in the mainly Chinese private motor vehicle sector and in the Malaysian Industrial Development Authority (MIDA), seen by some as too close to the latter, it would have "strengthen[ed] Malaysia's hand . . . with Mitsubishi." Bowie (1991: 134–135) makes the same argument. The case for the value of "growth coalitions" to national development is generally well taken. The kind of cooperation-derived expertise cited by Doner and Bowie can, however, only enhance a solidly based bargaining position, but it cannot significantly improve a fundamentally weak one. Malaysia could have made little really effective use of greater expertise in this bargaining situation. A somewhat hesitant MMC, controlling the capital and technology needed for the project and bargaining without competitors, was most unlikely to have made a deal any more advantageous to Malaysia than it ultimately did.

Most of the leverage Malaysia did have with Mitsubishi was expended to secure MMC's participation in the PROTON project. Malaysia's leverage derived primarily from the government's power to set terms and conditions of participation in the national economy in ways both more and less advantageous to Japanese firms. The Economist Intelligence Unit (1985: 24) reported that in promoting heavy industrialization, Malaysia was seeking to "obtain technological benefits . . . in return for . . . favorable consideration of Japanese interests in [its] trade and investment policies and . . . the award of contracts . . . (especially for construction . . . ) [and] to use its enormous natural resources to bargain for industrial assets." Mitsubishi Bank, Chemical, Electric, and Gas all operate in Malaysia. Mitsubishi Corporation also has a variety of interests there, including minority participation with PETRONAS (the national oil company) in the Malaysia Liquified Natural Gas project in Sarawak. Mitsubishi officials must certainly have understood the potential long-term group benefits of participating in a project so important to Mahathir, and the Malaysian side may have capitalized on this. According to one Japanese industry analyst highly knowledgeable about Mitsubishi affairs, terms being negotiated in the gas project were linked by Malaysia to MMC participation in PROTON, and from the group's point of view the profits from the gas project would cover its exposure in the car project. How bluntly such leverage may have been used is known to only a few. In any event, it appears that Mitsubishi Corporation's multiple interests in the country, contrary to expectation, may have enhanced rather than weakened Malaysia's leverage in this case.

The government's capacity to grant protection was of particular importance to MMC. To secure MMC participation and, it was presumed, the financial viability of the auto project, a 40 percent import duty was imposed on CKD kits, and PROTON was granted exemption from that duty as well as from the excise tax imposed on other assemblers. Thus, MMC was assured instant domination of the Malaysian passenger car market at the expense of its Japanese competitors. A Mitsubishi manager said that the company entered the venture expecting to take between 55 and 60 percent of the market. With this assurance, MMC could see Malaysian goals meshing with its larger regional and international strategies. The company had a relatively weak place in the Japanese and Malaysian markets in the early 1980s, and it was seeking to develop external markets as part of its strategy for gaining on the firms ahead of it at home and abroad. At that time, the ASEAN countries comprised Japan's largest Third World market and Malaysia was its largest ASEAN passenger car market (Economist Intelligence Unit, 1985: 13–14). In the longer run, MMC aimed to promote regionally based production of an auto for export to Western markets, and it was determined that Malaysian body parts might eventually be used in this scheme.

The formation of PROTON was only the first step in a process of ongoing bargaining between the Malaysian and Japanese sides. Bennett and Sharpe (1985: 92) point out that "because there are usually several ways of carrying out a decision, and because actors who lose out at the decision-making stage cannot be counted upon to desist from trying to alter or undermine the outcome, bargaining and the exercise of power continue through the implementation of policy." This is all the more true if, as in this case, conditions prevailing at the time of agreement change rapidly and substantially. Just as PROTON became operational in 1985, it was hit with multiple problems. Deepening recession resulted in a sharp decline in the demand for Malaysia's traditional exports. This event was soon translated into rapidly shrinking domestic demand for motor vehicles. With rapid yen appreciation, PROTON's all-yen debt soon doubled in Malaysian dollars. The cost of servicing it mounted accordingly, and it became a severe burden on the company. A multi-million-dollar difference (in M$) quickly developed between a losing PROTON and what proved to be a very profitable EON over what had been agreed concerning the transfer price of the Saga. As the companies were not under common control, this conflict proved quite intractable. By 1988, PROTON's accumulated losses were close to M$150 million (HICOM, 1983–1988). As PROTON foundered financially, it pushed for reduced interest on its debt, accelerated localization, export of the Saga to third countries, and other measures to improve its earnings. MMC cooperated with some initiatives but resisted others. In the context of negotiations over these matters, MMC placed its own people in top management positions in PROTON and pressed for its regional complementation scheme. UMW's majority shares in EON were transferred to the Ministry of Finance, Inc. (25 percent) and to a joint venture between MMC/MC and a *Bumiputera* company (15 percent each), thus giving Mitsubishi a voice in marketing operations and improving the coordination of PROTON and EON policies.

Table 9.2    Rationalization of the Malaysian Passenger Car Industry

|  | 1975 | 1980 | 1981 | 1982 | 1983 | 1984 | 1985 | 1986 | 1987 | 1988 | 1989 |
|---|---|---|---|---|---|---|---|---|---|---|---|
| Total passenger car production | 38.6 | 80.4 | 87.8 | 85.3 | 100.2 | 96.4 | 69.8 | 41.9 | 33.5 | 61.3 | 93.8 |
| PROTON Saga as percentage of total production | — | — | — | — | — | — | 12.3 | 59.5 | 71.6 | 72.9 | 70.1 |
| Total number of makes [a] | 19 | 15 | 15 | 16 | 13 | 13 | 12 | 12 | 10 | 11 | 11 |
| Top three makes as percentage of total production | 44.2 | 67.2 | 61.2 | 63.1 | 63.5 | 64.6 | 64.9 | 81.8 | 87.0 | 87.9 | 86.2 |

*Note:* a. With production of a least 100 passenger car units

*Sources:* Ariff (1982: 127); HICOM (1983–1989); and Malaysian Motor Vehicle Assemblers Association (1980–1989).

The recession finally abated for Malaysia in 1988. Demand for automobiles has increased steadily since that time, and Saga production has gone up correspondingly. With demand up and a more favorable pricing arrangement with EON, PROTON registered profits of M$32 million in fiscal year 1988/89 and M$159 million in 1989/90 (*Business Times*, 1990a). By late 1990, demand was such that PROTON was gearing up to expand plant production capacity. It appeared that PROTON would eventually attain a measure of economic viability as long as it continued to enjoy special protection and as long as the Malaysian economy continued to generate demand for what would, with that protection, remain a very expensive Saga. For example, in mid-1990 the cost of a new Saga ranged from M$26,000 to M$30,600 (*Business Times*, 1990b), whereas GNP per capita was less than M$5,500 (Ministry of Finance, 1990: 17).

Some of the other main objectives of the auto project were also being met. As Table 9.2 shows, a large measure of rationalization has taken place in the auto industry. The Saga by itself now accounts for 70 percent of all production, while the top three makes compose 86 percent. The number of parts makers has also increased, largely on the basis of supply to PROTON. The Saga is being exported with modest success to several markets and to the United Kingdom. Between 12,000 and 13,000 were exported in both 1989 and 1990. Most go to the United Kingdom, where the General System of Preferences (GSP) limit is 14,000 units a year before imposition of duty, a ceiling that easily could be reached. In any case, these advances are being accompanied by increasing rather than declining dependence. Malaysia has, at least temporarily, lost national management of PROTON to MMC, and its motor vehicle industry as a whole seems on its way to be being incorporated into Japanese-organized and Japanese-controlled regional production schemes. This process is in an early stage, it moves in fits and starts, and its outcome is still uncertain, but the die appears to have been cast.

*MMC takes management of PROTON.* By mid-1988, both the Mahathir administration and the MMC had become quite concerned about PROTON's problems. Malaysia's finance minister attributed these to management inadequacies and, given the state of the economy, made what seemed to be exaggerated and unusually harsh public criticisms of the project's managers. He told the press that "the recession is only part of the problem," and that if management cannot show results, "they should do what people in Japan do—commit *harikiri* [sic]" (*New Straits Times*, 1988). By this time, most of the original Japanese counterpart managers had returned to Japan, and PROTON was largely in the hands of Malay managers. MMC began pushing for management changes. The prime minister ordered the formation of a task force comprised of HICOM, PROTON, and MMC/MC to look into the company's affairs. This task force was primarily an MMC undertaking, however, and MMC assumption of the company's management was clearly to be the end result of its work. HICOM and PROTON managers were opposed to this but were unsuccessful in their effort to fend it off. The Malaysian managing director was relieved of his responsibilities and was replaced by a former MMC managing director in August 1988. Two additional MMC managers were made heads of the newly formed business and corporate planning divisions. This change was engineered in a face-saving way for the company but not for its top management. It was described as a Malaysian initiative. It was emphasized that the MMC managers were responsible to PROTON's board, not to MMC, and that this arrangement was to be for only two years while a "turn around" exercise was to be carried out. In light of the nationalistic thrust of Mahathir's heavy industrialization drive and its important part in the effort to promote the development of Malay entrepreneurs, the irony of this episode was lost on few politically attentive Malaysians.

The primary reason for the change was said by both sides simply to be to streamline PROTON's management and to bring it to profitability, but this was not a complete explanation. With local market contraction, PROTON began to push hard to export the Saga. MMC reluctantly went along with exports only to small markets (e.g., Jamaica, Bangladesh, and Sri Lanka) and was most displeased when Mahathir took independent initiatives to begin exports to the United Kingdom and the United States. With steep yen appreciation, PROTON also began to press for acceleration of localization and a search for suppliers outside of Japan. Locally produced parts had always been more expensive than Japanese ones because they were produced in such small numbers, but this situation changed rapidly as the value of the yen went up. With the rising costs of Japanese-made auto parts in world markets, MMC also became increasingly interested in promoting a complementation scheme in which there would be a measure of "agreed specialization" among regional states in making parts and subassemblies. These components would then be traded among MMC regional operations for use in vehicle assembly. The aim of producing components in one country for regional use was to take advantage of economies of scale. The MMC apparently found PROTON's management too keen on exporting the Saga and on hastening localization and not keen enough on regional complementation. Therefore, it wanted to be in charge while the details of all three were being worked out. According to one Japanese auto industry analyst, MMC officials had concluded that their company's degree of control over PROTON was not commensurate with what was going to be its increasing involvement in the project.

In pushing for the PROTON management change, MMC's leverage was increased because its cooperation was essential to improving PROTON's economic performance. MMC controlled the loan renegotiation process, the price of the CKD kit, the technology needed to make changes required if the Saga was to be exportable to markets with standards higher than Malaysia's, and the pace of localization. How bluntly MMC used this leverage is uncertain. PROTON efforts on the foregoing fronts were not progressing well. Mutual recognition of the strength of MMC's position could not have but helped to shape the outcome of discussions between the two sides. The intractability of the PROTON-EON conflict also strengthened MMC's hand, as it could be cited as evidence of a serious management problem. Malaysian acquiescence to the management change also appears to have stemmed partly from the belief that this conflict could be better resolved with persons not directly party to the dispute being in charge. In any case, soon after the change, the pricing dispute between PROTON and EON was settled. Impasses on other matters at issue were also soon broken. HICOM was able to renegotiate lower interest rates on part of PROTON's loans. A long-standing PROTON request for a small discount on the CKD kit was granted. An engine assembly line, long under negotiation, was started at the PROTON plant. This step would help boost the local content of the Saga over the 60 percent necessary to permit it to enter the United Kingdom under the GSP (for GSP purposes, local content includes labor costs). PROTON's new MMC manager stressed that one of his main priorities would be to make the Saga internationally competitive. Such facts are consistent with the observation of one Japanese auto industry insider that by putting a high-level person in the top slot at PROTON, MMC had given the Malaysians a hostage guaranteeing that the auto project would not be allowed to fail.

By early 1990, MMC personnel had assumed the five top positions in PROTON, and neither HICOM officials nor Japanese auto industry experts believed that their terms would, in fact, be limited to the originally specified two years. They were proven correct. In June 1990, MMC announced in Tokyo that Mahathir had asked them to stay on and that they would remain "for the next several years" (*Ward's Automotive International,* 1990: 4). It is now expected that the Japanese managers will remain in place at least until after a model change has been effected. The first model change was originally slated for 1993, but is now projected for 1994 or 1995. The timing and details of the bargaining over the duration of MMC management are known to only a narrow circle of participants. The extent of MMC's involvement in the PROTON project by August 1990 was such that it is hard to imagine it having been willing even to consider withdrawing its managers at that point. PROTON's technological dependence on MMC could have made it very costly for Mahathir to press for the departure of these managers even if he had been so inclined. The early export effort was enjoying modest success, but expanding on that would require MMC's cooperation. Introduction of a left-hand–drive model, for example, would be necessary to increase the potential overseas market for the Saga. A further increase in local content, perhaps to 80 percent, may be necessary to qualify for GSP in the European Community after 1992. These factors gave MMC leverage that would have been very difficult to counter in bargaining over the tenure of MMC management or other policy questions. In any case, the Japanese managers of PROTON were able to make decisions during this critical period on such matters as localization and complementation, which assured that MMC would set the direction and pace of these processes for some time.

***Localization.***      Increased localization of the Malaysian auto industry was a central goal of the national car project. The combination of Malaysian pressure and new departures in Japanese strategies following from yen appreciation have favored this development. Parts makers have grown in both number and strength, largely on the basis of supply to PROTON. At the end of 1988, PROTON was producing 337 parts in-house and procuring 46 parts from about thirty locally based companies. By early 1990, it was producing more than 450 parts in-house and about 370 parts were being supplied by close to seventy locally based vendors. PROTON was assisting an additional thirty vendors to begin production of more than another 100 parts. In mid-1990, local content of the Saga was reckoned to be 65 percent, and it is expected to reach 80 percent by GSP definition in 1994. Mahathir was said to be under pressure in the cabinet and from the parts makers to push MMC as well as HICOM and PROTON to hasten this process. The Toyota and Nissan affiliates have also expanded their capacity for in-house production and worked to develop suppliers. Both have become suppliers to PROTON. They are expected to achieve 60 percent local content within a few years. This is a sharp departure from the pre-1985 situation, but it is also somewhat deceptive. Such figures mask continuing conflicts over the nature and pace of localization. These are rooted in the very fundamental issues of where value is added and of how it is shared that help to determine the livelihoods and well-being of a great many people. Many Japanese worry that a rush of small and medium businesses or the transfer of higher value-added component production overseas will result in a "hollowing" of the nation's industrial structure (i.e., deindustrialization). Firms fear that loss of control over technology will harm their profits. Hence, the Japanese have strong motivations to limit the pace of localization.

Many auto components that count as local content under current regulations in Malaysia rely heavily on imported intermediate goods. This fact shows up clearly in the country's trade statistics. Malaysia enjoyed a modest trade surplus with Japan in the early and mid-1980s, but it became a small deficit in 1988, which was, it should be noted, after the peak of yen appreciation. The deficit increased six times to M$3.8 billion in 1989 and to M$5.6 billion in the first ten months of 1990 (*Far Eastern Economic Review*, 1991b: 53). The major items in the import bill were capital goods, mainly machinery and transport equipment, and a fair portion of these were bound for assembly and finishing plants. Imports have continued to surge in 1991. Foeign trade posted a deficit during the first four months of the year, and capital goods accounted for 67 percent of the import bill during this period (*Asian Wall Street Journal*, 1991). Much of this, of course, translates into exports, although their value is often only slightly in excess of the cost of the imported intermediate goods. The import of capital goods should eventually decrease with deepening industrial development. The basic point is, however, that many foreign participants in the Malaysian economy, including the Japanese parts suppliers that license technology to or are in joint ventures with Malaysian parts makers, have little reason to hasten change in these regards. The hostility of Japanese interests to autonomous Third World industrial progress was made clear in their government's 1989 submission to the Trade Related Investment Measures negotiating group under the General Agreement on Tariffs and Trade (GATT). It proposed worldwide abolition of requirements concerning local content, export percentages, and technology transfer, calling them restrictions on investment that distort trade. Although this frontal assault on localization is likely to fail, Japanese firms are in a good position to set the pace at which it occurs in the Malaysian motor vehicle industry. In negotiations on this issue, they have the upper hand primarily because they control the technology that must be transferred if localization is to take place.

Such localization centers on supply to PROTON, and progress can be sustained only by continuing government pressure on MMC to accelerate local sourcing of parts for the Saga. This is not an easy task. Absent a clear agreement with MMC on the specifics of localization, advances have to be negotiated on a case-by-case basis. PROTON echoes two standard complaints of assemblers of Japanese cars concerning the process of replacing CKD kit parts with local ones. The first is that MMC delays the testing of local parts proposed as replacements in order to slow the localization process. The other is that in itemizing the prices of parts in the CKD kit, MMC underprices the most easily replaced ones and overprices the others in order to keep its profits up when the former are deleted and replaced. To hasten localization, PROTON pressed MMC to begin engine assembly at the Saga plant. The latter argued that this was premature, but reluctantly agreed. By early 1990, all engine requirements were met with local assembly. Local content of engines was initially only 2–3 percent, but it was expected to rise with the opening of a HICOM Engineering Complex for casting and machining in 1991. Replacements for engine CKD kit parts will have to be negotiated on a part-by-part basis. There is little reason to suppose that this will be any easier than has been the deletion and replacement of auto CKD kit parts.

As MMC has come under added pressure on local content, it has taken new tacks to retain its control over the development of the Saga. With MMC managers at PROTON's helm, this has been comparatively easy. MMC has attempted to fragment control over technology. PROTON, for example, wanted to make the whole Saga brake assembly in-house, with the HICOM Engineering Complex taking the lead. PROTON's MMC managers opted instead to go to two outside companies to supply parts of the assembly. This decision was difficult to criticize because it advanced *Bumiputera* companies and because it represented localization. At the same time, it kept PROTON from controlling the technology for the whole assembly. This situation means that PROTON remains in the stage of making things up from subassemblies, and this is contrary to its larger goals. HICOM wanted to establish a joint venture with a local firm that had been supplying PROTON with some plastic parts, but a Japanese plastic company that is an MMC supplier in Japan made a better offer to the latter than HICOM could. This event was not purely an economic matter in HICOM's view, as it assured MMC continuing control over product technology.

As MMC's vendors in Japan have expanded operations in Malaysia to supply PROTON, concern is increasing that this is being done at the expense of established parts makers or national goals. A recent change in the sourcing of safety glass for the Saga provides a good example of the lengths to which Japanese firms may go to favor their own suppliers. A well-established and very successful company, itself in partnership with a Japanese firm, had been supplying PROTON with safety glass. MMC management apparently wished to shift some of this business to another company with ties to a Japanese glass company that is part of the Mitsubishi Group. MMC set a new standard for safety glass, which was that completed windows could have no handling equipment marks on the edges. The original supplier spent M$7 million for new equipment to meet this standard, but the other company did not match this investment and did not reach the standard. The standard was then relaxed, and the other company got 40 percent of the business anyway. It appears to private sector parts makers that PROTON's MMC managers give preference to Japanese companies even when MMC affiliates are not available as suppliers. One firm with very small Japanese participation claimed that it received a letter of acceptance to supply a specific part for the Saga and that it was then told that this was a mistake. The part was procured instead from a 90 percent Toyota-affiliated firm, which had not even made a bid to supply it. Such practices are bound to be more common if MMC succeeds in organizing and controlling a comprehensive regional auto production scheme.

## *Japanese Strategies, Malaysian and ASEAN Policies, and Regional Complementation in the Motor Vehicle Industry*

National governments and private businesses as well as transnational corporations (TNCs) operating in ASEAN states have long asserted interest in promoting regional economic cooperation. Governments and local businesses have, however, feared TNC domination of arrangements created to facilitate regional industrial cooperation. In 1971, ASEAN foreign ministers agreed to adopt an industrial complementation plan patterned on that of the Latin American Free Trade Area as recommended by a UN team. Among the first proposals considered was one by Ford for a motor vehicle "complementation, in which parts from participating . . . countries would be assembled into an 'Asian car'—a Ford." However, it was shelved by the ASEAN industry ministers who reviewed it (Young, 1986: 691). Several programs for regional industrial cooperation have subsequently been established. These include a 1981 ASEAN Industrial Complementation (AIC) scheme (ASEAN-CCI, 1987; Lim and Suh, 1988). AIC projects normally require the participation of industries in at least four member countries. To gain the benefits of producing in larger volume, industries in participating countries specialize in making selected components for the same end product and then trade these among themselves. The countries agree to tariff reductions on traded components and temporary exclusive production rights for the country making each of them. AIC proposals originate with national and regional industries but are advanced by the ASEAN Chambers of Commerce and Industry (CCI). Proposals are then evaluated and recommendations are made by the ASEAN Committee on Industry, Minerals, and Energy (COIME); and final decisions on them are made by the ASEAN economic ministers. The CCIs of some countries, Malaysia for one, include transnational firms, whereas others do not. The role of firms with foreign participation in these schemes has consistently been a source of conflict among various interests in the member states and among the states themselves. The only AIC proposal approved through 1987 was made by the ASEAN Automotive Federation, and five of the six items it included were produced by foreign-controlled or foreign-dominated firms (Young, 1986: 695). This effort ultimately foundered as a result of competing national concerns.

Japanese motor vehicle companies tended generally to be unenthusiastic about complementation schemes initiated by ASEAN. As complementation promised to make local production of auto parts economically viable by expanding the size of the market and thus production volumes, it could clearly cut into the profits the Japanese firms derived from the export of CKD kits. However, several factors combined to increase the interest of Japanese firms in this idea in the second half of the 1980s. Rapid yen appreciation upped the costs of Japanese-made auto parts and components in world markets. Parts could now for the first time be made more cheaply in ASEAN countries if they could be produced in sufficient volumes. They could then be used in vehicles assembled not only in ASEAN countries but also in Japanese firms' worldwide operations, and this step would help to keep increasing prices in Japan from hurting sales. ASEAN states were at the same time becoming increasingly assertive in demanding accelerated localization. Complementation offered Japanese firms the prospect of complying in a way that left much of the process under their control. Japanese firms might now also export ASEAN-made vehicles to North

America and the EC under GSP quotas for Third World–made vehicles with sufficient local content. With heightened interest in complementation, Japanese firms would attempt to organize and control it themselves.

MMC was the first to act. It had long been more receptive to the idea of complementation than any of its Japanese competitors, and it had already gone further than any of them in integrating regional production. It had operations in Indonesia, Thailand, and the Philippines—in addition to its PROTON involvement in Malaysia—and plants in the latter three countries were already exchanging parts among themselves on a limited basis without AIC benefits. In early 1987, MMC proposed a Brand-to-Brand Complementation (BBC) scheme to COIME under provisions of the basic agreement on AIC. This was simply to provide a general framework for specific agreements that would have to be worked out between interested companies. Complementation was to be on a brand-to-brand basis, meaning that parts for only one make of vehicle could be exchanged under any specific agreement. Diverging from the AIC formula, BBC agreements could be concluded between firms in as few as two countries. BBC's key features were to be a margin of tariff preference for ASEAN-produced auto parts traded among participating companies and, much more importantly for export potential, local content accreditation by each participating country for each traded part. MMC's immediate aims in taking the lead on BBC included boosting slumping sales in ASEAN markets. It hoped to secure an edge in price competition by eliminating duplication of investments in making the same parts at each ASEAN facility and gaining the cost advantages of higher volume production. More basically, however, according to the general manager of the Kuala Lumpur MMC office, BBC was meant to advance the firm's plan to use ASEAN as a production and export base (*Investors Digest,* 1988: 7). This was, however, to be developed within a much more extensive regional and international MMC network.[1] In any case, an idea that had, despite several efforts, not been implemented for nearly twenty years was again revived.

The ASEAN states and MMC carried on negotiations on the BBC proposal during 1987. Changed circumstances gave MMC some notable sources of leverage in this process. By 1987, new economic realities had made some in ASEAN more receptive to regional complementation under Japanese auspices than they would have been earlier. Yen appreciation had substantially increased the costs of imported CKD kits and thus changed the economics of motor vehicle assembly in the ASEAN states. In Malaysia, for example, 1.3 liter CKD kits that cost 550,000–600,000 yen in early 1985 had by 1988 dropped to 350,000–450,000 yen, due to deletion of parts due then being produced locally as well as discounting by the manufacturers. Nonetheless, with yen appreciation, this translated into an increase in the import price from M$5500–6000 to M$7000–8000 over the same period, and the parts deleted from the CKD kit during these years had to be purchased elsewhere at additional cost. The ASEAN states and motor vehicle assemblers were being pinched by this situation, and BBC appeared to offer some possibility of relief. Moreover, as the high yen and domestic economic considerations made Japanese auto firms more interested in production of parts and components in ASEAN countries for use in local assembly as well as in Japan and other countries, some in ASEAN began to see this development as containing promise for increased localization of the auto industry and increased exports. These facts clearly enhanced MMC's position as it pushed for BBC, and it was additionally in a position to offer inducements that were or at least appeared to be supportive of ASEAN states' interests in these regards to gain their assent to BBC.

The ASEAN states also had some leverage in these negotiations. This was based, first, on the fact that such ASEAN undertakings require full agreement. Hence, any one of the ASEAN governments could have killed BBC simply by refusing its assent. Furthermore, as already noted, each state has the power to set the terms and conditions under which foreign firms operate within its borders. How directly, if at all, the ASEAN states asserted such leverage to secure inducements is unknown, but their capacity to withhold assent was obvious to all participants in the negotiations. The ASEAN states had never been shy in making their interest in increased localization and exports known to the Japanese auto firms, and it seems only reasonable to assume that these interests were reaffirmed to MMC in connection with deliberations on its BBC plan. According to one report, the MMC agreement to produce gasoline engines in Thailand was in part to gain the Thai government's assent to BBC (*Tokyo Business Today,* 1988: 25). MMC announced several other decisions that appeared to further localization and/or exports around the time that its BBC plan and follow-up proposal for a specific complementation agreement were under consideration or soon after they were approved. It cannot be stated with certainty that any such decisions were explicit trade-offs demanded by the ASEAN states or proffered to them by MMC for signing off on its BBC plan. It can only be noted that MMC could and did offer some things that the ASEAN states wanted and that the latter did agree to BBC.

MMC shepherded a Memorandum of Understanding (MOU) on BBC through COIME and on to approval by ASEAN economic ministers in October 1988 (ASEAN, 1988; *Investors Digest,* 1988: 5–9), but it fell short of what MMC had hoped for. The ASEAN states clearly exerted their leverage in setting some critical features of the MOU. MMC wanted participation of the four ASEAN states where it had assembly operations. To its disappointment, Indonesia, the country with the largest potential market in the region, was unwilling to participate. The Indonesian government was concerned that it would have to buy far more from its much smaller neighbors than it could sell to them, and it believed that the scheme would limit its latitude in developing its own parts industry. It ultimately signed the MOU, which required agreement of all ASEAN governments, making it possible for other members to participate. MMC wanted a 90 percent margin of tariff preference on traded parts but had to settle for 50 percent. According to participants in the COIME deliberations, MMC's initial proposal gave the lead firm a very large measure of control over participating companies. It could specify which parts and components each participating company should produce and which it should buy. MMC clearly envisioned a single source per included component. This was unacceptable to ASEAN representatives, and they made it clear that they would not agree to it. They were concerned about the costs of supplier monopolies and about the prospect of Japanese auto firms giving such monopolies to Malaysian subsidiaries of their Japanese suppliers or local ventures tied to them. Hence, the final MOU leaves companies in a complementation agreement free to purchase included parts from any maker in a participating country, and it states emphatically that there will be "no mandatory single-sourcing of parts/components" (ASEAN, 1988: sec. 11). A firm proposing a complementation agreement is required to list the parts to be traded for specified vehicle models as well as the source and purchasing countries for each part. This proposal must be approved and formally certified by COIME and the ASEAN economic ministers. In subsequent deliberations on MMC's specific BBC proposal, it was further agreed informally that as a rule there should be no exchange of parts already being produced in an importing country.

Malaysian support for BBC came primarily from the Mahathir administration and local parts makers. HICOM and PROTON managers objected to MMC-led complementation because they believed it incompatible with the national car concept and feared that it would impede effective localization. Hence they played virtually no role in the COIME deliberations. Their lack of support for BBC was no doubt one reason that MMC wanted management control over PROTON. In any case, Malaysia's initial positions were formulated by concerned officials, primarily in the Trade and Industry Ministry and MIDA. As negotiations progressed, however, they received important input from the Malaysian Automotive Components and Parts Manufacturers' Association (MACPMA), the body representing private sector parts makers. Both government and many local makers shared the general ASEAN concern about the prospects of supplier monopolies and favored free choice in sourcing. The Malaysian parts makers' views on this and other matters were important in shaping the version of the MOU that was finally approved. The importance of this input supports Doner's (1991) point about the added negotiating leverage Third World interests may gain through private sector–government cooperation.

In negotiating the MOU on complementation, MMC advanced the

interests of Japanese and some European motor vehicle manufacturers as well as its own. This was not its objective, however, and it was clearly not consulting with its competitors. Its intention was simply to gain an edge on them. MMC had a specific BBC plan ready for submission as soon as the MOU was signed, and it was quickly approved in March 1989. Other Japanese automakers were anticipating approval of the BBC agreement, and as soon as it was announced, they turned to a MITI-sponsored research institute in Tokyo that, among other things, carefully tracks ASEAN economic developments to find out exactly what its terms were. Although not initially as keen on complementation as MMC, both Toyota and Nissan had become increasingly interested in the idea; they did not submit their plans for consideration until mid-1989, but these were approved in November 1989 and May 1990, respectively. Volvo and Mercedes Benz, both of which have assembly operations in several ASEAN states, also quickly launched BBC plans that include Malaysian affiliates.

Toyota and Nissan were, like MMC, very eager to incorporate Indonesia in their schemes, and when their plans were initially announced Indonesia was included. Their affiliates and the parts they would produce for exchange were named. It was then later announced that Indonesia had dropped out of both plans. According to one Toyota insider, the company did not, in fact, expect Indonesia to participate, given its government's well-known opposition to BBC. Its affiliate in Indonesia was quite willing to participate, however, so when Toyota announced its plan, Indonesia was named simply to make it clear that the company desired to include it and to give the Indonesian government something to ponder. It seems likely that Nissan's thinking was similar and that both were simply chipping away at Indonesia's resolve to go it alone.

Both Toyota and Nissan consulted with their regional affiliates on their BBC plans, but like MMC's scheme, their plans are widely perceived in Malaysian industry circles to have been wholly designed in Japan. Toyota has a significant stake and thus a management say in its local affiliate, UMW Toyota, whereas Nissan is far less involved in the affairs of its affiliate, Tan Chong Motors. In any case, both UMW Toyota and Tan Chong Motors were more favorably disposed to BBC than PROTON. First, as private firms, their chief purpose is profitmaking and not advancing national development. Unlike PROTON, they are not concerned with having an autonomous identity, and they are not defined as the vanguard of the national heavy industrialization drive. At the same time, they find BBC advantageous as they are obliged to adapt to the new national policy regime. Following the Industrial Master Plan–mandated push for rationalization of the motor vehicle industry, UMW and particularly Tan Chong expanded investment in parts making both in-house and in joint ventures. This was to insure their economic survival, and it meshes very well with the thrust of BBC. They must also comply with increasing local content requirements. Both also expect parts production to help keep their cars more affordable and, thus, to reduce the adverse impact on their sales of government protection for PROTON and yen appreciation.

MMC's regional complementation plan centers on Thailand (*Tokyo Business Today*, 1988: 24–25). In its initial stage, it has primarily involved incorporation of transmissions made by its Philippine affiliate and doors produced by PROTON into a Mitsubishi Lancer assembled in Thailand by MMC Sittipol (48 percent Mitsubishi owned) along with exchange of a few smaller parts. The immediate trade consequences of the plan for Malaysia have so far been limited. Malaysian industry insiders believe that MMC is not so keen on the plan that was finally approved and that the changes forced in the MOU slowed it down. Although that is no doubt true, MMC appears to hope for expansion of trade in parts both within ASEAN and beyond. Its initial proposal to COIME for the BBC plan for the Lancer listed more parts for exchange than were initially traded. For example, Malaysian companies were certified to sell twenty items to MMC Sittipol, and Thai companies to sell forty to PROTON. MMC also requested COIME certification for additional parts in May 1990. In any case, the general manager of MMC in Kuala Lumpur indicated that the company does not "expect [BBC] to be realized quickly" (*Investors Digest*, 1988: 7). Whatever the eventual extent of parts trade, by producing in these three countries, MMC is assured protection in all of them. At the same time, in conformity with its global strategy, the Thai-assembled Lancer acquires enough local content to qualify for export to North America and the EC under GSP provisions. In 1988, MMC Sittipol began fulfilling a six-year contract to sell 100,000 Lancers to Chrysler Canada, which markets them as Plymouth and Dodge Colts. Canada was intended primarily to be a way-station en route to the U.S. market following ratification of the U.S.-Canada Free Trade Agreement. It was no doubt with this possibility in mind that MMC Sittipol undertook to double its production capacity and began engine assembly during the following two years.

Neither Toyota's nor Nissan's schemes have progressed as far as MMC's. Toyota's, the more ambitious of the two, is initially to center on exchange of engines produced in Thailand, steering systems from Malaysia, and transmissions built in the Philippines for a range of Toyota four-wheel vehicles. In 1990, a 100 percent Toyota-owned management services company was established in Singapore to coordinate ASEAN operations and the BBC plan. Nissan's scheme involves exchange of engines and stamping dies made in Thailand, clutch and electrical components from Malaysia, and wiring harnesses from the Philippines for its small cars and light trucks. It also includes various subcomponents from Taiwan, which will not receive AIC benefits. Governments and local affiliates pressed successfully to make COIME approval of the Toyota plan conditional on Toyota investment in completely new plants for making the named components in Malaysia and the Philippines. These investments were consistent with Toyota's aims, so the leverage gained by imposing these conditions appears primarily to have been used to influence their details. In any case, combined with its establishment of a new engine assembly plant in Thailand and establishment of a new car assembly operation in the Philippines after a five-year absence, Toyota planned a total investment of US$215 million over three years beginning in 1989 to advance its BBC scheme. Although Nissan's plan places greater reliance on existing firms, Nissan has also invested in increasing the capacity of its regional affiliates and promoted a number of joint ventures between its parts suppliers and local companies.

Components produced by plants participating in both schemes are expected to be exported to Japan and to worldwide production sites. Nissan plans to do about 5 percent of its Japanese sourcing from ASEAN by 1992 and eventually to increase this to 10 percent. In 1989, Toyota Motor Thailand, the leading assembler in that country, was designated one of Toyota's few "global vehicle suppliers" and is projected to be an exporter of complete vehicles. Its 1989 output of 50,000 units is expected to triple to 150,000 by 1993. Toyota expects its plan to be well under way by 1992 or 1993, whereas Nissan's plan is developing more slowly. Nissan has not designated a lead exporting country as its two competitors have (i.e., Thailand), but its Malaysian affiliate has since 1989 exported vehicles to Singapore and Brunei with Nissan's approval. It is planned that BBC exchanges will boost the local content of both makers' ASEAN-produced vehicles from around 30 to 40 percent to the magic GSP number of 60 percent within a few years.

## Conclusion: Global and Domestic Factors in the Development of Malaysia's Motor Vehicle Industry

Both global and domestic factors have clearly shaped the recent development of the Malaysian motor vehicle industry. What remains is more systematically to analyze the mix of such factors in this case. It should first be stressed that although Mahathir's economic policies stemmed partly from Malaysia's long-standing problems in the world economy, these problems did not determine the specific strategy that he selected from among a variety of possibilities. Mahathir's emphasis on heavy industry was based largely on his reading of domestic political economic imperatives, particularly his understanding of the requirements for *Bumiputera* advancement and his desire to further specific NEP goals. It was also partly for such domestic reasons that Mahathir opted to rely primarily on Japan in pursuing his industrial strategy. In doing so, he tied Malaysia to the country whose government and transnational firms have the most elaborate and integrative global and regional strategies among the advanced capitalist states. In promoting the auto project, it was Mahathir, not MMC, that took the initiative. He was, however, able to secure MMC's participation in PROTON only because it served MMC's larger strategic purposes and because Malaysia was willing to underwrite most of the costs. This situation was still not without opportunities, but they existed within very circumscribed limits, and Malaysia had to push very hard and with great persistence to gain any advantages. This was particularly so both because PROTON's localization and export goals made it a potential challenge to industrial interests in Japan and because it was so heavily dependent on Japanese capital and technology. In any case, Mahathir had the will and the power to engage in some necessary pushing.

In the mid-1980s, trends in the world economy imposed severe constraints that heavily affected the auto project's outcomes. Indeed, one of the most apparent facts about Malaysia shown here is its continuing and extreme vulnerability to forces in the world economy over which it has no control. The vagaries of the business cycle in the advanced capitalist states, world commodity prices, and international currency fluctuations form a shifting matrix in which the country's industrial policy is pursued—sometimes for better, often for worse. The auto project was partly an effort to overcome the vulnerability inherent in its overdependence on world commodity markets, but this long-standing problem, along with new ones occasioned by yen appreciation, set this effort back and put it on a somewhat different track. The auto project's problems in the mid-1980s went beyond shrinking domestic markets and rapidly escalating debts. PROTON's economic troubles contributed greatly to the situation in which MMC was able to press the advantage it had thereby gained to assume management control and, thus, a larger role in setting the auto project's future direction. Economic troubles for all ASEAN states squeezed by yen appreciation, including Malaysia, created the context in which these states accepted a complementation scheme of which most had long been suspicious. Now, however, it will be organized and controlled by Japanese auto firms. Some of MMC's primary motivations for taking management control of PROTON and promoting BBC were its own problems with the rising yen and North American and EC market restrictions along with pressure for localization and exports from its regional affiliates, including PROTON.

External constraints weigh most heavily in the explanation of the outcomes to date of Malaysia's motor vehicle policies, but it is far from complete without reference to constraints of internal origin and to domestic capacity to make the most of some opportunities found in partnerships with Japanese transnationals. PROTON's ill-conceived arrangement with EON was based entirely on domestic considerations, and this greatly aggravated its economic problems. The intractability of the resulting domestic conflict also helped to justify, but did not determine, the decision for MMC's assumption of PROTON's top management. The PROTON-EON conflict affected the course of the auto project, but the effects were more of timing and detail than ultimate outcome. More positively, Malaysia undertook active efforts to shape the adjustments of the auto project to adverse trends in the world economy and to its own internal problems. It was very assertive in trying to extract concessions from MMC in order to gain more advantages for PROTON. The overriding fact is that MMC increased its influence over the direction of PROTON during the period of adjustment, but it also was obliged to accommodate certain Malaysian demands. Had the Malaysian side been less assertive in pursuing its interests, it is unlikely that the Saga would have reached the 60 percent local content required to enter Western markets under GSP provisions or that exports, particularly to the United Kingdom, would have gone ahead. Moreover, the aggressive national auto policy regime, which centers on the car project, is the primary factor driving desired changes in the private sector. It has, for example, pushed Toyota and Nissan assemblers to become substantial parts makers.

Malaysian reliance on Japanese transnational corporations for further development of its motor vehicle industry increased rather than decreased Malaysian dependence, at least for the foreseeable future. This survey of Japanese strategies and practices suggests that Japanese transnationals are unlikely to agree willingly to the changes in economic relationships that would be necessary to elevate Malaysia's place in the international division of labor significantly unless this development occurs within a framework largely of Japanese making. For PROTON, this reality was revealed earlier than it might otherwise have been as a result of the economic crisis, which induced Malaysian efforts to force the issue of Saga exports and accelerated localization. These issues would eventually have been joined, and it is difficult to imagine MMC assenting except on terms that made PROTON more dependent. MMC's promotion of regional auto complementation is exemplary of the larger Japanese regional integration strategy. Conditions were such that neither Malaysia nor other ASEAN states, except Indonesia, were inclined to reject this scheme; but at the same time, MMC could not simply force its terms on them. The ASEAN states were scarcely powerless in this situation, but they are now more tightly woven into an emerging Japan-centered regional production network. From now on they will have to negotiate such issues as localization and exports within this framework. Malaysia could derive significant economic benefits from this arrangement, but these benefits are likely to be concessions granted on MMC terms rather than gains securely anchored in national industrial strength. Malaysia has demonstrated considerable skill in winning such concessions, but whether the cumulative effects of these efforts can in the long term alter the asymmetric structure of its relationships with Japanese auto firms is at best problematic.

This summary highlights the value of focusing on the mix of global and domestic factors affecting the outcomes of specific Third World industrialization efforts. This approach produces better explanations of these outcomes than approaches that are limited by assuming the primacy of either global or domestic factors for all cases. The mix of factors differs from case to case, and their relative weight differs with a number of variables. There is no doubt that the capitalist world system imposes constraints on aspiring Third World industrializers. This study suggests that the nature and potency of such constraints is likely to vary with such factors as (1) the extent to which the advanced capitalist states' governments and transnational firms have and pursue integrative global and/or regional strategies through involvement in Third World industries; (2) the importance of industries that Third World countries attempt to promote to the national economies of the states in which leading firms are headquartered; (3) the capital and technology requirements of the industries that Third World countries seek to develop; (4) the characteristics of specific industrial joint ventures, such as their ownership, management, and financing arrangements; and (5) the global economic conditions at critical points in the development of specific industries. This study also suggests that the ability of Third World states to reduce the potency of such constraints is likely to vary with such factors as (1) their motives and strategies for industrialization and for promoting specific industries; and (2) the determination, skill, assertiveness, and independent power of their national political leaders. Third World industrialization efforts that vary in the foregoing respects from the pattern exhibited in the development of the Malaysian motor vehicle industry will also no doubt be shaped by a different mix of global and domestic factors than the one identified here.

## Notes

I thank the Fulbright Faculty Research Program Abroad, the California State University Northridge Foundation, and Waseda University for financial support; and the Institute of Strategic and International Studies, Malaysia, for institutional support for this research. I am particularly grateful to the numerous persons in Malaysia and Japan who granted the interviews between 1988 and mid-1990 on which much of this research is based. Most were government or private-sector employees and were assured that their responses were not for attribution. I have thus not cited interviews but, where appropriate, have identified the general position of sources in the text. I also thank Jane Bayes, Don Crone, and Jim Pletcher for their helpful comments on a preliminary draft, but I alone am responsible for the final product.

1. For a graphic portrayal of this, see the figure showing current, planned, and possible exchanges of motor vehicle parts and components among MMC

regional affiliates reported in the Japanese press (*Kikai Shinko Kyokai Keizai Kenkyujo*, 1988: 204–205).

## References

Akrasanee, N. (ed.). 1983. *ASEAN-Japan Relations: Trade and Development.* Singapore: Institute of Southeast Asian Studies.

Aoki, T. 1985. *Taiheiyo no seiki to Nippon (The Pacific Era and Japan).* Tokyo: Yuhikaku.

Ariff, M. 1982. "The Motor Vehicle Industry in Malaysia." In United Nations, Economic Commission for Asia and the Pacific (ed.), *The Scope for Southeast Asian Subregional Cooperation in the Automotive Sector.* Bangkok: author.

ASEAN. 1988. "Memorandum of Understanding: Brand-to-Brand Complementation in the Automotive Industry Under the Basic Agreement on ASEAN Industrial Complementation." Mimeo.

ASEAN-CCI (ASEAN Chambers of Commerce and Industry). 1987. *ASEAN: The Way Forward.* Kuala Lumpur: Institute of Strategic and International Studies.

*Asian Wall Street Journal.* 1991. July 8.

*Asian Wall Street Journal.* 1989. December 20.

Bennett, D. C., and K. E. Sharpe. 1985. *Transnational Corporations Versus the State: The Political Economy of the Mexican Auto Industry.* Princeton, N.J.: Princeton University Press.

Bowie, A. 1991. *Crossing the Industrial Divide: State, Society, and the Politics of Economic Transformation in Malaysia.* New York: Columbia University Press.

*Business Times.* 1990a. November 23.

*Business Times.* 1990b. March 6.

Caporaso, J. A. (ed.). 1987. *A Changing International Division of Labor.* Boulder, Colo.: Lynne Rienner Publishers.

Cardoso, F. H., and E. Faletto. 1979. *Dependency and Development in Latin America.* Berkeley, Calif.: University of California Press.

Deyo, F. C. (ed.). 1987. *The Political Economy of the New Asian Industrialism.* Ithaca, N.Y.: Cornell University Press.

Dobashi, K. 1988. "Restructuring of Japanese Industries and the Impact on Asian Economic Development." *Asian Perspectives* 5: 2–28.

Doner, R. F. 1991. *Driving a Bargain: Automobile Industrialization and Japanese Firms in Southeast Asia.* Berkeley, Calif.: University of California Press.

Economist Intelligence Unit. 1985. *The ASEAN Motor Industry: Problems and Prospects.* London: author.

Ellison, C., and G. Gereffi. 1990. "Explaining Strategies and Patterns of Industrial Development." In G. Gereffi and D. L. Wyman (eds.), *Manufacturing Miracles: Paths of Industrialization in Latin America and East Asia.* Princeton, N.J.: Princeton University Press.

Evans, P. B. 1979. *Dependent Development: The Alliance of Multinational, State, and Local Capital in Brazil.* Princeton, N.J.: Princeton University Press.

*Far Eastern Economic Review.* 1991a. May 2.

*Far Eastern Economic Review.* 1991b. March 28.

*Far Eastern Economic Review.* 1991c. February 28.

Frieden, J. A., and D. A. Lake (eds.). 1991. *International Political Economy: Perspectives on Global Power and Wealth,* 2nd ed. New York: St. Martin's.

Frobel, F., J. Heinrichs, and O. Krey. 1980. *The New International Division of Labour: Structural Unemployment in Industrialized Countries and Industrialization in Developing Countries.* Cambridge: Cambridge University Press.

Gomez, E. T. 1990. *Politics in Business: UMNO's Corporate Investments.* Kuala Lumpur: Forum.

Government of Malaysia. 1981. *Fourth Malaysian Plan, 1981–1985.* Kuala Lumpur: author.

Haggard, S. 1990. *Pathways from the Periphery: The Politics of Growth in the Newly Industrializing Countries.* Ithaca, N.Y.: Cornell University Press.

Haggard, S. 1986. "The Newly Industrializing Countries in the International System." *World Politics* 38: 343–370.

HICOM (Heavy Industries Corporation of Malaysia). 1983–1989. *HICOM Annual Reports, 1983–1989.* Kuala Lumpur: author.

Hoffman, K., and R. Kaplinsky. 1988. *Driving Force: The Global Restructuring of Technology, Labor, and Investment in the Automobile and Components Industry.* Boulder, Colo.: Westview.

Hollerman, L. 1988. *Japan's Economic Strategy in Brazil: Challenge for the United States.* Lexington, Mass.: Lexington Books.

*Investors Digest.* 1988. November. Kuala Lumpur: Kuala Lumpur Stock Exchange.

*Japan Times.* 1990. January 18.

Jesudason, J. V. 1989. *Ethnicity and the Economy: The State, Chinese Business, and Multinationals in Malaysia.* Singapore: Oxford University Press.

JETRO (Japan External Trade Organization). 1991. *Business Facts and Figures: Nippon.* Tokyo: author.

Khor, K. P. 1987. *Malaysia's Economy in Decline.* Penang: Consumers' Association of Penang.

Khor, K. P. 1983. *The Malaysian Economy: Structures and Dependence.* Kuala Lumpur: Marican & Sons.

*Kikai Shinko Kyokai Keizai Kenkyujo* (Machine Industry Promotion Association Economic Research Institute). 1988. *Kikai sangyo no kozo henka to ajia to no sogoison no genjo—21 seiki e mukete no waga kuni kikai sangyo no doko* [Current Changes in the Structure of the Machine Industry and Interdependence with Asia—Trends in Our Country's Machine Industry as We Face the 21st Century]. Tokyo: author.

Kitazawa, Y. 1987. "Setting Up Shop, Shutting Up Shop." *AMPO: Japan–Asia Quarterly Review* 19: 10–29.

Kojima, K. 1970. "An Approach to Integration: The Gains from Agreed Specialization." In W. A. Eltis, M. F. G. Scott, and J. N. Wolfe (eds.), *Essays in Honor of Roy Harrod.* Oxford: Clarendon Press.

Lim, C. P. 1984. "The Malaysian Car Industry at the Crossroads: Time to Change Gear?" In L. L. Lim and C. P. Lim (eds.), *The Malaysian Economy at the Crossroads: Policy Adjustment or Structural Transformation.* Kuala Lumpur: Malaysian Economic Association.

Lim, C. P., and J. W. Suh (eds.). 1988. *ASEAN Industrial Cooperation.* Kuala Lumpur: Asian and Pacific Development Centre.

Machado, K. 1989–1990. "Japanese Transnational Corporations in Malaysia's State Sponsored Heavy Industrialization Drive: The HICOM Automobile and Steel Projects." *Pacific Affairs* 62: 504–531.

Machado, K. 1987. "Malaysian Cultural Relations with Japan and South Korea in the 1980's: Looking East." *Asian Survey* 27: 638–660.

Mahathir, b.M. 1981. Interview, *Far Eastern Economic Review* 33: 38–39.

Mahathir, b.M. 1970. *The Malay Dilemma*. Singapore: Asia Pacific Press.

Malaysian Motor Vehicle Assemblers Association. 1980–1989. *Annual Report*. Kuala Lumpur: author.

MIDA/UNIDO (Malaysian Industrial Development Authority/United Nations Industrial Development Organization). 1985. *Medium and Long Term Industrial Plan—Malaysia, 1986–1995*. Kuala Lumpur: author.

Milne, R. S. 1986. "Malaysia—Beyond the New Economic Policy." *Asian Survey* 26: 1364–1382.

Milne, R. S., and D. K. Mauzy. 1986. *Malaysia: Tradition, Modernity, and Islam*. Boulder, Colo.: Westview.

Ministry of Finance, Malaysia. 1990. *Economic Report 1989/90*. Kuala Lumpur: author.

*New Straits Times*. 1988. June 28.

*New Straits Times*. 1985. September 2.

Ohata, Y. 1989. "The Developing Countries of the Pan-Pacific Region: The Interdependence of Economic Relations with Japan." *Waseda Journal of Asian Studies* 11: 1–18.

Ozawa, T. 1979. *Multinationalism Japanese Style: The Political Economy of Outward Dependence*. Princeton, N.J.: Princeton University Press.

Phongpaichit, P. 1988. "Decision-Making on Overseas Direct Investment by Japanese Small and Medium Industries in ASEAN and the Asian NICs." *ASEAN Economic Bulletin* 4: 302–315.

Puthucheary, M. 1984. "The Political Economy of Public Enterprises in Malaysia." In L. L. Lim and C. P. Lim (eds.), *The Malaysian Economy at the Crossroads: Policy Adjustment or Structural Transformation*. Kuala Lumpur: Malaysian Economic Association.

RIM Studies Group. 1988. "International Division of Labor in the Pacific Rim Area." *RIM—Pacific Business and Industries*. August, pp. 5–19.

Saravanamuttu, J. 1988. "Japanese Economic Penetration in ASEAN in the Contest of the International Division of Labour." *Journal of Contemporary Asia* 18: 139–164.

Sekiguchi, S. (ed.). 1983. *ASEAN–Japan Relations: Investment*. Singapore: Institute of Southeast Asian Relations.

Shiode, H. 1989. *Japanese Investment in Southeast Asia*. Hong Kong: Center for the Progress of Peoples.

Smitka, M. J. 1991. *Competitive Ties: Subcontracting in the Japanese Automotive Industry*. New York: Columbia University Press.

Steven, R. 1990. *Japan's New Imperialism*. Armonk, N.Y.: M.E. Sharpe.

Sudo, S. 1988a. "Japan-ASEAN Relations: New Dimensions in Japanese Foreign Policy." *Asian Survey* 28: 509–525.

Sudo, S. 1988b. "From Fukuda to Takeshita: A Decade of Japan-ASEAN Relations." *Contemporary Southeast Asia* 10: 119–143.

*Tokyo Business Today*. 1988. April.

Unger, D. 1990. "Japanese Manufacturing Investment and Export Processing Industrialization in Thailand." Mimeo.

*Wall Street Journal*. 1990. August 20.

*Ward's Automotive International*. 1990. June.

Womack, J. P., D. T. Jones, and D. Roos. 1990. *The Machine That Changed the World*. New York: Rawson.

Young, E. 1986. "The Foreign Capital Issue in the ASEAN Chambers of Commerce and Industry." *Asian Survey* 26: 688–705.

# 10

# Lessons from East Asia
## *Cal Clark & Steve Chan*

The chapters in this book present a complex view of the Pacific Basin political economy. At the most macro and perhaps stereotypical level, the conventional image is of tremendous economic dynamism among the Asia Pacific countries, which have capitalist economies and generally authoritarian governments (Japan, the "Little Dragons," the ASEAN members with the notable exception of the Philippines, and southern coastal China under Deng Xiaoping's reforms). Their rapid economic growth and movement up the international product cycle or "East Asian dynamism" (Chan, 1990), in turn, are viewed as presenting an increasing commercial challenge to the traditional democracies in North America and Oceania (the United States, Canada, Australia, and New Zealand), which at present can take cold comfort from the severe economic and political dislocation of their communist rivals.

This image of success certainly implies that we should try to draw some lessons from the East Asian political economy. However, before we can even attempt such a task, we need to move far beyond the stereotype of a simple East Asian political economy to understand the nuances and even contradictions that can be found in the region. The chapters included in this volume indicate two important drawbacks to the conventional image of East Asia. First, very significant variations exist among these political economies; and these differences themselves tell us something about the recipe for national progress in the contemporary world economy. Second, the glow of aggregate regional statistics hides considerable failure, which must be taken into account as well.

Most obviously, these nations differ quite substantially in terms of their place in the international division of labor. Although many capitalist countries in the region can claim strong export drives based on manufactured products, what they make and sell differs very substantially in terms of labor intensity, technological sophistication, and value-added domestic content with Japan, the Little Dragons, and the "third wave" NICs, each occupying a distinct niche in the international product cycle. Moreover, this hierarchy is far from stable because each group is under pressure from the group beneath it as the international product cycle inexorably undermines national competitiveness in specific industries as economic change pushes up wage rates and induces technological obsolescence. As Russell Mardon and Won Paik argue in Chapter 8, therefore, long-term success depends upon an ability for continuous economic upgrading and transformation.

The development strategies of even countries with similar positions in the world economy may differ quite significantly as well. For instance, the role of foreign capital in the four Little Dragons is quite divergent: Singapore actively recruited multinational corporations (MNCs); Hong Kong treated both domestic and foreign businesses in a generally laissez-faire manner; Taiwan limited foreign capital to certain key export sectors and promoted linkages with the internal economy; and South Korea strongly regulated MNCs and pushed the eventual "indigenization" of the industries in which they were allowed. Consequently, the nature of enterprises within these economies differed radically. Because of explicit government policy, two very different types of large-scale firms (MNCs and domestic *chaebols*) led the economic drives in Singapore and South Korea, respectively. In sharp contrast, as explicated by Danny Lam and Ian Lee in Chapter 6, small and medium firms dominated the export sectors in Hong Kong and Taiwan, in large part because of the Chinese variant of Confucianism. These very different strategies, however, have produced fairly similar overall results, at least so far.

In addition, despite their generally authoritarian hue, the political differences among Asia Pacific countries are quite substantial in such important areas as the bureaucracy's role in the "developmental state" and the regimes' responses to popular pressures. Japan, South Korea, and Taiwan are usually cited as the best examples of "hard" developmental states; yet, the role of the technocracy varies radically among them. Japan has very weak executive leadership, whereas the presidents in Korea and Taiwan exercised strong central direction of policy, at least until recently; interagency infighting and conflict are much more muted in Korea than in the other two; business-bureaucratic relations are relatively warm and consensual in Japan, somewhat more selective and government-dominated in Korea, and relatively "cool and distant" in Taiwan. Moreover, technocratic power over the economy is limited, but in quite different ways in all three countries. Taiwan really has no bureaucratic equivalent of Japan's MITI (Ministry of International Trade and Industry) or Korea's EPB (Economic Planning Board) that concentrates sufficient power for economic leadership; the power and policies of Korean technocrats have, at least until the late 1980s, been at the mercy of military leaders; and Japan's developmental state has been sharply segregated from important sectors (e.g., agriculture, small business, and construction), in which rampant patronage politics are employed to maintain the power of the ruling Liberal Democratic party (Amsden, 1989; Calder, 1988; Cho and Moon, 1991; Chu, 1989; Haggard, 1990; Lam, 1992; Moon, 1988; Wade, 1990).

The governments in the region have responded to growing popular pressures in a wide variety of ways, as well. Japan has maintained the pattern of what Kent Calder (1988) felicitously calls "crisis and compensation" (i.e., when economic stress creates popular political pressures, patronage support is extended to new constituencies without attacking the basic industrial sectors). In South Korea and Taiwan, democratization reforms have provoked intensified domestic disputes and raised fears about whether the no longer insulated regimes will be able to pursue "rational" developmental strategies (Chan and Clark, 1992). Hong Kong and Thailand basically opened their economies in the hope (which proved well founded) that rapid growth would satisfy most of the population. Singapore (and, to a lesser extent, Hong Kong) provided subsidized housing and social support through the Central Provident Fund, which can be considered an inspired combination of enforced savings, welfare net, and source of patronage (Castells et al., 1990; Schiffer, 1991). Malaysia instituted preferential policies for the Malay majority and recruited foreign capital in part as a way of controlling the country's Chinese business community (Bowie, 1991).

The myriad differences among the East Asian political economies extend into very substantial variations in economic performance. The growing economic deterioration in the communist "garrison states" of North Korea and Vietnam is widely recognized. Moreover, in China the tragedy of Tiananmen Square, as James Hsiung notes in Chapter 4, was at least partially the result of a growing contradiction between the vibrant market and stagnant state sectors (also see Harding, 1987; Vogel, 1989). When contrasted with the rapid development in much of capitalist East Asia, this situation superficially suggests the failure of the communist model of state-sponsored and state-planned economic development focusing on heavy industries. Yet, this is far too simplistic a conclusion for two reasons. First, similar failures are easy to discern in several capitalist countries in the region; and second, the communist states, in particular the PRC, had some notable achievements, especially in promoting the popular quality of life.

The Philippines and—to a lesser extent—Indonesia can be considered examples of "capitalist" failure in several regards. They continue to rely on exports of agricultural goods and raw materials; their populations remain impoverished and subjected to fairly high levels of income inequity (albeit not at Latin American–like levels); and their governments have been widely cited as examples of misrule. The political economies underlying these sorry conclusions resemble in some important ways "dependency" and "dependent development" in Latin America (Cardoso and Faletto, 1979; Evans, 1979; Frank, 1969), but they are also different in significant ways. In the Philippines, a traditionally landed elite expanded its "extraction" to locally controlled industry under Ferdinand Marcos's "crony capitalism." The democratic revolution that brought the Aquino government to power, however, did little to change the social composition of the regime; consequently, only marginal progress has been made in promoting social and economic change. Indonesia has been ruled by nationalistic military regimes of varying political hues—leftist under Sukarno and rightist under Suharto. For the last twenty-five years under the latter, a system very much like the "triple alliance" in Brazil, described by Peter Evans (1979), has evolved, with the military rulers using contacts with foreign and a few domestic businessmen to control the economy for their mutual benefit (Hawes, 1987; Higgott and Robison, 1985; Robison et al., 1985).

Failures or problems can occur in much less dramatic forms as well. First, even in the most putatively successful developmental states, government policies can be misguided or ineffectual. For example, Japan's attempts to promote a greater concentration in the machine tool industry have failed time and again, very probably contributing to this sector's successful pattern of "flexible production" (Friedman, 1988); the problems created by South Korea's push in the heavy and chemical industries during the 1970s stimulated the political crisis of the 1980s (Moon, 1988); and Taiwan's attempts to promote its automobile industry led to outright failure (Arnold, 1989; Chu, 1991; Noble, 1987). Second, the short-term and long-term implications of a situation might be quite different. This explains, for example, the somewhat different evaluations of the Thai political economy in Chapter 5 by Gerald Fry, who focuses upon the contemporary dynamism while noting some emerging problems, and in Chapter 8 by Russell Mardon and Won Paik, who are more concerned with future "structural impediments" generated by the current economic strategy.

In addition to citing problems in capitalist East Asia, the accomplishments of some Asian communist states should not be overlooked. In particular, the People's Republic of China provided a quality of life for its people—as indicated by such standard indicators as life expectancy and infant mortality—far higher than would be expected of a nation at its level of development. The PRC had one of the most dynamic economies in the world during most of the 1980s. Until the market reforms of the 1980s, the government provided substantial subsidies for housing, food, and other services through industrial employment in what the Chinese call the "iron rice bowl." In the wake of Deng's market economics, the growing incompatibility between the state and private sectors has posed a major dilemma for the regime (Clark, 1992). Rising price inflation and widening income inequity have been major causes of the regime's unpopularity.

Given this more nuanced overview of the East Asian political economy (or, more accurately, economies), what lessons can be drawn? To use a phrase we coined earlier (Chan and Clark, 1992), East Asia's success evidently devolves from an "eclecticism beyond orthodoxies" that, in turn, reflects a combination of "flexibility, foresight, and *fortuna*." That is, these political economies cannot be adequately conceptualized in terms of any single theoretical paradigm, such as the three outlined in Chapter 1, or the prescriptions for developmental strategy that can be derived from them. The modernization approach touts laissez-faire capitalism and cultural change; in contrast, although markets have played a key role in East Asian dynamism, the state and Confucian culture are also essential elements in this development pattern. Dependency theory decries capitalist exploitation of the Third World; in contrast, the East Asian nations have explicitly and vigorously sought incorporation into the global economy (although many East Asian states have also tried to manage foreign capital as if they believed *dependencia* warnings). Finally, statists trumpet governmental leadership of the economy; in contrast, the economic problems of Asia's planned economies, mistaken governmental initiatives throughout the region, private entrepreneurial successes, and blatant corruption (especially in Southeast Asia) indicate the need to do more than (in the words of Evans et al., 1985) "bringing the state back in."

Thus, in their different ways the East Asian states have "unbundled" and selectively recombined the bimodal injunctions of these various approaches—to leave everything to the market, to escape the tentacles of international capitalism, or to put the state in charge of a nation's development project. Rather, we argue that much of the recent social, economic, and political accomplishments of the East Asian capitalist countries can be traced to their effective combination of the admonitions embodied in the various models of political economy. They have thus encouraged private entrepreneurship and at the same time insisted on governmental economic tutelage. Vigorous market competition has accompanied active statist intervention, and private firms have coexisted and indeed developed a symbiotic relationship with public enterprises. Similarly, while pursuing a policy of active commercial expansion abroad, these countries have not necessarily eschewed the option of import substitution and indeed protectionism (most notably in the agricultural sector) as a matter of doctrinaire principle. As another example, efforts to recruit various foreign contributions (for example, capital, technology, and arms imports) go hand in hand with other efforts to regulate and contain the influence of their providers (for example, various requirements regarding domestic contents, export quotas, joint ownership, and technology transfer). Accordingly, this pragmatic flexibility—eclecticism, if you will—seems to be a hallmark East Asian economic success. A reluctance to be boxed in by any given orthodoxy, and a concomitant sensitivity to the "received wisdom" presented by competing paradigms offer an important insight into the policy capacity of these nations.

Turning to the explicit lessons from East Asia, these countries by and large have subscribed to what might be termed "comprehensive national security." That is, they view the primary goal of national security to include not just defense matters, but economic development and popular welfare as well. Examples of this include the stress on foreign economic relations by Japan and most of the East Asian NICs; the indirect promotion (i.e., subsidy) of the popular standard of living and low-cost labor by public housing in Hong Kong and Singapore; and the iron rice bowl that the PRC provides to industrial workers. Successful as these policies have been in the past, however, the post–Cold War order is providing new challenges. Thus, as the chapters by Tsuneo Akaha and James Hsiung illustrate well, the two large nations in East Asia—Japan and China—are now facing considerable pressure to integrate their economic policies with their traditional "security" concerns. Moreover, most of the NICs are facing growing demands for more political participation and larger social welfare nets that imply an even broader mandate of what should be included in a "comprehensive" definition of national security.

A central feature of East Asian development has been *flexibility*—the ability to find new niches of comparative advantage in the global economy which, as the data presented in Chapter 2 by Chan and Clark show, is rapidly evolving and transforming itself. Three variants of economic flexibility can be found in East Asia. First, particularly for the more dynamic Japanese firms, flexible production has meant a continuous and innovative upgrading of both products and production processes to create high-quality goods aimed at specific market niches (Friedman, 1988; Okimoto, 1989; Piore and Sabel, 1984). Second, Chapter 6 by Lam and Lee describes another approach to flexible production as practiced by the small-scale Chinese firms in Hong Kong, Singapore, Taiwan, and most recently southern coastal China. This involves extremely aggressive marketing based on cost and speed of fulfilling contracts, flexible use of production facilities, expanding capacity through informal subcontracting networks, exploitation of low-cost labor, and so forth (for more detail, see Lam, 1992). The final type of flexible production involves a major reorientation of an entire domestic economy. For example, the PRC quickly constructed an orthodox Marxist heavy industrial structure under Mao Zedong in the 1950s and then, conversely, enacted sweeping market reforms under Deng Xiaoping in the 1980s. Other examples of rapid restructuring are provided by the wholesale invitation of foreign capital into Singapore in the 1970s and Thailand in the 1980s.

Such economic flexibility, of course, operates within the broader framework of the domestic polities and international linkages. The different types of flexibility exhibited by East Asian businessmen, therefore, must be matched by government policies that facilitate rapid economic adaptation. That this has evidently been the case in many of the capitalist states of East Asia represents an ironic "standing on its head" of Marxist theory, which predicts that capitalism would fail because the bourgeoisie would use its power to retard economic progress.

Moving beyond the national level, intense economic interactions are creating "natural economic territories" (NETs)—Hong Kong, Taiwan, and southern coastal China; Shandong Province in the PRC, South Korea, and perhaps Japan; or Singapore, Johore in Malaysia, and Batam Island in Indonesia. These NETs cut across traditional political lines (involving in the first example mutually contradictory sovereignty claims by Taipei and Beijing), so that their emergent success indicates a new type of "internationalist flexibility." Their success may also reinvigorate broader regional bodies, such as ASEAN, whose ability to promote regional integration has been limited by its members' pursuit of relatively similar economic strategies. In fact, as Chapter 9 by Machado well demonstrates, further integration in ASEAN will be a complex and time-consuming process, which runs the risk of increasing unwanted dependence upon the Japanese conglomerates that have extensive subsidiaries throughout the region. The most inclusive Asia Pacific Economic Cooperation forum (APEC) has yet to move much beyond a "debating society," although its simultaneous admission of China, Hong Kong, and Taiwan in November 1991 was a major diplomatic stroke, which validated the logic of a Fujian–Guangdong–Hong Kong–Taiwan NET. Still, it has the potential to integrate both sides of the Pacific Rim by promoting trade, investment flows, and developmental assistance (Scalapino, 1991/92).

The inevitable impact of government upon the economy, then, implies that the East Asian governments have exercised foresight to promote (or at least not retard) economic flexibility and adaptability. This can be seen in a variety of state roles or policies. First, most of these states have strong records in developing infrastructure and especially in promoting mass education, which creates the "human capital" necessary for the various types of flexible production. Second, a good general business environment has been created in a number of ways—conservative macroeconomic policies that promote stability, significant but limited periods of import substitution that create a foundation for domestic enterprises, overall tax and regulatory policies favorable to business, suppression of strong labor movements, resistance of pressure to protect "sunset" industries, and the limitation although certainly not elimination of corruption and bureaucratic harassment of businessmen. Third, targeting specific "sunrise" industries has met some selective successes—for example, the Malaysian automobile project described in Chapter 9 by Machado, the Korean petroleum and automobile industries analyzed by Mardon and Paik in Chapter 8, the Japanese semiconductor industry (Prestowitz, 1988), or the national steel corporations in Korea and Taiwan (Wade, 1990). Fourth, many of these governments have proved quite adept at negotiating with trade partners and MNCs in the advanced industrialized world (Bobrow and Chan, 1987; Chan, 1990, 1987; Yoffie, 1983).

Finally, *fortuna* has affected the East Asian political economies in the sense that many have evidently benefited from factors over which they had little, if any, control. For example, Chi Huang's statistical comparison of regime change in South Korea and Taiwan implied that his hypothesized causal factor—how radical the change was—had far less impact on overall fiscal policy than did external pressures emanating from the global economy. In fact, the region's position in the international system is often cited as a contributing factor to "East Asian dynamism"—from U.S. security interests during the 1950s and 1960s in creating strong client states, to the fortuitous timing of export drives at times of global expansion, to the long-term workings of the "Northeast Asian product cycle" (Chan, 1990; Chan and Clark, 1992; Cumings, 1984).

This ability to benefit from the international system is also relevant for evaluating current alternatives for structuring the world economy, in particular the choice between maintaining an open trading system and moving toward three regional trading blocs in Asia Pacific, North America, and the European Community. Clearly, the trading bloc approach would be quite harmful to many East Asian economies, given their success on world markets. Beyond simply constricting their markets, it would almost certainly freeze the division of labor in Asia Pacific into a "flying geese" pattern with Japan as the lead goose. Thus, Malaysia's proposal for an exclusive East Asian Economic Group could be self-defeating to its developmental program, as demonstrated by Kit Machado's argument in Chapter 9 about growing Japanese leverage in the Malaysian national automobile project.

For the United States, inviting itself out of the increasingly competitive Pacific Basin economy would probably be disastrous in the long run. The United States could probably retain short-term prosperity by dominating the economies of North and South America. The collapse of state socialism, however, indicates that walling oneself off from international competition almost certainly results in what James Millar (personal comment) has called a "woolly mammoth" economy—one that is increasingly obsolete and inefficient. Both the United States and Japan need to manage a partial "power transition" in their relationship. The end of the Cold War has, if anything, enhanced the global leadership position of he United States in the diplomatic and security realm (Nye, 1990). However, the eroding U.S. economic position means that it can no longer afford to "go it alone" and must treat Japan as much more of a respected equal. Conversely, Japan, as an emergent economic superpower, can no longer expect some of the benefits it formerly derived as a U.S. client state (e.g., tolerance of closed markets and provision of security support). Unfortunately, Peter Peterson's proposal (1991, cited in Holbrooke, 1991/92: 53) is probably premature: "Japan would be senior partner on economic issues and the United States the senior partner on political and military ones [with] Japan becoming more open [and] the United States putting its economic house in order." Still, the current domestic pressures on the struggling Bush and Miyazawa administrations should not obscure the long-term complementarity of interests between these two nations, as Akaha implies in Chapter 3.

There also may be some *fortuna* in even internal structures. For example, comparisons of East Asia and Latin America often focus upon the land tenure system as an explanation for the differing economic trajectories of the two regions—agro-exports based on a concentrated land ownership and a plantation system of production in Latin America create a festering inequality that inhibits the development of entrepreneurial talents and human capital in general (Chan and Clark, 1992). In fact, in Chapter 5, Gerald Fry credits the smallholder land tenure system in Thailand with stimulating economic growth, but explains its existence in terms of natural and geographical factors. Similarly, agricultural success in Japan, South Korea, Taiwan, and China under the responsibility system reflects a combination of both explicit land reform policies and the methods for wet rice farming.

Another internal factor that might be considered *fortuna*, because it reflects the broader context-shaping business activities and state policy, is a nation's political culture. Thus, Confucian culture has widely been seen as promoting both economic dynamism and political stability in East Asia. The chapters in this book provide several widely varying examples of cultural impacts—the difference between the U.S. and Japanese patterns of political economy found by Chan and Clark; the impact of culture on Thai dynamism adumbrated by Fry; the pattern of Confucian capitalism conceptualized by Lam and Lee; and, perhaps more indirectly, the different government styles described by Mardon and Paik and by Machado.

In fact, Hung-chao Tai (1989) specifically argues that Confucianism encompasses an "affective" culture, which can present an alternative basis for development to the Western cultural traditions of individualism, efficiency, and rationality. This affective culture has proved an important stimulus to economic innovation and entrepreneurship in several important ways. First, loyalty to the family as a kinship unit stimulates efforts to increase family wealth and defer present consumption in favor of future benefits. Second, these norms emphasize education, hard work, and investment. Third, the affective culture encourages a paternalistic management style and a reliance on personalized business networks that form a distinctive East Asian business environment. Although such practices contravene conventional

Western management theory, they are increasingly seen as key ingredients in the East Asian success story. Fourth, the respect for authority and government in a Confucian society undoubtedly has promoted political stability and the acceptance of "strong" developmental states. And finally, the willingness of the political elites to forgo maximizing their own material benefits, rather than engaging in "crony capitalism" and "squeeze," might also be explained by the Confucian value system, which gives the highest status to "scholar bureaucrats" in contrast to money-grubbing businessmen (Hofheinz and Calder, 1982; Pye, 1985; Tai, 1989; Zeigler, 1988).

The dynamism of Confucian capitalism should not make us forget, however, the experience of nineteenth-century China where a conservative Confucian bureaucracy stifled political and economic change, giving rise to the "received wisdom," until lately, that Confucian culture inhibits development (Weber 1951). Similarly, official corruption was rampant during the 1930s and 1940s. This recognition should certainly make us wary of simplistic explanations focusing on cultural determinism, as should the ability of non-Confucian nations, including Thailand and Malaysia, to follow the way blazed by Japan and the four Little Dragons (see the chapters by Chan and Clark, Fry, Mardon and Paik, and Machado).

Still, it seems safe to say that some cultural traits are more advantageous than others in specific situations. For example, Kit Machado's description of Malaysia and Russell Mardon and Won Paik's comparison of South Korea and Thailand present pictures of great variation in governmental ability to control and channel foreign capital. South Korea emerges as quite successful, Thailand as relatively unsuccessful (which could well inhibit its ability to climb the product cycle), and Malaysia as somewhere in between. These differences may not simply mirror state resolve and efficacy. Rather, these three policies may well have been constrained by the nature of the indigenous societies in terms of entrepreneurial skills and human capital, which, in turn, could at least partially derive from broader cultural factors.

Flexibility, foresight, and *fortuna*, therefore, seemingly interact. To cite an example from Chapter 6 by Lam and Lee, the high-tech industry in Taiwan resulted from the fortuitous combination of a state-supported project to develop integrated circuit production, the existence of a low-tech guerrilla capitalist electronics industry that owed little to state support, and a U.S. court decision to break up AT&T. Perhaps the most essential lesson from East Asia, therefore, is the axiom that a successful political economy will probably be an open-ended one ready to pursue many options when faced with international competition and opportunities—a lesson the United States should take to heart when making the choice between bashing or learning from Japan and the other East Asian dynamos.

# References

Amsden, A. H. 1989. *Asia's Next Giant: South Korea and Late Industrialization.* New York: Oxford University Press.

Arnold, W. 1989. "Bureaucratic Politics, State Capacity, and Taiwan's Automobile Industrial Policy." *Modern China* 15: 178–214.

Bobrow, D. B., and S. Chan. 1987. "Understanding Anomalous Successes: Japan, Taiwan, and South Korea." In C. F. Hermann, C. W. Kegley, Jr., and J. N. Rosenau (eds.), *New Directions in the Comparative Study of Foreign Policy,* pp. 111–130. Boston: Allen & Unwin.

Bowie, A. 1991. *Crossing the Industrial Divide: State, Society, and the Politics of Economic Transformation in Malaysia.* New York: Columbia University Press.

Calder, K. 1988. *Crisis and Compensation: Public Policy and Political Stability in Japan, 1949–1986.* Princeton, N.J.: Princeton University Press.

Cardoso, F. H., and E. Faletto. 1979. *Dependency and Development in Latin America.* Berkeley: University of California Press.

Castells, M., L. Goh, and R. Y. W. Kwok. 1990. *The Shek Kip Mei Syndrome: Economic Development and Public Housing in Hong Kong and Singapore.* London: Pion.

Chan, S. 1990. *East Asian Dynamism: Growth, Order, and Security in the Pacific Region.* Boulder, Colo.: Westview.

Chan, S. 1987. "The Mouse That Roared: Taiwan's Management of Trade Relations with the U.S." *Comparative Political Studies* 20: 251–292.

Chan, S., and C. Clark. 1992. *Flexibility, Foresight, and Fortuna in Taiwan's Development: Navigating Between Scylla and Charybdis.* London: Routledge.

Cho, M. B., and C. I. Moon. 1991. "State Structure and Policy Choice: Japan and South Korea in Comparative Perspective." Paper presented at the annual meeting of the International Studies Association, Vancouver.

Chu, Y. H. 1991. "Industrial Change and Developmental State in the East Asian NICs: A Case Study of the Automobile Industry in South Korea and Taiwan." Paper presented at the annual meeting of the American Political Science Association, Washington, D.C.

Chu, Y. H. 1989. "State Structure and Economic Adjustment of the East Asian Newly Industrializing Countries." *International Organization* 43: 647–672.

Clark, C. 1992. "The Search for Chinese Modernization: The Political Economies of Taiwan and China." Paper presented at the symposium on Chinese Modernization, National Cheng Kung University, Tainan, Taiwan.

Cumings, B. 1984. "The Origins and Development of the Northeast Asian Political Economy: Industrial Sectors, Product Cycles, and Political Consequences." *International Organization* 38: 1–40.

Evans, P. B. 1979. *Dependent Development: The Alliance of Multinational, State, and Local Capital in Brazil.* Princeton, N.J.: Princeton University Press.

Evans, P. B., D. Rueschemeyer, and T. Skocpol (eds.). 1985. *Bringing the State Back In.* Cambridge: Cambridge University Press.

Frank, A. G. 1969. *Capitalism and Underdevelopment in Latin America.* New York: Monthly Review Press.

Friedman, D. 1988. *The Misunderstood Miracle: Industrial Development and Political Change in Taiwan.* Ithaca, N.Y.: Cornell University Press.

Haggard, S. 1990. *Pathways from the Periphery: The Politics of Growth in the Newly Industrializing Countries.* Ithaca, N.Y.: Cornell University Press.

Harding, H. 1987. *China's Second Revolution: Reform After Mao.* Washington, D.C.: Brookings Institution.

Hawes, G. 1987. *The Philippine State and the Marcos Regime: The Politics of Export.* Ithaca, N.Y.: Cornell University Press.

Higgott, R., and R. Robison (eds.). 1985. *Southeast Asia: Essays in the Political Economy of Structural Change.* London: Routledge & Kegan Paul.

Hofheinz, R., Jr., and K. E. Calder. 1982. *The Eastasia Edge.* New York: Basic Books.

Holbrooke, R. 1991/92. "Japan and the United States: Ending the Unequal Partnership." *Foreign Affairs* 70: 41–57.

Lam, D. K. K. 1992. *Explaining Economic Development: A Case Study of State Policies Towards the Computer and Electronics Industry in Taiwan (1960–80).* Ph.D. dissertation, Carleton University, Ottawa.

Moon, C. I. 1988. "The Demise of a Developmentalist State? Neoconservative Reforms and Political Consequences in South Korea." *Journal of Developing Societies* 4: 67–84.

Noble, G. W. 1987. "Contending Forces in Taiwan's Economic Policy-Making: The Case of Hua Tung Heavy Trucks." *Asian Survey* 27: 1003–1022.

Nye, J. S., Jr. 1990. *Bound to Lead: The Changing Nature of American Power.* New York: Basic Books.

Okimoto, D. I. 1989. *Between MITI and the Market: Japanese Industrial Policy for High Technology.* Stanford, Calif.: Stanford University Press.

Peterson, P. G. 1991. "The 1990s: Decade of Reckoning or a Decade of a New Partnership?" Paper for the Commission on U.S.-Japan Relations for the Twenty-First Century.

Piore, M. J., and C. F. Sabel. 1984. *The Second Industrial Divide: Possibilities for Prosperity.* New York: Basic Books.

Prestowitz, C. I., Jr. 1988. *Trading Places: How We Allowed Japan to Take the Lead.* New York: Basic Books.

Pye, L. W., with M. W. Pye. 1985. *Asian Power and Politics: The Cultural Dimensions of Authority.* Cambridge, Mass.: Harvard University Press.

Robison, R., K. Hewison, and R. Higgott (eds.). 1985. *Southeast Asia in the 1980s: The Politics of Economic Crisis.* Sydney: Allen & Unwin.

Scalapino, R. A. 1991/92. "The United States and Asia: Future Prospects." *Foreign Affairs* 70: 19–40.

Schiffer, J. R. 1991. "State Policy and Economic Growth: A Note on the Hong Kong Model." *International Journal of Urban and Regional Research* 15: 180–196.

Tai, H. C. 1989. "The Oriental Alternative: A Hypothesis on East Asian Culture and Autonomy." *Issues and Studies* 25: 10–36.

Vogel, E. F. 1989. *One Step Ahead in China: Guangdong Under Reform.* Cambridge, Mass.: Harvard University Press.

Wade, R. 1990. *Governing the Market: Economic Theory and the Role of Government in East Asian Industrialization.* Princeton, N.J.: Princeton University Press.

Weber, M. 1951. *The Religion of China: Confucianism and Taoism.* Glencoe, Ill.: Free Press.

Yoffie, D. B. 1983. *Power and Protectionism: Strategies of Newly Industrializing Countries.* New York: Columbia University Press.

Zeigler, H. 1988. *Pluralism, Corporatism, and Confucianism: Political Association and Conflict Resolution in the United States, Europe, and Taiwan.* Philadelphia: Temple University Press.

# The Contributors

*Tsuneo Akaha* is an associate professor of international policy studies and director of the Center for East Asian Studies at the Monterey Institute of International Studies. His primary teaching and research interests include Japanese foreign policy, security studies, the political economy of Asia Pacific, and international cooperation in ocean management. He is the author of *Japan in Global Ocean Politics* and coeditor of *International Political Economy: A Reader* and *Japan in the Post-hegemonic World*. His work has appeared in such journals as *Asian Survey, Pacific Affairs,* and *Ocean Development and International Law,* and in such books as *The International Relations of Japan, U.S.-Japan Trade Frictions,* and *Ocean Yearbook.*

*Steve Chan* is a professor of political science at the University of Colorado. His teaching and research interests focus upon international relations theory and international political economy. He is the author of *East Asian Dynamism,* and *International Relations in Perspective,* and coauthor of *Flexibility, Foresight, and* Fortuna *in Taiwan's Development.* His work has appeared in such journals as *American Political Science Review, Comparative Political Studies, International Studies Quarterly, Orbis,* and *World Politics.*

*Cal Clark* is a professor and head of the Department of Political Science at Auburn University. His primary teaching and research interests are international political economy and comparative public policy. He is author of *Taiwan's Development,* coauthor of *Flexibility, Foresight, and* Fortuna *in Taiwan's Development,* and coeditor of *State and Development.* His work has appeared in such journals as *American Political Science Review, Comparative Political Studies,* and *International Studies Quarterly.*

215

*Gerald Fry* is a professor of political science and director of the Center for Asian and Pacific Studies at the University of Oregon. His teaching and research interests focus upon the politics and political economy of Southeast Asia. He is the coauthor of *The International Education of a Development Consultant* and cocompiler of *Pacific Basin and Oceania: A Bibliography*.

*James C. Hsiung,* professor of politics at New York University, teaches international politics theory, international law, and East Asian politics. He is the author of *Ideology and Practice: The Evolution of Chinese Communism* and *Law and Policy in China's Foreign Relations.* He is editor or coeditor of thirteen other volumes, including *U.S.-Asian Relations: The National Security Paradox* and *Beyond China's Independent Foreign Policy.* His latest work is *China's Bitter Victory: The War with Japan, 1937–1945.*

*Chi Huang* is an associate professor of political science at the University of Kentucky. His research interests focus on political methodology and the political economy of development. He is author or coauthor of articles published in such journals as *American Political Science Review, American Journal of Political Science, Comparative Political Studies, Journal of Conflict Resolution, Defense Economics,* and *Journal of Politics.*

*Danny Kin-Kong Lam* is an assistant professor of management at Seton Hall University. His primary teaching and research interests focus upon business organization, international competitiveness, and East Asian political economy. His work has appeared in such journals as *Asian Affairs, Journal of Northeast Asian Studies, Canadian Business Review, Science, Technology, and Politics,* and *International Studies Notes.*

*Ian Lee* is an assistant professor of business strategy at Carleton University. His primary teaching and research interests include strategic management, business policy, and government-business relations. His work has appeared in such journals as *Canadian Public Administration* and *Naval Research Logistics,* and in such books as *Communications in Canada.*

*Kit G. Machado* is a professor of political science at California State University, Northridge, where he teaches courses on Southeast Asian and Japanese political economy. He has recently completed a year of research in Malaysia at the Institute of Strategic and International Studies and a year of research and teaching at Waseda University in Tokyo. His work has appeared in such journals as *Asian Survey, Journal of Asian Studies,* and *Pacific Affairs.*

*Russell Mardon* is an assistant professor of political science and the director of graduate programs in international relations at California State University, Fresno. His principal research interests are industrial-finance relations and foreign investment policy in East Asia. His work has appeared in such journals as *World Politics, Journal of Social, Political, and Economic Studies,* and *Pacific Focus.*

*Won K. Paik* is an assistant professor of political science at Central Michigan University. His primary teaching and research interests are international political economy, trade policy, and political methodology. His work has appeared in such journals as *International Studies Quarterly, Pacific Focus,* and *Journal of Southeast Asian Studies.* He is currently serving as assistant secretary general of the International Society of Korean Studies.

# Index

Index                    223

Organized labor, 5, 10, 13, 110, 163
Pakistan, 36–37, 52
Panama, 52. *See also* Latin American countries
Park Chung Hee, 17, 130–131, 139, 142
PC revolution. *See* Personal computer (PC) revolution
People's Republic of China. *See* China
Periphery countries. *See* Dependency theory; International division of labor
Personal computer (PC) revolution, 121–123
Peru, 6, 8, 9, 100. *See also* Latin American countries
Phaichitr Uathavikul, 88
Philippines, 51, 61, 78, 205–206; crony capitalism in, 7, 41, 206; and international division of labor, 9, 43; and multinational corporations, 6, 8
Phin-Phao Clique, 89
Poland, 39, 52
Political conflict, 51, 60, 74, 205; Tiananmen Square incident, 3, 5, 13, 49, 59, 73–74, 205. *See also* Authoritarianism
Political economy: Chinese reforms, 2, 3, 13, 16, 73–76; and colonial legacy, 39, 41, 43, 44; and end of Cold War, 2, 20; interdependence, 14–15; variations in, 12–14, 20–21, 204–208. *See also* specific countries and topics
Political stability, 29
Population control, 96, 97
Portugal, 28–29. *See also* European Community
PRC. *See* China
Prem Tinsulanonda, 85, 88, 89
Prestowitz, Clyde, Jr., 31
Privatization, 94, 99
Production flexibility, 4, 5, 20, 108, 109, 208; and capital ownership, 113–114, 119–120; Japan, 206, 208; and state policies, 208–210; vs. flexible manufacturing, 123(n1). *See also* Chinese capitalism; Guerrilla capitalism
Protectionism, 8, 28, 29, 51, 62, 163; and guerrilla capitalism, 120–121, 124(n5)

Rationalization, 170, 174
Reagan, Ronald, 73, 100
Regional Groupings, 100–101, 209, 210. *See also* Association of Southeast Asian Nations
Republic of Korea. *See* South Korea
Roh Tae Woo, 58
Russia, 55, 56

Saisuree Jutikul, 88
Saiyud Kerdphol, 88
Sanga Sabhasri, 88

Sanoh Unakul, 88
Saudi Arabia, 37, 39
Savings, 12, 14
Security policies: deterrence, 68–70; economic emphasis, 14, 15, 69–70, 208; Japan, 50, 51, 60, 62, 63; Korean peninsula, 58; regional security framework proposals, 15, 54; and U.S.-Japanese relations, 50–51, 60–61; U.S. policies, 11, 50–51, 60–61. *See also* Defense spending
Singapore, 5, 11, 29, 59, 61, 101; ethnic minorities, 43, 44; and international division of labor, 9, 33, 38, 43; labor costs, 10, 208; and Malaysia, 43–44; and multinational corporations, 6, 121, 122; political economy, 13, 41, 43, 44, 204, 205. *See also* Chinese capitalism; East Asian newly industrializing countries; Guerrilla capitalism
Sippanondha Ketudat, 88
Small firms. *See* Chinese capitalism
Social integration, 40. *See also* Income distribution
Socialist countries, 2, 3–4, 12–13, 14, 38. *See also* China; Soviet Union
Southeast Asia, 61–63, 62, 147–148. *See also* Association of Southeast Asian Nations; East Asian newly industrializing countries; *Specific countries*
South Korea, 8, 10, 12, 44, 49, 211; exports, 10, 152; foreign investment in, 6, 155–157; and international division of labor, 33–34, 43; and international product cycle, 11, 18, 149; and Japan, 56–58, 64(n2); leadership change in, 17, 129–131, 132–133, 135–137, 139–144; oil industry, 157–159; political conflict in, 5, 205, 206; political economy, 13, 18, 20, 28, 40–41, 42, 151–159, 204–205, 212; and Soviet Union, 3, 49, 56; state policies, 4, 153–155, 209–210. *See also* East Asian newly industrializing countries
Soviet Union, 1, 12–13, 53, 70, 100; defense spending, 11, 51; economic decline, 10, 69–70; GATT observer status, 68; integration with world economy, 3, 14; and Japan, 16, 49, 51, 53–56, 59; 1991 coup attempt, 3, 55–56; political leadership, 126, 127; and South Korea, 3, 49, 56. *See also* Cold War, end of; Socialist countries
Spain, 38
Sri Lanka, 28–29, 38
State enterprises, 6–7, 60, 94, 99, 173–174. *See also* State policies
State policies, 2–5, 29, 30; and Chinese capitalism, 4–5, 17, 107–108, 123; and ethnic minorities, 7, 170–171, 173–174; and foreign investment, 6–7, 161–162, 207; and free enterprise, 12, 40,

# About the Book

Challenging and revising traditional perspectives with new evidence, this collection addresses the new international role of the Pacific Basin nations and the political and economic forces that are influencing their growth and stability.

The book is organized around two dominant themes. The first examines the general nature of the Pacific Basin's regional system and looks at how the evolving international context of increasing interdependence is impinging on national policy conduct. The second evaluates the domestic contexts of selected countries, comparing policy conduct and outcomes either across countries or across time for a single country. Among the contributions of the book is a reevaluation of the dominant image of the factors underlying the "economic miracles" in the East Asian NICs.